TEACHING
ISAIAH

Unlocking Isaiah for the Bible Teacher

SERIES EDITOR: DAVID JACKMAN

PTMEDIA

CHRISTIAN
FOCUS

Contents

Contents – expanded

SERIES PREFACE

Isaiah is a 'big' book in every sense! Teaching Isaiah is, therefore, an important contribution to the series. As preachers and Bible teachers we need help in handling the different genres of Scripture, not least the prophetic literature. This volume will be valuable, therefore, not simply in unlocking Isaiah, but the prophetic literature in general.

David's many years of preaching and teaching Isaiah have been distilled in a book that is purposefully practical, seeking to offer real help for those involved in teaching the Bible to others. The preacher or teacher, the sermon or talk, and the listener are the key 'drivers' in this series.

The Introductory Section contains basic 'navigation' material to get you into the text of Isaiah, covering aspects like structure and planning a preaching series. The 'meat' of the book then works systematically through the major sections of Isaiah, suggesting preaching or teaching units, including sermon outlines and questions for Bible studies.

These are not there to take the hard work out of preparation, but as a starting point to get you thinking about how to preach the material or prepare a Bible study.

Teaching Isaiah brings the number of published volumes in the series to nine. We are encouraged at how the series is developing and the positive comments from the people that really matter – those at the chalk face of Christian ministry, working hard at the Word, week in week out, to proclaim the unsearchable riches of Christ.

Our thanks to Sam Parkinson at The Proclamation Trust for his unstinting editorial work and, as ever, to the team at Christian Focus for their committed partnership in the project.

David Jackman & Robin Sydserff
Series Editors, London & Edinburgh, March 2010

AUTHOR'S PREFACE

It was not long after the start of the Cornhill Training Course in 1991 that I began trying to teach the prophecy of Isaiah. I had preached sections of it, while in local church ministry, but it was a challenge to try to see the book as a whole and to think through its contemporary relevance to the wider church. Gradually as the message of Isaiah gripped me, that part of the course became a foundation unit for many successive year groups, and I have benefited enormously from visiting its pages, known and less well known, over and over again. I am convinced that there is still a great need to preach Isaiah from our pulpits, since its themes are so central to God's majestic purposes in the revelation of his character and the accomplishment of his salvation. So my hope and prayer is that this book may encourage a much wider and perhaps deeper use of this giant of Old Testament prophecy.

This book is not a commentary. Since I started teaching Isaiah, a number of excellent commentaries have appeared,

from which I have benefited extensively, as will be seen
from the footnotes and from the appendix at the end of the
book. I have tried to summarise main lines of thought and
argument in the different sections which comprise the whole,
but this is at best a bird's-eye view of a detailed landscape,
so I wholeheartedly recommend that the preacher buy and
work through one of the first-class commentaries now
available. Nor is this book a collection of sermons. There are
sermon outlines and group Bible study questions here; but
they are only suggestions in the form of outlines and would
all need more flesh on the skeleton, in terms of practical
application. Because I believe every teaching/preaching
context to be unique, I would much prefer the individual
to develop applications that are particularly suited to that
unique context, rather than be content with less specific
generalisations. I hope the book provides signposts, but
they do not in themselves accomplish the journey.

My hope is that this book will prove to be a useful way
into Isaiah's magnificent teaching and vision for the pastor-
teacher. On the principle that you can eat an elephant if you
tackle it slice by slice, I have tried to divide the book into
its major sections and their subsections, so as to focus on
manageable teaching units. Since all good preaching begins
with good listening, I have concentrated on the major
thought content of these units, set in their historical, literary
and theological contexts, in the hope that as we hear Isaiah
more clearly, we shall preach his message more convincingly
and effectively. So this book's aim is to be a preacher's guide
to Isaiah, which I hope may help to spark increased spiritual
perception and more powerful proclamation of Isaiah's
divinely inspired content.

I am grateful to those who have inspired and helped me in this task, especially Dr Alec Motyer, who was my theological college principal and through whose love of the Old Testament, and of the Lord whom it reveals, my own spiritual life has been immeasurably enriched over the past thirty-five years. It was his work which first gave me, and then developed in me, some pale reflection of his own enthusiasm for the prophet of justification by faith in the Old Testament. Many years worth of Cornhill Students have sharpened my understanding and given me new insights, through their astute questions and reflections. I would like to express my appreciation to Nancy Olsen, who typed and re-typed my handwritten manuscript, to Jess Richards, who spent considerable time checking it with great thoroughness, and to Sam Parkinson, whose editorial skills, shrewd questions and biblical insights have combined to make the end-product a much better and more useful book than it would ever have been without him.

I acknowledge my indebtedness to many other scholars and preachers of Isaiah's great book, who have influenced my thinking at various stages and in more ways than I can actively remember. The weaknesses are, of course, all my own, but I trust that what follows may encourage more of my contemporaries and especially those starting out as biblical preachers to put Isaiah centre stage in their thinking and in their teaching practice.

David Jackman
London, March 2010

How to Use this Book

This book aims to help the preacher or teacher understand the central aim and purpose of the text, in order to preach or teach it. Unlike a commentary, therefore, it does not go into great exegetical detail. Instead it helps us to engage with Isaiah's own themes, to keep the big picture in mind and to think about how to present it to our hearers.

1. 'Part One: Introductory Material' examines Isaiah's context, purpose and structure. This material is crucial to our understanding of the whole book, which will shape the way we preach each section to our congregations. As a preliminary to the rest of the book, it divides the sixty-six chapters up into manageable units. This preliminary work leaves us with five major sections: 1–12, 13–23, 24–39, 40–55 and 56–66. Each of them will form the successive parts of this book, and each can readily be treated as a sermon series in its own right.

This section also discusses different ways to plan preaching series from Isaiah, and how they might suit different congregations. It suggests one set of series suitable for preaching through the whole book, which is the pattern that the sermon outlines in the rest of the chapters will follow.

2. Parts one to five, each a major portion of Isaiah, begin by examining 'Context and Structure' – laying out the thought-content, as well as the structure, of each section of the book. This will enable the preacher to put his passage properly in context and so to approach it with the right emphases and aims.

3. They then continue with 'Preaching Notes.' These examine the main issues with preaching the texts in the unit, as well as the main lines of application. This will be useful to those preaching individual sections of the unit, and especially to those who are planning a series covering the section.

4. The bulk of each unit is in 'Working through the Text.' Here the text is broken up into individual, preachable chapters, and lays out the thought-content of each part of the prophecy. All good biblical preaching begins with careful, detailed listening to the text. Nowhere is this more the case than in a long and complex book like Isaiah, where it is all too easy to plunder the context for favourite 'gems', or simply to ignore the development of themes and ideas which do not suit the preacher's own purpose.

5. The chapters that are covered by the example teaching series suggested in the introductory section are followed by a sermon outline in 'Preaching the Text.' This is a suggestion designed to help the preacher think about his own division of the text and the structure of the sermon. I am a great believer in every preacher constructing his own outlines, because they need to flow from our personal

encounter with God in the text. Downloading other people's sermons or trying to breathe life into someone else's outlines are strategies doomed to failure. They may produce a reasonable talk, but in the long term, they are disastrous to the preacher himself since he needs to live in the Word and the Word to live in him, if he is to speak from the heart of God to the hearts of his congregation. However, these sections provide a few very basic ideas about how an outline on some of these passages might shape up.

Note also that not all chapters have an outline: the series suggested here are designed to cover the material of Isaiah quite thoroughly, without covering very similar material repeatedly over a short space of time.

6. In the same way, most chapters are then followed by '**Leading a Bible Study**.' The aim of good questions is always to drive the group into the text, to explore and understand its meaning more fully. This keeps the focus on Scripture and reduces speculation and the mere exchange of opinions. Remember the key issues are always 'What does the text say?' and then 'What does it mean?' Avoid the 'What does it mean to you?' type of question. It is much better to discuss the application more generally and personally after everyone understands the intended meaning, so that the Bible really is in the driving seat of the study, not the participants' opinions, prejudices or experiences! These studies will be especially useful in those churches where Bible study groups are able to study the book at the same time as it is preached. This allows small groups to drive home understanding, and especially application, in the week after the sermon has been preached, ensuring it is driven home and applied to the daily lives of the congregation.

Part I

Introductory Material

Getting our Bearings in Isaiah

In a world of preaching 'mini-series' and sound bites, like ours, teaching Isaiah can seem an impossibly difficult task. The book is vast; its structure is complex; the material is often historically remote from our own times. Not surprisingly, contemporary excursions into Isaiah tend to be restricted to the passages predicting the incarnation at Christmas (Chapter 7, 9, 11 and perhaps 35) and the songs of the servant (especially chapter 53) at Easter. But we miss so much, as a result, and we deprive our congregations of so much benefit and nourishment, which we all desperately need.

It is being convinced of the benefits that will motivate the contemporary preacher to put in the hard work which Isaiah's magnificent book will undoubtedly demand. We are unlikely to preach it well 'on the backstroke,' without considerable diligence and effort, because its treasures are not given up easily to the casual observer or skim-reader.

But think of what characteristics you would like to see developed in your church-life and Christian discipleship, and you will find a remarkable match with Isaiah's own concerns. Once that connection is made in your own mind and heart you will need no further persuasion to teach Isaiah.

For example, one of our greatest weaknesses in contemporary Western Christianity is the poverty of our knowledge of God. This is not only doctrinal, in terms of our ability to articulate God's character and attributes, but essentially practical – we do not know this relationally in all the challenges and changes of our lives. Where would you go to strengthen your understanding of God's sovereignty as the ruler of the world he has created, to deepen your understanding of his essential nature as the faithful covenant-keeping God, who promises and fulfils? Where would you find Scriptures which build confidence in God's commitment to his people and the absolute certainty of his eternal kingdom of righteousness and peace? The answers are in Isaiah.

How would you seek to be a faith-builder for your congregation? How would you try to woo them away from the siren voices of our contemporary culture, with its superficial understanding of human nature, glib 'fix it' remedies which cannot mend broken hearts and lives, reductionist and materialist ways of life in this world which fail their adherents over and over again? If you want to encourage faith in God's promises, rather than a desperate resort to human policies, whether political, social, ecclesiastical or personal, you will preach Isaiah.

In a pluralist culture, with its many faiths and ideologies demeaned and reduced to mere variations on an out-of-date theme, how will you build up your people to believe in and defend the uniqueness of the Lord Jesus Christ as the only son of God, the only Saviour of the world? How will you equip your hearers to share the non-negotiable essentials of the gospel, in a warm-hearted and relational way, with those who do not yet share their faith? What tools will you put in their hands to construct confident structures of faith in the unique accomplishments of the Lord Jesus, and so to give them a strong undergirding for their witness by life, as well as lip, in an unbelieving world? You will need to preach Isaiah.

What ought to be the priorities of the church at this point in world history? How should we regard the competing ideologies of the global village in an age of instant information? If much of what Isaiah prophecies has already been fulfilled, what should be our attitude between the first and second comings of the Messiah? How should we occupy the 'waiting time,' in which we live, looking towards the eschatological completion of God's salvation plan? What are the values that should predominate, both within the Christian community and also in its relationships with others, whether structurally or personally in the light of what we know about the end of all things? These vitally important issues constitute just another reason to preach Isaiah.

So many of our current needs, problems and deficiencies are met in this magnificent book. We shall need to think carefully and prayerfully about how best to divide this word of truth, in view of the uniqueness of the particular congregations we each serve. Short series, with frequent breaks, may well be the answer. But there is a deep mine of theological and practical treasures here to explore, so that the time and energy put into its study and proclamation will be more than rewarded by its powerful impact on our own lives and on those whom we serve. My hope is that what follows will both strengthen your resolve and equip you with the tools to preach Isaiah.

1. Isaiah and His Times
Isaiah's place in the Bible

The book stands at the head of the last major section of the Old Testament, which we call the Prophets, sometimes the 'writing prophets', or in Hebrew terminology the 'latter' prophets. Of these fifteen books, twelve are grouped together as the 'minor' prophets (Hosea to Malachi), so called because of their shorter length, not their comparative importance. This leaves the three longer or 'major' prophets, led by Isaiah, who comes first in chronological order, followed by Jeremiah and Ezekiel. It is important to see Isaiah's ministry as exercised near the start of the prophetic period, which spanned approximately three hundred years. It acts as something of an overture to the whole, laying out God's agenda for his purposes in the present and immediate future, as well as stretching forward to the Babylonian exile and the return. There is a remarkable sweep of events foretold in Isaiah's prophecy – some of which we have yet to see fulfilled (e.g. 65:17-25).

Isaiah's place in his time

The heading of the book (1:1) dates Isaiah's prophetic ministry to the reigns of four kings of Judah – Uzziah, Jotham, Ahaz and Hezekiah – a period spanning about one hundred years, from the 790s to the 680s BC Historical detail can be found in both Kings and Chronicles, which helpfully explains the background to Isaiah's work. After his calling in 740 BC, the year that Uzziah died (6:1), Isaiah's early ministry focused on the hidden, unacknowledged sins of Judah at the end of a long reign of peace, prosperity and security. (See 2 Kings 15:1-7 and 2 Chron. 26:1-23 for the details of Uzziah's 52-year reign.) For the last eight years of his life he was a leper, and his son, Jotham, ruled as regent, after which he succeeded his father for a further eight years (see 2 Kings 15:32-38 and 2 Chron. 27:1-9). Most of Isaiah's ministry was exercised in two contrasting reigns: Ahaz, who 'walked in the ways of the kings of Israel and even sacrificed his son in the fire, following the detestable ways of the nations' (see 2 Kings 16:1-20 and 2 Chron. 28:1-27), for sixteen years; and Hezekiah, who 'did what was right in the eyes of the LORD just as his father David had done' (see 2 Kings 18–20 and 2 Chron. 29–32), for twenty-nine years. Both Ahaz and Hezekiah feature in historical events in the first half of Isaiah's book, which the history writers fill out in further detail. Isaiah's own ministry may well have spanned fifty of those hundred years, from 740 BC onwards. Hezekiah's death is usually dated in 687/6 BC.

Isaiah's place in the world

What was going on in the wider world during that century had a profound effect on Isaiah's message, as it was destined to do on the whole nation of Judah. To tell the story in one word, it was Assyria. With the accession of Tiglath-Pileser III (Pul) in 745 BC, the nation began to stir itself, solve its internal problems, build up its formidable war-machine and, under its able and powerful leaders, fill the power vacuum in the whole region. The glory days of comparative prosperity and independence enjoyed by Israel and Judah, along with all the other smaller nation states, were numbered. Menahem, king of Israel, became Assyria's vassal (2 Kings 15:17-20), as did Ahaz, king of Judah (2 Kings 16:7-9), in events which Isaiah deals with in chapter 7 of the book. But this was only the beginning. Assyrian incursion into Israel increased during the reigns of Pekaliah (Menahem's son), who was assassinated by the usurper Pekah, who was himself killed and usurped by Hoshea (see 2 Kings 15:29). In 722 BC, after a three-year siege, Samaria, the capital of the northern kingdom, fell to Shalmaneser (2 Kings 17:3-6), and the northern kingdom was finished. 2 Kings 17:7-23 provides a very important theological perspective on this enormous tragedy.

But Isaiah's primary concern was of course with the southern kingdom, Judah, and its capital Jerusalem. Here too the Assyrian incursion would be felt, in all its remorseless, invasive power. Isaiah warns of 'the mighty floodwaters of the River—the king of Assyria with all his pomp. It will overflow all its channels, run over all its banks and sweep on into Judah, swirling over it, passing through it and reaching up to the neck' (8:7-8). This culminated in the attack on Jerusalem by the armies of Sennacherib in 701 BC, recorded in some detail in chapters 36-37 of Isaiah's prophecy. Yet as 39:6 makes clear, immediately after that account, it was not Assyria that Jerusalem and Judah needed to fear, but Babylon. God miraculously delivered Jerusalem from the Assyrians (37:36-37), but an equally terrifying conqueror was waiting in the wings, albeit over one hundred years still distant.

The second half of the book, from chapter 40 onwards, has its focus firmly on the Babylonian exile, which took place in stages, but climaxed in the destruction of the temple and city and the mass deportation of the people in 587 BC. Nevertheless, Isaiah predicts a political deliverance when proud Babylon will bow to the conquering forces of the Medo-Persian armies, under their leader, Cyrus, whom God identifies as 'my shepherd' (44:28–45:4). The restoration of at least a remnant of the people to the land is clearly prophesied, but a greater servant-shepherd dominates these chapters as the political rescue of Judah pales alongside the spiritual rescue of a righteous remnant, from all over the world, created and redeemed by the work of God's suffering servant-Messiah.

2. Isaiah's Prophetic Purpose

We must not divorce Isaiah's unified book from the biblical genre of prophecy, of which he is arguably the leading exponent. So, it may be helpful to remind ourselves of the purpose of prophecy in the Old Testament. Today, prophecy is mainly thought of as prediction of the future. God inspires the prophet to see and speak the future realities of his plans and purposes, whether for his covenant community and/or for the whole human race and the cosmos he has created. These may involve judgement and salvation, which are often viewed as the two sides of the same coin, predicting God's intervention in the history of planet earth. But at the same time it is important to remind ourselves that the prophets also look back to what Yahweh has already revealed in the Torah, the instruction that constitutes the Pentateuch, the five books of Moses (Genesis–Deuteronomy) and which is the seed bed for everything else in the rest of the Bible.

In their excellent introduction to biblical interpretation, *How to Read the Bible for All Its Worth*, Gordon Fee and Douglas Stuart have a wonderful description of the prophets, whom they define as 'covenant enforcement mediators'.[1] They become prophets through the Word of the Lord which comes to them, not so much to reveal hitherto unknown facts about his character, but to apply revelation already given with divinely granted insight and penetration to the situation of their contemporary hearers. They are preachers of the covenant: its terms, its blessings for obedience and curses on disobedience (see Deut. 28:1-14 and 15-68). They are sent as God's mediators, to explain the often perilous situation of the covenant people in their unfaithfulness and rebellion, to summon them to repent and renew their trust. They come to reiterate, apply and enforce the covenant relationship, with all that it involves, to the people who belong to Yahweh because of his steadfast faithfulness and loving kindness.

Isaiah provides a major example of this ministry. He comes to a people who are relatively prosperous, at the end of Uzziah's long reign and who by the end of his ministry are again increasing in prosperity under Hezekiah (2 Chron. 32:27-29), having survived the crisis days of attack and invasion during the rule of Ahaz and the earlier part of Hezekiah's reign. But prosperity is not necessarily a sign of God's pleasure, not least because much of the wealth is in the hands of an increasingly rich elite, who oppress and exploit their fellow citizens, whom they should regard as their covenant brothers.

Isaiah is shown the inevitable outcome of this course of action, in considerable detail, by the Lord whose wrath against sin and rebellion must express itself in judgement. He is sent, therefore, to summon Judah to fresh repentance

---

1. Gordon Fee and Douglas Stuart, *How to Read the Bible for All Its Worth* (Grand Rapids, USA: Zondervan, 2003), p184

and renewed faith, but with the chilling knowledge that there will be no mass repentance (6:9-10).

We might say that the prophet's role is to warn of an impending disaster, an accident of huge proportions just waiting to happen, and to call people to hear, to heed and to act now, while there is still time. But in addition we are to see the 'accident' not as the random product of historical forces outside of Judah's control, but as the predetermined plan and purpose of the God who rules the whole of his creation according to the counsel of his will and the perfection of his character.

The prophet speaks from God to his covenant people to inform them of what God is going to do, whether in the immediate or more distant future, and to call for amendment of life in the present. God yearns jealously over his people and loves them so steadfastly that he cannot allow them to sin with impunity or to rebel and get away with it.

For those who lived as Isaiah's contemporaries during the known historical parameters of his ministry, from the death of Uzziah (740 BC) to the siege of Jerusalem by Sennacherib's armies (701 BC), the message is plain and urgent. Assyria, the rod of God's anger, is being raised against Judah's rebellion, not yet in a terminal sense, but as a fearful prototype of an even more devastating future judgement in the coming exile at the hands of the Babylonians. But Isaiah's focus does not end there. Chapters 40-55 deal with the period 605–538 BC, when the Babylonian attack and destruction of Jerusalem and the temple led to the exile actually happening. This material was designed as a warning to Isaiah's first hearers and to their succeeding generations, whether in Judah or later in Babylon. Not only does it affirm the truth of God's Word, but also looks beyond the events themselves to a more glorious fulfilment of God's promises, in the universal salvation procured by the suffering servant. This would be a source of great strength to the believing 'remnant' through all those intervening years, as they held on to the sure and certain hope culminating in new heavens and a new earth (65:17).

There is, however, a third setting which is the major focus of the final section of the prophecy, chapters 56-66. This deals with the period following the restoration to the land at the hand of Cyrus (538 BC), and could be characterised as 'the waiting time'. It looks forward not only to the replanting of a faithful covenant people in Israel, but beyond its borders, geographically and ethnically, to the gathering-in of believers in the Lord and his salvation, from across the world: 'all mankind will come and bow down before me, says the LORD' (66:23). Since that day is still future for us too, this final section has a particularly direct application to our 'waiting time', living, as we do, between the first and second comings of Christ, in what the New Testament calls 'the last days'.

As we discern Isaiah operating in these three distinctive contexts, we begin to see that we too need to keep three horizons, or points of reference, in view when we come to teach this material. This will help us to 'cut with the grain', to use Scripture for the purposes God intends, not trying to make it do something for which it was not given.

As always, in biblical interpretation, we need to go back to the original writer, hearers and their context – 'them and then' – before we can move with confidence and integrity to our own very different situation – 'us and now'. However, we must never preach this in a detached, merely academic way, as though its purpose is simply to present us with interesting historical background information.

We relate to the original context in at least two basic ways. Firstly, because the biggest picture of the Bible is that God is preaching himself to us, we recognise that everything the unchanging Lord reveals of his nature and character in the Old Testament text is still true for us as its twenty-first century readers. Secondly, because human nature does not change, we can only too easily see ourselves reflected in the deceitful hearts of the people of Judah and learn from their mistakes how our own divided hearts may equally lead us astray. All of this stems from careful reading of the text and sensitive immersion of ourselves in the circumstances and world-view of Isaiah's original hearers.

But we are not in the same position as they were. Our second reference point must be the great divide of human history, in the coming of our Lord Jesus Christ, to bring about God's great rescue plan. It was Christ himself who told his disciples, 'Everything must be fulfilled that is written about me in the Law of Moses, the Prophets and the Psalms' (Luke 24:44). His post-resurrection ministry was characterised by his appearance to the two disciples on the road to Emmaus, when, 'beginning with Moses and all the Prophets, he explained to them what was said in all the Scriptures concerning himself' (Luke 24:27).

The text of Isaiah has more specific references to the Messiah than any other Old Testament prophet, but what was future to him is past to us, so that we must always view his message through the lens of Christ's person and work. Theologically, the expositor must consider carefully where there are points of continuity and discontinuity between the Old and New Covenants, and especially where our position as members of the universal church, indwelt by God's Spirit, differs from that of the physical sons of Abraham living as members of a theocratic nation-state.

Our third point of reference will be future for us too, in that it will embrace the 'eschaton', the culmination and fulfilment of all God's promises and purposes in the eternal kingdom, at the end of time. As Isaiah's hearers waited for the first coming of the Messiah, so the prophets themselves 'searched intently and with the greatest care, trying to find out the time and circumstances to which the Spirit of Christ in them was pointing when he predicted the sufferings of Christ and the glories that would follow' (1 Pet. 1:10-11).

Similarly, we await his second coming and will learn from Isaiah many lessons about how to live in the waiting time. Indeed 'waiting' is a widespread theme throughout his book. In any specific passage we preach from Isaiah, we shall need to apply the three horizons or reference-points in our preparation, so as to hear his intended message clearly for our generation and then be able to preach it to ourselves and to others with integrity and clarity.

3. Isaiah's Theological Agenda

Paying attention to the historical context will always mean that the theological purpose becomes clearer, which, in turn, matters very much if the living Word of Scripture is going to impact our lives today. We have noted that Isaiah's time was one of immense political upheaval across the ancient near east, when all the traditional spiritual and moral values were being questioned and reassessed. The long period of peace and prosperity under Uzziah began to break up after his death, and new challenges faced the kings of the Davidic dynasty – Jotham, Ahaz and Hezekiah – in Jerusalem.

Judah had always been a comparatively small nation, forced to depend on Yahweh for her security. Indeed, she was always strongest when she was most dependent. But with the people of the land increasingly exploited by the rich elite, and the rulers consumed with greed and self-seeking in both the religious and political life of the community, the challenge of Assyrian domination of the area posed serious questions. Though these issues were often viewed as essentially political or social, Isaiah's ministry uncompromisingly defined them as spiritual. What will Judah, the people of the covenant, ultimately put their trust in? Where will they look for help? On what will they base their confidence? The question is posed in precisely those terms in 36:4, at the climax of the first section of the book. However, it is asked numerous times in various forms throughout the prophecy, and its realities are never very far away.

The choice is a stark one. Will Judah follow the ways of the nations all around her, trusting in diplomacy and alliances, relying on her own political wisdom and shrewd policies to preserve her status and security? Or will she rely on the promises of her sovereign Lord, Yahweh, bound to her by covenant oath, and so put her confidence in God alone? It is a choice with which every Christian is familiar, whenever life becomes challenging, whether at a personal level, or in a congregation, or on a national or international scale. Whom will we trust – God or ourselves?

Isaiah has often and rightly been designated the Old Testament prophet of justification by faith, the gospel prophet. We tend to narrow such a reference down to the proclamation of God's justifying grace on the basis of the substitutionary atonement of the suffering servant (e.g. Isa. 53:4-6). That is of course the heart of the doctrine, as it is the heart of God's great rescue plan, and Isaiah expounds it with great clarity as he calls for the response of repentance and faith. But we should also remember that justification by faith is a way of life, since being a justified sinner, a Christian believer, consists in a single and exclusive reliance upon the promises of God for the whole of one's earthly existence.

The way into the Christian life is also the way on. The title of Scott Hafemann's study *The God of Promise and the Life of Faith*[2] sums it up so well, and the book itself is a magnificent whole Bible exposition of this great theme. So, this was the lifestyle question Judah had to face, as do we all. Are the promises of God a true and reliable foundation for life in this world (and the next), or do we have to look elsewhere for our confidence and security? In a nutshell, the choice is between divine promises and human policies.

By way of illustration, we can note that in the part of the book devoted to Isaiah's own context (1–39) there are two parallel historical incidents, each given considerable coverage, which illustrate the issues facing the king of Judah and his people. They are dealt with in two diametrically opposite ways. The first comes from the reign of Ahaz and is the content of chapter 7. Syria and the northern kingdom of Israel had formed a coherent policy against Assyria in the form of an alliance that they wanted Judah to join. Her refusal led to a determined attempt to liquidate Judah as an independent dynasty, to topple the Davidic line and impose the son of Tabeel as a puppet king, draining all of Judah's considerable resources into the alliance (7:1-6). Ahaz faces a very powerful force and is staring his own downfall in the

---

2. Scott Hafemann, *The God of Promise and the Life of Faith* (New York, USA: Crossway Books 2001).

face. But he is given a word from the Lord through Isaiah: 'keep calm and don't be afraid. Do not lose heart... It will not take place, it will not happen' (7:4-7).

As with every word of God, there comes a great accompanying challenge. Will Ahaz believe it and so act upon it, or not? The issue could not be expressed more clearly than by Isaiah's statement on behalf of God in 7:9b (which might be a strong candidate for the big idea of the first part of the prophecy), 'If you do not stand firm in your faith, you will not stand at all.' Faith is the only way to be established.

Ahaz, however, has already rejected the way of faith and is not going to turn back now. 2 Kings 16:5-9 tell us that he ignored God's gracious promises and chose instead to commit himself to Tiglath-Pileser, the king of Assyria, as his vassal, using the silver and gold from the Lord's temple to buy his assistance. It could hardly be clearer. He rejects the covenant Lord of his fathers, in order to submit himself to a pagan overlord. Judah can only suffer terribly as a result.

Ahaz even refuses God's gracious offer of a sign to strengthen his faith (7:10-13), but by embracing Assyria as his help he has invited in a swarm of bees to ravage every part of the land, 'to shave your head and the hair of your legs, and to take off your beards also' (7:18-20) – total humiliation and subjugation. The history of the reign of Ahaz is the commentary on this text.

In contrast, Hezekiah, his son, later faces an Assyrian invasion of even more terrifying proportions, mopping up the fortified cities of Judah and advancing on Jerusalem itself (36:1-2). He too receives a gracious word from the Lord, 'Do not be afraid of...those words with which the underlings of the king of Assyria have blasphemed me.'(37:6) Instead,

God promises deliverance and the imminent assassination
of Sennacherib, Hezekiah's tormentor (37:6-7).

We know from chapters 30 and 31 that Hezekiah
has been dabbling in an attempted alliance with Egypt,
disparagingly referred to by Isaiah as 'Rahab the Do-
Nothing' (30:7), in order to attempt to extricate himself
from being Assyria's vassal. But now, to his great credit,
he believes God's promise and affirms his faith by laying
out the whole perilous situation in prayer (37:15-20).
In response, God gives more detailed promises, a sign to
strengthen faith and a clear divine affirmation, 'he will not
enter this city…I will defend this city and save it, for my
sake and for the sake of David my servant!' (37:34-35).
And he does! 'Then the angel of the LORD went out and
put to death a hundred and eighty-five thousand men in
the Assyrian camp' and Sennacherib returned to Nineveh
where his sons cut him down with the sword in the temple
of his god (37:36-38).

In this way, Isaiah presents the central theological issue
facing him and his hearers at the very heart of his prophecy.
But we must also note that from the beginning to the end,
this particular historical event is set in the wider context of
God's promises and purposes for his people, not just in the
restricted environment of Jerusalem in the eighth century
BC, but universally and eternally.

Isaiah 1 presents us with a summary of the situation
in Judah, both as to its symptoms and causes. There is
corruption in every area of her national life: political,
religious and social. 'Your whole head is injured, your whole
heart afflicted' (1:5b). The climax of this devastating exposé
is its focus on Jerusalem as representative of the whole

people of Judah. 'See how the faithful city has become a harlot!' (1:21).

Unfaithfulness to her covenant obligations will produce two divine responses. The first is, 'I will turn my hand against you', but that is immediately shown to initiate a purging away of dross and removal of all impurities. 'Afterwards you will be called the City of Righteousness, the Faithful City' (1:25-26). Here are the two cities, the unfaithful and the faithful city, so that one way of understanding the theological agenda of the prophecy is to trace its answer to the question, 'How is the faithless city to become the faithful city?' Or, on the broadest canvas, 'How is the earthly Jerusalem to become the New Covenant?' One Bible study book on Isaiah's prophecy is entitled *Two Cities* for very good reasons.[3]

It will take the whole of the Bible to spell out God's detailed answers to that question, but it is all here, in embryonic form at least, in Isaiah's amazing book. The immediate answer is only by a miraculous intervention of God's compassionate grace, which centres on the Messianic figure, who dominates the whole book, as Immanuel, the suffering servant and the conquering warrior.

3 Andrew Reid and Karen Morris, *Two Cities: Isaiah* (St Matthias Press, 1993).

4. The Structure of Isaiah's Book

(1)	1–12	Promise and threat – the early years (i) Introduction: Judah's perilous situation (1–5) (ii) Isaiah's call and commission (6) (iii) The Ahaz disaster and the promise of Immanuel (7–12)	**The Davidic King**
(2)	13–23	God's universal sovereignty affirmed	
(3)	24–39	Judgement and rescue – the later years (i) God's sovereignty over the whole earth and humanity (24–27) (ii) The vanity of trusting men (28-35) (iii) Hezekiah's vindication…but the prediction of exile (36–39)	
(4)	40–55	The new exodus and the universal salvation (i) The situation: spiritual and political bankruptcy (40–48) (ii) The servant's work of redemption (49–55)	**The Suffering Servant**
(5)	56–66	The New World Order and the waiting time (i) The contrast: human frailty and divine enabling (56-59:17a) (ii) The anointed conqueror and his mighty work (59:17b-63:6) (iii) The ultimate fulfilment: rescue and judgement (63:7-66:24)	**The Anointed Warrior**

We have already noted the three different historical settings of Isaiah's prophecy: his own lifetime, the exile to Babylon and the return. The chronological development determines the arrangement of the material into the three major sections, 1–39, 40–55 and 56–66. But in each of these sections there is a different portrait of the central figure, the Messiah, who will be the agent of God's purposes in rescue and restoration of his people. In 1-39, he is the Davidic king, the fulfilment of God's promise of an eternal dynasty to David (2 Sam. 7:11b-16). In 40–55, he is depicted as the servant of the Lord suffering vicariously for the sins of God's people, and in 56–66, as the anointed warrior, conquering God's enemies and finally vanquishing all evil.

These portraits will enable us to preach Christ very directly from Isaiah's text.

However, at this stage it will be most helpful to work out the structure of the book as a whole (using the threefold division mentioned above), each section of which can be subdivided into smaller units. Of course, this process of subdivision can go on to chapters and segments of chapters, even to sections of oracles, which form the basic building blocks of the book as a whole. At every stage, we should be looking for the internal dividers, the marker-posts, which the author has included as a way of ordering his material. These will be much more reliable than our chapter divisions, which sometimes seem almost arbitrary, even perverse.

1–39 *The new revelation and the challenge to faith*
Taking the unit 1–39, we can observe that there are three larger blocks of material: 1–12, 13–23 and 24–39. This division is established by reference to the contents of chapters 13–23, which constitute a series of prophecies against the nations. Either side of this distinctive focus are units which can themselves be readily subdivided.

1–12 *Promise & threat – the early years*
Chapters 1-5 serve as the overture to the book, where the major themes are introduced with special reference to the contemporary situation. The famous call narrative in chapter 6, which can either be attached as the climax to 1–5 (which I prefer) or as the prelude to 7–12. In the latter, the challenge to faith in the reign of Ahaz is followed by what is sometimes called the Book of Immanuel, or the Book of the King, because of its dominant prophecies of the Messianic figure in 7:14; 9:1-7 and 11:1-16. This is probably the substance of the earliest period of Isaiah's ministry.

13–23 God's universal sovereignty affirmed

The central section of this unit is chapters 13–23, a series of prophecies of judgement against the nations, beginning with Babylon, Judah's arch-foe (13:1ff.), and concluding with Tyre (23:1ff.). They seem to be presented in no particular chronological order and probably are drawn from different periods in Isaiah's ministry. Their main purpose is to demonstrate Yahweh's government of the whole earth, as he superintends the rise and fall of nations. He is no tribal deity, but the sovereign creator whose rule extends throughout his world. The twin purpose is to give confidence that his promises will therefore be fulfilled and to underline the folly of trusting any merely human agency for support or deliverance.

24–39 Judgement & rescue – the later years

Chapters 24–27 focus on God's future universal judgement, on the last day, when the whole of humanity will appear before the creator. As such, they form something of a climax to the series of oracles in 13–23, but it is probably best to see them as a bridgehead to chapters 28–29 since their form is less national and temporal, and more universal and eschatological. But for the people of faith this is a great day of rescue, by God's grace, and is marked with great rejoicing in the experience of the New Covenant, the faithful city.

Beyond these chapters lies the third and last section of the first 'half' of Isaiah's book, chapters 28–39. The end of the section is clearly marked by the largely prose accounts, from Hezekiah's reign, of the Assyrian invasion of Judah and attack on Jerusalem under Sennacherib. There are additional significant events from Hezekiah's reign and together they constitute the unit chapters 36–39. Before this, chapters 28–35 consist of a series of six oracles, each beginning with the Hebrew exclamation of sorrow 'Ho' (translated 'Woe'), which are rooted in the political events of Hezekiah's day, as he is tempted to look to Egypt's false promises of help in a putative rebellion against his Assyrian overlords. Chapters 34 and 35 form a contrast between the desert (34) and the garden (35), as the two outcomes between which the people of God have to choose, as they determine to live either by human policies or divine promises. The actual historical events and the lessons learned are then featured in 36-39.

40–55 The new exodus & the universal salvation

Moving now to chapters 40–55, this section can be divided into two parts, by noting 48:22 as the marker. "'There is no peace," says the LORD, "for the wicked."' This verse will be repeated at 57:21. Here it comes at the end of a long section (40–48) promising restoration after exile and that Yahweh will ultimately deal with the spiritual as well as the political needs of Judah. Spiritual blindness and political slavery go hand-in-hand, since the former is the cause of the latter. But political solutions are insufficient, hence 48:22. The wickedness of the heart still has to be dealt with, and chapters 49–55, with their sustained focus on the suffering servant of the Lord, expound how this will be accomplished. The repeated motif of the song of universal rejoicing, in praise of the saving work of Yahweh's Anointed, signals the end of the unit at 55:12-13, as it did the end of earlier units, at 12:4-5 and 35:10.

56–66 The new world order & the waiting time

The final section, 56–66, is by far the most difficult to analyse, but it can be divided broadly into three parts, due to the third Messianic portrait, this time of the warrior king, which begins with a description of his person and work at 59:17b. This is then taken up again and elaborated at 63:1-

6. So, if we accept that these two pictures effectively serve as 'book-ends' to the unit (59:17b–63:6), we can identify either side of it, two other sections, 56–59:17a and 63:7–66:24. The first of these deals with how the people of God are to live in the waiting time before the warrior-king finally eliminates evil, illustrating the contrast between human inability to live in a way that is pleasing to God and the divine enabling. In New Testament terms, this parallels the life of righteousness by faith, energised by the Spirit not legalism. Isaiah's final section then looks forward to the fulfilment of God's purposes in his universal sovereignty within the eternal kingdom. There are great blessings ahead, when God will dwell in all his glory among his repentant people, and when the whole earth will be united in its recognition of his total authority and awesome righteousness. Finally, the New Covenant is established as the city of righteousness, the faithful city, in which representatives of all the nations will be found, but for the unrepentant, the only alternative is unremitting judgement, which is where Isaiah's book ends (66:24).

5. Planning a Series on Isaiah

A book of this length can appear daunting to both reader and congregation, especially when we are committed to consecutive exposition as our homiletic method. I know at least one church where the whole book was taught recently by that method, over sixty-six or more sermons, with great benefit to all. But for most congregations we shall need to consider how to divide the material, without doing violence to the original contextualisation. What follows provides some suggestions about how the book might be approached.

There are, of course, many and varied theological themes running through the whole prophecy. This can be a concern for the expository preacher since he may feel that the major themes recur so frequently that he will be in danger of losing the interest of his congregation, if he preaches consecutively through sections of the book. There are two possible ways to deal with this problem.

The first is to recognise that the Holy Spirit's wisdom in both the inspiration and preservation of the Scriptures is far superior to our own. God knows what his people need to be told and how often they need to hear it, whether in Isaiah's generation, our own or all the generations in between. If we follow the division and emphases of the book in its canonical form, we can be confident that God's Spirit will use his own word to accomplish his intended work. Though the general message of the material may be similar week by week, careful attention to the detail of each passage will mean our sermons are different every time. The language, examples, imagery and contexts always will be different, so that there always will be new light on old, familiar themes.

The second is to preach some thematic sermons in a series on a particular section of the book, which can draw together Isaiah's material on major theological subjects, in order to sharpen the focus and augment the contents of our contemporary understanding. It has to be recognised that this is a much more difficult challenge for the preacher to meet well. There is a great danger of confusion and boredom in preaching that can become merely a string of references. 'Concordance preaching' of this sort is hard to follow and difficult to sustain. But there may be a case for it occasionally in a complex book like Isaiah, provided the preacher is still driven by the emphasis of the text as given, not by doctrinal or ethical bees buzzing in his bonnet.

Chronological series from Isaiah

This approach to preaching the book allows the chronological development of the historical events to which the prophecies are connected to determine their context. It is also governed by the theological grouping and application of major teaching materials, as the message of the prophecy develops progressively through the book. As I shall attempt to show, both sorts of development dictate the shape of Isaiah's book, and so it is well worth following the chronological pattern, since it holds the whole together. However, the length of the series must be conditioned by the congregation's ability to cope both with the length of individual passages and with the number of sermons in a particular sequence. I suspect most congregations can cope with far more than is often imagined, but we do need to be sensitive to their capacities and ease people gradually into less accessible passages of Scripture.

At this point, we need to remind ourselves that a long and complex book like Isaiah needs to be tackled 'slice by slice'. Each of the five main sections listed above could readily provide a preaching series of considerable length. There is certainly no shortage of material! Perhaps it would be best for the preacher to tackle Isaiah in a series of series. In this case, it would be important to keep the chronological line clear and to use 1–12 as the first ingredient, at whatever pace and in however much detail you think would be appropriate to your own congregation. The ten oracles of chapters 13–23 could all be treated as separate sermons, of course, but for many congregations it would probably be better to take one or two representative passages, perhaps those dealing with Babylon (13), Egypt (19) or Tyre (23). This could be combined with a series expounding chapters 24–27 in more detail since they have so much to teach about the ultimate realities of salvation and judgement, heaven and hell. Another series could then be preached on 28–39, contrasting Hezekiah's dalliance with Egypt with the glorious promises of Yahweh to those who trust in him. This could culminate in the deliverance of Jerusalem from the Assyrian invaders, but with a look at the greater horror of the Babylonian threat if Judah remains unrepentant.

The section 40–55 contains some of the most well-known and loved passages of Isaiah and could well repay a slower pace and more attention to detail. The songs of the servant (42:1-4; 49:1-7; 50:4-9 and 52:13–53:12) provide obvious material for a preaching focus, as do the explanations and commentaries which follow each of these great poems. We shall examine a more detailed breakdown of this material later on, but the portrait of the servant certainly deserves careful coverage. There are many other important subjects, however, in this section. It is especially strong on the doctrine of God and of the uniqueness of Yahweh in contrast with the emptiness of idolatry. These are areas in which we are comparatively weak within contemporary evangelicalism. The material of chapters 40–45, for example, is especially important in countering the modern fallacy of the so-called 'openness of God.' The two sections of this unit, as indicated in the outline above, would therefore provide two very worthwhile preaching series exposing the vanity of all our human substitutes for God (40–48) and then teaching us the necessity and glories of the servant's work in accomplishing salvation and so providing the only solution to the greatest needs of humanity (49–55).

In preaching a series of 56–66, it might be wisest to focus on the central passage (59:17b–63:6) with its powerful portrait of the anointed warrior and his ultimate conquest of evil. Around this are grouped many great promises which find their ultimate fulfilment in the gospel, such as 60:1-3; 62:1-5 and especially the section 61:1-2, which Jesus chose to use as the proclamation of the beginning of his Messianic ministry in the synagogue at Nazareth (Luke 4:16-21).

The preceding material could be preached in summary form as godly priorities in preparation for the final coming of the kingdom, how God's people are to live in faith and expectation (56–59:17a). Similarly, the great prayers of faithful waiting (63:15–64:12) in response to the rehearsal of all God's faithfulness (63:7-14) could be expounded, followed by the Lord's response in 65:1ff. and broadening out into the visions of the new heavens and the new earth with which the book concludes (65:17ff.).

One might well decide to have an Isaiah 'quarter' or 'term' each year, for four or five years, as a keystone of an expository preaching programme. The benefits would be great, since the prophecy addresses so many of our contemporary issues of faith and obedience. Most of all, it will focus our attention with profundity on the character and purposes of the only true and living God. It will exalt the person and work of the Lord Jesus Christ, as 'great David's greater Son,' Immanuel, the servant of the Lord and the conquering warrior-king. In addition, it will lead us to be more fully dependent on the work of the Holy Spirit to enable us to live godly lives in this present world. For all of these reasons, and many others, teach and preach Isaiah!

A series in five parts

With the exception of the section on 40–55, see p. 46, this series is followed by the sermon outlines in this book.

Promise & Threat – the early years (1–12)		
Sermon 1	God's overture to his people	1:1-31
Sermon 2	Lament for God's vineyard	5:1-30
Sermon 3	When things are at their worst	6:1-13
Sermon 4	Waiting for the Lord	8:11–9:7
Sermon 5	Cosmic hope	11:1–12:6

King of the Nations – Yahweh's universal sovereignty (13–26)		
Sermon 1	The end of human pride	13:1–14:2
Sermon 2	Beware! God is at work	19:1–20:6
Sermon 3	The folly of short-sightedness	22:1-25
Sermon 4	The poverty of human wealth	23:1-18
Sermon 5	Something to shout about	25:1–26:21

Trust & Obedience in Hezekiah's reign (29–39)		
Sermon 1	Understanding God's perspective	29:1-24
Sermon 2	The God who waits	30:1-33
Sermon 3	Our God is a consuming fire	33:1-24
Sermon 4	Which way?	34:1–35:10
Sermon 5	Where is your confidence?	36:1–37:38
Sermon 6	To be or not to be…?	38:1–39:8

The Servant King – a new exodus & the restoration of Zion (40–55)		
Sermon 1	Here is your God!	40:1-31
Sermon 2	A light for the Gentiles	42:1-17
Sermon 3	Good News for everyone	49:1-13
Sermon 4	Walking in the fear of the Lord	50:4-11
Sermon 5	Salvation accomplished	52:13–53:12
Sermon 6	Eternal certainties	55:1-13

The Sovereign Conqueror – waiting for the fulfilment of God's purposes (58–65)		
Sermon 1	True or false?	58:1-14
Sermon 2	Portrait of the sovereign conqueror	59:15b-21 and 63:1-6
Sermon 3	God's glory revealed	60:1-22

Sermon 4	Gospel realities – now and forever	61:1-11
Sermon 5	The prayer of faith	63:7–64:12
Sermon 6	Two ways to live	65:1-25

A longer series on 40–55

The outline we have just reviewed would enable a congregation to acquire the major teaching of the book over five series of six or so weeks each. Obviously, these sections could be grouped together to provide a longer programme. But with a specially rich section, such as 40–55, it might be profitable to run a much longer series, which covers all the material and builds sequentially on the major themes already outlined.

This four-month series is followed by the sermon outlines in part five of this book.

The Servant King – a new exodus & the restoration of Zion (40–55)		
Sermon 1	Here is your God!	40:1-31
Sermon 2	Glory in the Holy One of Israel	41:1-29
Sermon 3	A light for the Gentiles	42:1-17
Sermon 4	The God who makes things new	42:18–43:21
Sermon 5	The God who redeems	43:22–44:23
Sermon 6	The God who rules	44:24–45:25
Sermon 7	What is your bottom line?	46:1–47:15
Sermon 8	The mystery of mercy	48:1-22
Sermon 9	Good News for everyone	49:1-13
Sermon 10	Objection over-ruled!	49:14–50:3
Sermon 11	Walking in the fear of the Lord	50:4-11
Sermon 12	Great expectations	51:1-16
Sermon 13	God's wake-up call	51:17–52:12
Sermon 14	Salvation accomplished	52:13–53:12
Sermon 15	Future perfect	54:1-17
Sermon 16	Eternal certainties	55:1-13

Some possible mini-series

At the opposite end of the spectrum, there are shorter units of Isaiah which lend themselves to more detailed exposition, but in a shorter series format.

For example, chapter 1 could be divided into three sections, as God exposes the failure and rebellion of the people in the three spheres of national life: political (vv. 2-9), cultic or religious (vv10-20), and social (vv21-31). Remembering that this is to be applied to the covenant community and not to contemporary secular nation-states, it could provide a valuable mini-series check-up on our spiritual health – or lack of it.

Another unit is 2:1-4:6. The matching oracles (2:2-5 and 4:2-6) which begin and end the section focus on the idealised city of God, the faithful city which is yet to be. In-between, 2:6–4:1 provide a devastating exposure of how far from this the current city was. Although our circumstances are very different, we share the same characteristics of our human falleness and need to understand how these sinful actions and propensities can deprive us of our joy in God and hinder our effectiveness. A valuable mini-series of four could be developed expounding this searching material.

Chapters 40–41 might form a mini-series as we witness God's rescuing and restoring work firstly for the covenant people (chapter 40) and then explaining the desperate need of the pagan Gentile world (chapter 41) to which the introduction of 'my servant' (42:1) is the ultimate answer. The servant songs themselves would also provide an excellent series portraying the person and work of the Lord Jesus.

All of these, and many others, are valid ways of giving some of the different flavours of Isaiah's prophecy in a short compass. The main danger is distortion and a resort to topical or agenda preaching, so that the passage is 'used' rather than expounded. But with close attention to the detail of specific texts and careful contextualisation of the message there is no reason why such mini-series should not be faithful, accurate and powerfully effective.

Thematic series from Isaiah

There are many rich themes in Isaiah which could form the bases of short series. For example, consider the title 'the Holy One of Israel,' which is Isaiah's favourite designation of Yahweh, occurring twenty-nine times in the book. An explanation of its significance, linguistically and contextually by its use, since Bible words have Bible meanings, could yield a very profitable sermon on the character of God. Or again, one could take the concept of 'waiting for (or on) the Lord,' in its several references throughout the book, with great profit to our knowledge of God and living the life of faith.

Further comment on these areas will occur throughout the text, but there is a fine section in the introductory material to John Oswalt's commentary on Isaiah where he reviews the major theological themes of the prophecy (God, humanity and the world, sin, judgement and redemption), with great help to the preacher. One of his most telling insights is that Isaiah is a book of contrasts, in which polar opposites are played off against one another: divine glory and human degradation, judgement and salvation, the wisdom of God and the vacuity of human idols, prosperity and desolation, arrogance and humility.

Part 2

PROMISE AND THREAT

Isaiah 1–12

'The content of Isaiah 1–12 alternates between the motifs of promise and threat, effectively introducing the outline of chapters 1–39 as mainly threat and 40–66 as predominantly promise.'

William Dumbrell, *Faith of Israel*
(Leicester, UK: Apollos 1988) p100

Introduction

This first section of the prophecy is in many ways a microcosm of the whole. Introducing the theme of the whole book, the opening chapter poses the central dilemma, which is how the faithless, sinful city of Jerusalem, symbolising the people of God, is to be transformed into the faithful city in which righteousness dwells (1:21-26). How can men and women, who are sinners by nature, be transformed into the faithful, obedient people of the loving and powerful Lord, 'the Mighty One of Israel,' who is the only true and living God?

In preaching chapter 1–12, we are made to face the duplicity and ungracious evil of the human heart and to recognise the desperate nature of our human condition before God's holiness. The exposure of sin, in the religious, social and political areas of Judah's national life is relentless. But we need these chapters to hold a biblical mirror to our hearts and to see ourselves reflected in their cynical self-justification and wilful disobedience. The oscillation between judgement and salvation, threat and promise, is a feature of this section. God is more than willing to 'reason together' with a people who are prepared to listen and to repent, but disaster and destruction inevitably await those who harden their hearts and become entrenched in their rebellion, because this God who rules the universe is holy. The threat of Assyrian invasion with its devastating body blows to Judah's very existence is contrasted with the hope of the coming of Immanuel and the establishment of his eternal Davidic dynasty in righteousness and peace. Everything depends on whether God's people choose to rely on the divine promises or resort to independent human policies (7:9b).

All this is founded historically in the events of the early crisis in the reign of Ahaz, when he faces the threat of the Israelite-Syrian alliance and makes the fatal choice of fleeing to Assyria for assistance, rather than depending on Yahweh. The underlying spiritual issues are fleshed out in real-life history and provide a dramatic teaching context in which the principles of God's covenant relationship are affirmed (7–8). But at the heart of the unit is another historical event – the call of Isaiah as a result of his vision of the Lord. Here, by contrast with Ahaz, is a man who reacts rightly before the majesty of God's holiness. Isaiah is humbled and convicted of his sin. He repents and is cleansed. He is strengthened and commissioned. He then becomes the representative of what God is willing to do for all his people if they will receive the revelation of his holiness and seek his forgiveness. There has to be a radical shift in the control-centre of their everyday living if they (and we) are to enter into the fulfilment of God's magnificent, eternal purposes which chapter 11-12 expound.

Every part of this section is therefore highly relevant to our lives in God's world, in this twenty-first century. Here is the spiritual analysis showing why the church is so weak and how things might be different, both in the content of God's self-revelation and this call he makes to turn back and trust him. There could be few greater benefits from contemporary preaching than to find ourselves brought to our knees in deep-seated repentance and practical faith and obedience. Nothing less than that is what we should be prayerfully expecting God to accomplish, as we preach and teach these opening twelve chapters.

1. Context and Structure

Almost every commentator agrees that Isaiah divides into the two 'halves' of 1–39 and 40–66. Subdividing further, we can observe that in the first 'half' the text is concerned exclusively with oracles concerning the nations (including Judah) from chapters 13–23 inclusive. This central section provides us with the threefold division of 1–12, 13–23 and 24–39 which we shall follow, as indicated above. While we shall see that the unit 1–12 contains within itself a wide variety of themes and issues, we can be confident in treating it as a major section, in its own right, and can therefore legitimately expect to be able to discover a structure to the flow of its content and coherence to its message.

Our first step is to work through the chapters, noting their content in summary form and identifying significant subdivisions and particularities of their literary structure.

1   God reasons with his people, calling them to repent
2–4 God's city examined – future ideal and actual state
5   The lament for God's vineyard
6   Isaiah's call – the beginning of the remedy
7–11 God's people examined – future hope and present
       despair
12   God's salvation declared and his glory proclaimed.

Or, at its most basic, we could represent the unit as:
1   Prologue
        2-5   Problem and remedy
            6   Fulcrum: Isaiah's call
        7-11   Problem and remedy
12   Epilogue.

Chapters 1-6

Chapter 1 – following the introductory verse, identifying the author and the historical context of his prophecy (1:1), 1:2 throws us in straight away to the realities of the situation from God's point of view. Heaven and earth are summoned to hear the Lord's indictment against his covenant children, who have become ignorant, foolish rebels (1:2-3). The 'sinful nation' is then addressed, through to the end of the chapter (1:4-31), as Yahweh spells out their condemnation in the three major areas of their national life – political (1:4-9), religious (1:10-20) and social (1:21-31). In each section, we can observe the motif of judgement and mercy, threat and promise.

At the very start of the message all that is spoken is from the LORD. This translation in capital letters is always indicative of the name Yahweh (YHWH) in the original Hebrew text. It will occur many times in Isaiah and should always drive us back to its first explanation in Exodus 3:13-15 and 6:2-8. 'I am who I am' signifies the unchanging nature of the present-tense God, who can always be relied upon to be the same, now and forever. He is the God who establishes his covenant with Israel, in promises which he will always keep and fulfil, and especially in his great act of salvation, in the relationship he establishes with his people and in his preservation of them and provision for all their needs. When we see 'the LORD,' we should think covenant, think of the God who makes and keeps his promises, and reckon on the rock-solid certainties of his word and his will, rooted in his very nature. The exposure of the nation's rebellion in chapter 1 is even more devastating on the lips of such a faithful covenant-keeping God.

Chapter 2 abruptly shifts the focus to 'the last days' and 2:2-5, set in an unspecified future time, envisage a reformed Judah and Jerusalem at the centre of God's worldwide purposes. But at 2:6 we are back in Isaiah's present, where the unfaithful city is again exposed in its conformity to the surrounding nations, its worldliness (2:6-9) and warned of the inevitability of the coming judgement at the hands of the covenant LORD (2:10-22). Chapter 3 continues the theme of the outworking of God's judgement on Judah for her religious apostasy, here in terms of social instability and collapse (3:1–4:1). But the short section which is chapter 4 (4:2-6) takes us again to the glorious future which had been described in 2:2-5. The renewed city is revealed as 'holy' and cleansed, the dwelling-place of the LORD himself.

This repetition and expansion of these ideas, from chapter 2 onwards, alerts us to the fact that 2:2-5 and 4:2-6 act as 'book-ends' at either end of this mini-unit, chapters 2 to 4. As Jerusalem is examined, the actual state of the faithless city is ruthlessly exposed, but against that dark background, the hope of the future faithful city, God's ideal, shines out. We might well decide that chapters 2-4 form a suitable mini-series, given the clearly intended coherence of their composition – see page 47 'Some possible mini-series', for more details.

Chapter 5 begins with a famous lament poem (5:1-7), where under the image of the fruitless vineyard, the people of God are again warned of their coming day of reckoning with great urgency in the light of the devastating destruction which must occur. The following section (5:8-30) is structured as a series of six pronouncements of 'Woe' (see verses 8, 11, 18, 20, 21, 22), which detail not only the sins for which God's rebellious children must be judged, but also the horrific nature and means of the coming judgement at the hands of foreign invaders (5:25-30).

However, chapter 6 seems to belong to another world, as it presents to us the narrative describing Isaiah's call and commission to be God's prophet. If the predominant note of chapters 1–5 has been the threat of judgement, then Isaiah's call stands at the heart of the unit as the first step in God's gracious answer to Judah's terrifying predicament. What God is able to do for and with Isaiah is perhaps proto-typical of what he is willing to do for the whole nation. Certainly, chapters 7–12 have a stronger emphasis on the promises of grace, and chapter 6 appears to be the introduction to the second part of the unit made up by chapters 1–12, with its emphasis on salvation. So, by the time we reach 12:1-3 we see God doing for the whole people what he began by doing for the one man in 6:4-7. From either perspective, 1–5 or 7–12, chapter 6 is the bridge passage, linking the promises of God to the threats, demonstrating the salvation which he offers in the face of his righteous judgement. This helps to explain why the call narrative is not at the very start of the book, as in Jeremiah (1:4-19) or Ezekiel (2:1–3:15). For Isaiah what happened to him was a key to what God would yet bring about for his people and needed, therefore, to be kept centre-stage in this introductory overture section to the whole prophecy.

Chapters 7-11
These chapters bring us right into the historical particularity of Isaiah's own time, in eighth-century Jerusalem, during the reign of the ungodly king Ahaz (732–715 BC). First, we are presented with a moment of immense crisis (7:1-17) as armies from Syria and Israel (the northern kingdom) muster

against Judah and march on Jerusalem. Ahaz is facing the loss of his kingdom, his throne and probably his life. Yet he refuses to turn to God (7:11). Although Isaiah's message is predominantly about the impending Assyrian invasion (7:18–8:8), it is preceded by the mysterious 'sign' (7:14) – the virgin birth of a son to be named Immanuel (God with us) – which is clearly designed to be in direct contrast with the faithless behaviour of the current Davidic king, Ahaz. This Immanuel owns the land of Judah (8:8) and thwarts the plans of the nations (8:10). He is the guarantee that God will fulfil his promises and purposes, however much the present occupant of David's throne may seem to deny it.

Although Assyria is to be very powerful against Judah, her plans will not succeed (8:9-10) because God will not allow his people to be destroyed. His plans are the ones that will be carried through, so the reality is that the enemies of God's people are those who are ultimately doomed to destruction, while his own people will be secure. But this raises the very important questions as to who are 'his own' and on what terms are they secure. 8:11-22 introduces us to the first use of a concept, which will become very central to the message of the whole book, namely that of the righteous 'remnant'. As Isaiah's emphasis is upon justification by faith, believing God's promises, it is not surprising that the remnant of God's people is characterised by saving faith. They believe the promises of God and build their lives upon them, unlike the unbelieving and rebellious Ahaz. It is this faith which accredits them as righteous in God's sight and so as acceptable to him, just as in the New Testament gospel.

There is clear continuity between God's method of dealing with people under both the Old and New Covenant periods – it is always dependent on his grace, declared in his promises and appropriated by faith. From the very beginning, the pattern has been clear. As early as Genesis 6:8-9, we are taught that it was only because grace found Noah and laid hold of his life that Noah was regarded as a righteous man. The same pattern is here in Isaiah, as it will be in Romans 3:21–4:25 and countless other New Testament references. However, in Isaiah's day too many of his contemporaries had appropriated God's gracious promises to the Davidic dynasty (2 Sam. 7:11b-16) as a blanket approval and security for the nation, irrespective of their behaviour, whether godly or sinful. They wrongly assumed that God would never visit Zion with destruction, thinking this would be to renege on his promises. Isaiah's task (6:9-10) was to declare to stubborn, rebellious children, who only hardened their hearts in response to God's call to repentance and faith, that such a judgement would most certainly fall. But through it, God would fulfil his promises by preserving a faithful remnant of believers, from which the holy seed would shoot into a new branch and become a tree by which God's glory was to fill the whole earth, in the fulfilment of all the promises covenanted to Abraham and David. The rest of chapter 8 provides a pen-picture of what it looks like to be a member of that remnant.

This in turn leads on to the proclamation of hope, in the form of the great gospel promises of 9:1-7, which centre on the child to be born, who will be both human and divine (9:6). As Alec Motyer has pointed out in his magisterial commentary, *The Prophecy of Isaiah*[1], the same pattern is then repeated, with special reference to the northern kingdom of Israel (here called Ephraim) and its capital Samaria, which

---

1. Alec Motyer, *The Prophecy of Isaiah* (Nottingham, UK: Inter-Varsity Press 1993).

was to fall to the Assyrians in 722 BC. This indicates that these chapters are rightly placed in the early years of Isaiah's ministry. Again, there is a moment of crisis (9:8–10:4) as God confronts Israel with her sin, presenting perhaps one final opportunity to turn in repentance, to these hardened rebels. The four short poems of woe and judgement each end with the same refrain, stressing the urgency of the issue and the unavoidable nature of the coming destruction. 'Yet for all this, his anger is not turned away, his hand is still upraised' (9:12, 17, 21; 10:4). Next, the declaration of judgement is repeated (10:5-19 cf. 7:18–8:8) but now not only Israel and then Judah, but also Assyria herself 'the rod of my anger' will fall to Yahweh's judgement, in view of her pride in her own strength and wisdom as though she were responsible for her conquests.

However, once again the righteous remnant appears, returning to the mighty God (10:20-34), liberated from the fear of the Assyrian invasion and oppression, and then follows a renewed proclamation of hope (11:1-16) as the focus falls on the perfect king of Davidic descent, the Immanuel figure, in whom they place their trust. This righteous ruler will reverse the curses of a fallen world, reconcile the nations to one another, and bring men and women from every nation together under his sovereign rule (cf. 2:2-5).

No wonder chapter 12 ends the unit with a song of praise, reminiscent of the doxology in Exodus 15, after Israel's crossing of the Red Sea. God's anger is turned away and he has become his people's salvation (12:1-3). No longer is this narrowly confined to ethnic Israel but his glory is extolled throughout the world, as the whole earth joins in the universal proclamation of Zion's glorious king (12:4-6)

In concluding our survey of the structure of chapters 1-12, there are two issues to note. The first regards Isaiah's repetitive structure, which balances God's word to Judah (7:1–9:7) with his word to Israel (9:8–11:16). Although the two kingdoms were long divided by Isaiah's day, he addresses both, since God's purposes for his whole people cannot be thwarted by human rebellion. But the two sections of chapters 7-11 also introduce us to a feature of Isaiah's literary style, 'doublets,' in which the author covers similar ground twice or repeats a structural form. Alec Motyer draws attention to this characteristic structure also in chapters 28–35; 42:18–44:23; 44:24–55:13 and within that section 51:1–52:12, and comments, 'In all these cases the second statement is not a mere repetition but also a development of the first.'[2]

This last comment also encourages us to note the differences or developments between the two sections, which have important historical implications for our understanding of what was going on in Isaiah's own day. So although the northern kingdom will fall to Assyria, it is clear that Judah will not. She will feel the discipline of God's 'rod' through the Assyrian invasion, but she will survive.

Indeed, it is Assyria who will feel a blow from which she will not recover, at Jerusalem (Zion). These references in 10:12, 16-19, 27-34 are later fulfilled in the events of chapters 36–37.[3] God has different purposes for the two kingdoms, though by the end of chapter 11 they will be reunited under the rule of the Branch from Jesse's roots, the perfect king of David's line.

---

2. Alec Motyer, *The Prophecy of Isaiah* p75
3. *IBID.* p106.

2. Preaching Notes

There are several issues of interpretation and application which the preacher needs to tackle, if the word of God in Isaiah is to be rightly handled and its inherent implications for twenty-first century believers to be drawn out with authenticity and authority. We cannot be content simply with accurate exegesis of the text, accompanied by historical explanation. These are foundational ingredients of our preaching which must not be ignored, but what is God's message to us today? This is what our congregations rightly long to hear, but which is so often lacking from exposition of the prophets, or imposed arbitrarily from outside by the preacher, according to the bees that are currently buzzing in his bonnet. How can we do better?

One important consideration is that Isaiah's book is a formative ingredient in the biblical genre of prophetic writing and that we must handle the text carefully in terms of its own literary context. Prediction constitutes a vitally important part of prophecy, but it is misleading to imagine that it is primarily a coded message about the future, waiting to be 'cracked'.

The predictive ingredient is strongly persuasive, spiritually and ethically, because the prophet draws attention to what will be the likely (sometimes inevitable) future outcome of present attitudes and actions. His purpose is to call his hearers to repentance and amendment of life now, in the light of God's declared character, plans and promises. Because the prophet has been shown God's mind and will, he has an urgent message for God's people – and, at times, for those who are not yet his people. We need to recover this immediacy and urgency as we preach the prophetic literature, to rescue its contents from the merely academic or theoretical, and to bring its message with all its challenge, conviction and hope into the present-tense experience of ourselves and our hearers.

Central to this confidence is the recognition that Old Testament prophecies may have multiple fulfilments. There is a real significance and relevance for the original recipients which spoke to them in their day about the actual circumstances of the history in which they lived. We need to understand that first, to go back to them then, if ever we are to bring this living and enduring word with power and authority into our today. Hence, we have tried to spell out the historical realities which are totally integrated into the spiritual truths of chapters 1–12.

For Isaiah's hearers, all the predictions were future. Examples could be drawn from the past (e.g. the exodus) that are illustrations of unchanging principles, but the events prophesied are all in the future. That is the whole point of the prophecy. However, for us they are nearly all in the past. The Assyrians and Babylonians have long since come and gone, buried in the sands of time. Even the prediction of the birth of Immanuel, the Branch of the Lord, the great Messianic king in David's line, which was still more than seven hundred years distant in Isaiah's day, is two thousand years in the past for us. So, if there was one level of fulfilment in Isaiah's day and the times immediately following, there was another in the coming of Christ and the breaking into time and space of the eternal kingdom of the heavens, through the gospel. All this means that much of the value of the prophecy to us is generating our faith in the consistent character of this God, whose promises are still being worked out. We look back and take heart from all the fulfilments we have already seen.

However, when we look at the prophecies in chapter 11 about the nature of that eternal kingdom, it becomes obvious that much of that fulfilment is still in the future, even to us. It awaits the return of Christ in glory at the parousia and the appearance of the New Covenant. But whatever stage we find ourselves along the chronological timeline, the purpose of the prophecy – to generate faith and lead to right living – remains the same. As we look back on what must have seemed an impossible future to Isaiah's hearers, we know that it all happened – the defeat and scattering of the northern kingdom, the exile of Judah, the return, the coming of Christ, the birth and growth of the universal church. For us, these predictions, now fulfilled, enormously strengthen our faith to go on believing God's word in its entirety. It encourages us to go on living our lives according to its instruction, and to go on waiting in active faith for the 'not yet' fulfilments which will be ours when the Lord Jesus comes again in glory. Looking back strengthens our faith to go on trusting, as we look forward.

At the heart of this response lies the knowledge of the character of God, which the prophecies both reveal and confirm. This is why the contemporary church needs the preaching of the prophets so badly and why their absence from our pulpits is so weakening. One of the most challenging areas of ignorance among Christians today is that of the knowledge of God. So often we hear from inside the churches, almost as much as from the outside world, statements such as 'I like to think that God is…' or 'I could never believe in a God who…' followed by flat denials of what God teaches us about God in Scripture, especially in the prophets. No-one who has immersed themselves in Isaiah could begin to imagine that God needs advice from us in our intercessory prayers about his governance of the world! All too often we have domesticated God, reduced him to a convenient pocket-size, or simply recreated him in our own image. As George Bernard Shaw once quipped, 'God made man in his image and man has returned the compliment'. That is one reason why we need to preach the prophets.

But we need to be acutely aware of another pitfall here. When the prophets are preached, their analysis is often pressed into service to draw parallels to the state of our contemporary culture. In other words, their message is used to address the absent and unbelieving world and to confirm the saints in their distinctiveness. Sometimes the prophets do address the surrounding nations, or at least speak about them, showing that they will not be immune from God's judgement, as in the case of Assyria (chapter 10). In fact, our next section, chapters 13–23, is entirely given over to this theme. However, it is undeniable that the bulk of Isaiah's message is directed to covenant people, as God warns them of the violation of their relationship with him and the impending consequences. It is precisely because there is so little difference between Israel and the nations that they are heading for the same judgement destination.

For contemporary preachers, this must mean that the major applications of Isaiah's message will be to covenant people now. But if we have avoided one pitfall, we must not fall into another. We must not use the prophets and the law which they came to teach and apply, as a big stick, with which to try to beat our congregations into being more holy. There are few more debilitating experiences than sitting under preaching which substitutes law for grace, threat for promise and which treats the whole congregation as though they were all apostate, like Ahaz and the rulers of Judah. It is the task of the pastor-teacher, as a physician of souls, to diagnose the spiritual ills of his people from Scripture so that the disease is recognised and accepted. Against that background, he then seeks to apply the remedies of grace to preach for life-change, while recognising that this will be neither quick nor easy because the stubbornness of the human heart is so resistant to recognising its true spiritual state.

In preaching Isaiah, then, we shall not use his diagnosis of sin and warnings of God's wrath to berate ourselves and our congregation into being better Christians. That is not the purpose of the law and so it has never achieved that goal (see Galatians 4–5). The conviction of sin, which Isaiah sought to generate, was designed to move his hearers to cast themselves upon the grace and mercy of God, which for us is so clearly displayed in the person and work of Christ. If ever Isaiah's readers are to embrace the glories of the suffering servant's work, to accept God's redemption and restorative grace and to proclaim his gospel to the nations, there needs to be total realism about our human depravity and need. As chapters 1–12 shine the spotlight of God's righteousness into our own covenant relationship with him, we find that, in spite of all the blessings of the gospel, we have to declare ourselves guilty of covenant violation over and over again, in ways that are exactly parallel in heart and motivation to those of Judah.

Such healthy teaching brings a much-needed injection of spiritual reality into our congregational life. It prevents us from the conspiracy, which grips many evangelical churches, of agreeing to pretend that we are all a good deal more godly than is actually the case. It saves us from succumbing to the pressures of our so-called tolerant society, which generates a spiritual equivalent of political correctness, where any real dealings with our sinful natures or exposure of our double-mindedness become unacceptable.

For Isaiah, the exaltation of God's holiness and the recognition of our deep sin are inextricably bound together as inseparable strands of the same spiritual reality. Judah's rebellion (and ours) is not just a matter of breaking God's rules, but of breaking our relationship with him. The more we understand the true nature of the God of the Bible, the more horrific and serious that possibility becomes to us.

It will also preserve us from the popular contemporary fallacy of seeing our preaching as predominantly life-coaching, where the sermon provides top tips and principles to follow rather than bringing us face to face with a living Lord. Isaiah has a different agenda. He will not allow us to turn the pulpit into a platform for advocating models of ministry, purpose statements or church goals we have articulated and around which congregational life is structured.

Preaching Isaiah faithfully will mean humbling ourselves in the dust before the exalted Holy One of Israel. More than that, it will demand the disappearance of our own idols (2:17-18). That is why the contemporary church is in desperate need of the preaching of this great book and why it needs to be done well. All our issues are in its pages, and all God's remedies lie there to be rediscovered and applied.

3. Working through the Text

It is not the purpose of this book to be a commentary on the text of Isaiah, but to help the preacher and teacher to understand and communicate the richness of Isaiah and to feed their hearers with it. There are several excellent commentaries on the whole book, detailed in the appendix of further resources, each of which provides invaluable help in our teaching of this great prophet. My only plea would be to do as much of the work of exegesis and exposition as is possible before running to the commentaries. They are much-valued aids, but there is no substitute for hearing God speak directly to us from the text itself. That message, burned into the preacher's mind and heart, and worked out in the preacher's own life, will produce a sermon which will have a degree of personal involvement and vitality through first-hand encounter with the Lord in his Word, which even the most erudite and helpful of commentaries can never replicate.

Working on our structural analysis, let me suggest that we could very beneficially divide chapters 1-12 into seven sermons or studies. These sub-units would be chapters 1; 2–4; 5; 6; 7:1–9:7; 9:8–10:34 and 11–12. I have chosen this last unit because although chapter 11 rounds off the section beginning at 9:8, it can stand on its own and is ultimately related to the short chapter 12, which is really the outworking of Messiah's kingly rule. We shall examine each in turn.

1. God's overture to his people (1:1-31)

This chapter is an overture to the whole book since it explores so many of its central themes. The charge of 1:2-3 is serious and needs careful exposition. Note the Lord's dismay at this unnatural rebellion and the sad irony that the verb 'to know' – used of intimate fellowship and affection (Gen. 4:1) – is now used in its negative form to reduce God's children to a status worse than that of a brute beast.

Explore the political consequences in 1:4-9. The verbs of apostasy in 1:4 show that the nation is like a beaten-up, broken slave (1:5-6). They are vivid and merit careful attention. Note the effect on the land (1:7-9), a covenant blessing, which now lies under the covenant curses (cf. Lev. 26:14-39 and Deut. 28:15-68). The most galling reference is to Sodom and Gomorrah, destroyed by direct intervention from heaven for their gross evil. Where is the difference (1:9)? Indeed, 1:10 indicates there is none.

1:10-20 explores the religious sins of the faithless city. There is too much religion (1:11), because it is merely formal. Look at God's violent rejection of it in the various phrases he speaks in 1:11-15. The climax in 1:16-17 reveals that their religion is devoid of reality because their lives are devoid of morality. But note the move from judgement-threat to gospel-promise, so characteristic of these opening chapters, at 1:18. 'It doesn't have to be like that,' God is saying. 'Reasoning together' picks up a courtroom metaphor in the covenant context. Choices always have implications.

1:21-31 major on the social repercussions of this spiritual rebellion. 1:21-26 are a clear unit in the Hebrew text, bound together by a common rhythm throughout. Beginning with the faithful city (1:21) and ending with the same words (1:26), it presents Isaiah's agenda for his book. The social sins are graphically listed, but the root is unfaithfulness ('harlot' 1:21). Yet alongside the threat of judgement is the purpose of restoration and renewal (1:25-26), and in the final section 1:27 is a key verse. The only hope lies in the Lord's gracious redemptive intervention, which will lead to penitence by some (the first hint of a remnant). 1:29-31 refer to Canaanite religion, with its 'imitative magic' and fertility cults, all of which is ready to go up in flames when God comes to judge. 'The fundamental cause of disaster is false, inadequate religion.'[4]

---

4. Alec Motyer, *The Prophecy of Isaiah* p51.

Preaching and Teaching the Text

Title: **God's overture to his people**

Text: **Isaiah 1:1-31**

Structure: The Holy One of Israel exposes the nature of his people's sin and its consequences in judgement

    (1.) Politically (vv. 2-9)

    (2.) Religiously (vv. 10-20)

    (3.) Socially (vv. 21-31)

Leading a Bible Study

1.   1:2-4 What are the charges God brings against his people, to which he summons the whole creation to listen? Why are they so important?

2.   1:5-9 Use these verses to build up a picture of Judah's national predicament. Why has all this happened and why is that a shock (v. 9)?

3.   1:10-17 What is it about Judah's religion which disgusts and angers God? What does this reveal of their true state before him?

4.   1:18-20 These verses match the problem outlined in verses 16-17. What is the solution and what is Judah's choice?

5.   1:21-26 What do these verses reveal of God's big-picture agenda both in the present and the future? What is his ultimate goal?

6.   1:27-31 What is the future for those who persist in their rebellion and what is the alternative?

Application: Only a heart commitment to the Lord secures true values in life. Godliness is always revealed in behaviour, not external religion. When commitment declines, values are quickly eroded. How do we measure up to our covenant commitment (John 14:15, 23)? Are there roots of unreality in our apparent devotion?

2. God's city examined (2–4)

This should be regarded as one unit, due to its carefully worked structure. But in preaching it may be helpful to unite 2:1-5 with 4:2-6, contracting these great promises of God's ultimate blessing with the terrors of his judgement (2:6-22). These could form two separate expositions, in which case 3:1–4:1 will stand on its own as a diagnosis of why God's anger is being turned against his people.

If the hopeless situation of chapter 1 is to be reversed, it can only be by divine intervention in redemptive grace. Only Yahweh can change the harlot into the faithful city. That fulfilment is described in 2:2-4. Jerusalem is already God's chosen city, the home of the ark of the LORD (2 Sam. 6), and already the Gentile world has come in the person of the Queen of Sheba to learn divine wisdom from the Davidic king, Solomon, and to marvel at his splendour (1 Kings 10:1-13). However, this is much greater. The New Covenant is the centre of the world, the locus of divine revelation and the seat of Yahweh's universal government. Who would not respond positively to the exhortation of 2:5?

But from 2:6 to 3:26 there is a catalogue of woe. The elect nation, designed to model the distinctiveness of Yahweh in her devotion and likeness to him, has become like all the other nations. Note the details in 2:6-8. The judgement which must follow is announced in 2:9 and detailed in 2:10-22. The last verse is an especially powerful summary ('Stop trusting in man'), as chapter 3 demonstrates, because the social stability of the kingdom of Judah is under immediate threat. This is the area where the whole populace will feel God's judgement: in the removal of 'both supply and support' (3:1). The infrastructure of experienced government will be removed and the vacuum filled by 'mere children' (3:4), resulting in social anarchy (3:5) and despair (3:7). The message is that proud rebellion is self-destructive, because it triggers the righteous retribution of the covenant LORD (3:8-11). This will particularly affect the rulers, whose oppressive greed has plundered the people (3:12-15) and the 'women of Zion' (3:16-26) whose arrogant, luxurious lifestyle has been sustained by these injustices. The city and kingdom are ripe for destruction (3:25–4:1).

Yet it is at this very point of judgement-declaration that the promises of redemption and renewal occur again (4:2-6). God's discipline had a cleansing, restorative purpose. Covenant blessings will be restored. The covenant remnant will be cleansed. God will once again dwell among his people, 'in that day' (4:2). This will be associated with the 'Branch of the LORD,' later described as the 'shoot from the stump of Jesse (11:1). Later, this image would be used as a Messianic title (Jer. 23:5-6; Zech. 3:8; 6:12), but while that is not yet explicit, all the blessings of Messiah's reign are already being listed in this chapter, though in distinctly old covenant terminology, as one would expect. With such a glorious future prospect, guaranteed by God's promises, the present challenge which Isaiah poses is whether God's people will believe his Word and follow in his ways, or persist in their arrogant defiance and reap his wrath.

Leading a Bible Study

1. 2:1-5 Unpack the ingredients of this glorious future vision for Jerusalem. Why is the actual situation such a contrast (v. 5)?

2. 2:6-9 Why has God abandoned his people?

3. 2:10-22 Why must God's judgement fall on the whole human race? Why is Judah no different and what should she do about it (v. 22)?

4. 3:1-15 How does God seek to bring his people to their senses? What evidence does he produce to undergird his righteous actions?

5. 3:16–4:1 What is the heart of God's controversy with the women of Zion? Why is there so much detail in these verses?

6. 4:2-6 As we return to the ideal city (cf. 2:1-5), what are the blessings which the Branch of the LORD will bestow? How does this relate to Christ and ourselves?

Application: There is so much detail because it is in these areas of everyday life that devotion or rebellion are revealed. What might be our own areas of compromise with the clear teaching of Jesus? Examine this, not to induce guilt, but to show where our confidence and values are being misplaced. But even human sin cannot thwart God's saving purposes. He will have a faithful city, through the work of the Branch.

3. Lament for God's vineyard (5:1-30)

The song of the vineyard (5:1-7) and the subsequent 'woes' (5:8-25) can be seen as the climax of God's controversy with his people and his denunciation of their sin. There are two related theological questions to be asked. Has God's grace been so abused that there is now only judgement remaining? This would certainly seem to be the case in

5:5-6, if those verses were to stand alone. But if there is any hope, how does it relate to the judgement and how will it come to fulfilment? How can the faithless city become the faithful city? The sorrow and poignancy of the situation is a penetrating ingredient of the lament, with its authorised interpretation in 5:7.

The 'woes' which follow spell out the justice of God's condemnation. Here the important ingredient is the content of the sins which God must judge. The accumulation of personal wealth by oppression of the weak and poor (5:8-10) reveals a refusal to recognise that the land belongs to God (see Lev. 25:23-24, 35-43; Deut. 6:10-12). The social symptoms reveal a spiritual disease. The same is true of the indulgent, luxurious lifestyle exposed in 5:11-17. Exile is the consequence (5:13), but its root is a refusal to understand and take seriously the righteous character of Yahweh (see 5:16). The remaining 'woes' all focus on the childish stupidity of Judah's behaviour. Deceived by sin (5:18-19), reversing God's moral absolutes (5:20), they are foolish enough to imagine themselves to be self-sufficient (5:21) but are merely self-indulgent (5:22-24). Note at the end of 5:25, a judgement refrain that chapters 9 and 10 repeat four times. The remaining verses (5:26-30) indicate the horrors of the invading Assyrian army, the agent of Yahweh's chastisement, as a war machine against which Judah has no self-generated defences. It is no wonder that the chapter, and with it the overture to the whole book, ends in unremitting 'darkness and distress' (5:30).

Preaching and Teaching the Passage

Title: **Lament for God's vineyard**

Text: **Isaiah 5:1-30**

Structure:

1. Why God's heart is breaking (vv. 1-7)
    – what God did (vv. 1-4)
    – what God will do (vv. 5-7)
2. Why Judah's judgement is coming (vv. 8-30)
    – what God sees
    – what God must do

Leading a Bible Study

1.   5:1-7 Why is God's vineyard the subject of this lament? What has gone wrong? What is going to happen?
2.   5:8-25 Look through each of the 'woes,' beginning at verses 8, 11, 18, 20, 21, 22. Each one is a pronouncement of judgement, but what is the essence of each offence and what is the nature of God's response?
3.   5:26-30 What response is the detailed description of the Assyrian invasion intended to evoke from the hearers? (Consider the New Testament greater parallels – e.g. Mark 9:43-48; Luke 12:4-5; Rev. 20:10-15.)

Application: Although this is a chapter of 'darkness and distress' (v. 30) we need its sombre message because God not only exposes sin but must act against it. It is against this dark background that the hope of a new start shines out in chapter 6.

Discuss the New Testament parallels in question 3 – how do they apply these truths to the Christian life? How does the exposure of sin and the threat of judgement work in our lives to bring hope?

4. *When things are at their worst (6:1-13)*

This, one of Isaiah's most popular chapters, needs to be understood and preached in this specific context. It is extremely important for the development of the whole prophecy and, as we have seen, is in this position in the book as the answer in prototype to the questions posed by chapters 1-5. So it forms a bridgehead between the inevitability of God's righteous judgement and the hope of which Immanuel is revealed as the focus in chapters 7-12.

The reference to the death of Uzziah (6:1) is pointed, since in many ways the good king's downfall reflects and encapsulates the nation's decline. The historical background is found in 2 Chronicles 26. The answer, however, lies not in Isaiah, who is himself a ruined sinner (6:5), but in a new vision of the LORD, who is superlative in his holiness (6:3). The seraphs sing his praise, but the human prophet is silenced – his lips are unclean, as are his people's (6:5). This identification with Judah is significant, because Isaiah becomes representative of the nation, excluded by sin, but able to be cleansed (6:6-7). The holiness of God, symbolised by the altar fire, is satisfied by the substitutionary sacrifice burning on the temple altar, and it is from this source alone that cleansing and atonement are provided. The cleansed prophet is now no longer excluded, but commissioned to speak for this holy God to his recalcitrant people, although the fruit of this ministry will be calloused hearts and deaf ears (6:9-10). Although this commission will persist until the exile (6:11-12), yet beyond any human hope, the chapter ends with a glimmer of light in its reference to 'the holy seed' (6:13). This is not the end of God's promises and purposes for his people. What he has done for the one man, Isaiah, becomes that man's divinely given message for the nation.

Preaching and Teaching the Text

Title: **When things are at their worst**

Text: **Isaiah 6:1-13**

Structure: Background of chapter 5, Uzziah's death. All this is the context for grace to intervene.

1.   A new encounter with God (vv. 1-4)
     – holiness
2.   A new awareness of sin (vv. 5-7)
     – conviction, confession, cleansing
3.   A new realism in service (vv. 8-13)
     – commission, reaction, hope
     What God does in Isaiah, he can do in his people.

Leading a Bible Study

1.   Reflect on the first five chapters and consider why Isaiah has delayed the call narrative to this point in the book.
2.   6:1-4 Isaiah's commission begins with a vision of the Lord himself. Observe the details of these verses as they relate to God's nature and character. Do we have such a view of him?
3.   6:5-7 The 'woe' of chapter 5 is repeated, but related by Isaiah to himself. What does he discover about himself when he sees the Lord? How does he react, and what does God do about it?
4.   6:8-10 What is the nature of Isaiah's commission? What is encouraging and discouraging about it? How might it relate to all gospel proclamation, in the light of Mark 4:9-12?
5.   6:11-13 How do these verses provide not only information about Isaiah's ministry, but also encouragement to sustain it?

Application: At this turning point in Judah's history (6:1), Isaiah is, in a sense, representative of the nation (needing cleansing, renewal, being recommissioned). What happened to him could happen to all. God offers that choice by sending his prophet, who has seen his glory. Relate this to our New Testament gospel parallels – e.g. John 1:14; 12:23; 27-28; 32-33.

5. *The Hope of Immanuel* (7:1–9:7)
This section picks up the historical theme from Isaiah's own situation, in the reign of Ahaz. We have already considered the general themes of this section in our overview earlier. Overall, it is the contrast between the unrelieved gloom of Ahaz in his unbelief and the eschatological hope of Immanuel which provides the motor-power of this section. (For further historical background, see 2 Chron. 28.) Although the occupant of David's throne is so different from his forefather, God nevertheless sends Isaiah to speak his word of deliverance to the unbelieving king (7:3-9). The end of the oracle (7:9b) provides a key verse for the historical context of the whole book. There is only one rock, one secure foothold, but to trust oneself to the promises of Yahweh requires faith and the renunciation of the alternative imagined securities of human policies and politics. That is the issue Ahaz and Judah are facing – divine promises or human policies? Which will they choose to put their faith in?

Graciously, knowing that Ahaz is so weak, God offers him a sign to confirm the divine origin of the promises and the Lord's commitment to his word (7:11). But Ahaz is a true unbeliever (7:12), so God declares his own sign of the virgin birth of Immanuel (7:14-17), though it is somewhat obscure and difficult to understand. One possibility is that the virgin ('alma' means young woman) is Zion, already referred to as 'daughter Zion' in 1:8, and that her son would then be 'the faithful remnant who will emerge from her sufferings. That is why he is given the name Immanuel, 'God with us'. This vindicates Matthew's use of the promise with reference to the Lord Jesus Christ in Matthew 1:23, since Jesus is 'the perfectly faithful and righteous one'. He is the personification and fulfilment of the remnant promises. This view is suggested and given a detailed and well-argued presentation by Barry Webb in his excellent commentary *The Message of Isaiah* in The Bible Speaks Today series.[5]

There are, of course, alternative views, such as that expressed by Alec Motyer in his commentary, that 'it is impossible to separate this Immanuel from the Davidic king whose birth delivers his people (9:4-7)…Isaiah foresaw the birth of the divine son of David and also laid the foundation for the understanding of the unique nature of his birth'[6]. While all evangelical commentators declare the ultimate fulfilment in Christ's birth, since the latter revelation must interpret the former for us as New Testament believers, the problem lies in the apparent dating of the child's birth to the days of Ahaz (7:16). Motyer explains this by drawing attention to 'a tension between the immediate and the remote'[7] throughout the section.

Another view, which relates the prophecy much more closely to Isaiah's own circumstances, is suggested by John Oswalt.[8]

5. Barry Webb, *The Message of Isaiah*, *The Bible Speaks Today* (Nottingham, UK: Inter-Varsity Press 1996), p62ff.
6. Alec Motyer, *The Prophecy of Isaiah* p86
7. *IBID.* p87
8 John N. Oswalt, *Isaiah: The NIV Application Commentary* (Grand Rapids, USA: Zondervan, 2003) p140-141

Whichever interpretation the preacher adopts, the devastating nature of the imminent judgement at the hand of Assyria, not Syria and Israel, is abundantly clear and was historically fulfilled in the fall of Damascus (732 B.C.), Samaria and Israel (722 B.C.) and the attack on Jerusalem (701 B.C.). The humiliation and shame of the devastated land occupy 7:18-25 but this is not (yet) genocide nor exile for Judah. However, the imagery of 8:5-8 sees Judah 'up to the neck' in the Assyrian floodwaters and the land which belongs to Immanuel inundated and overwhelmed by the invasion. But 'Immanuel' is a present reality, not just a pious hope (8:9-10). God is with his people, and in 8:11-22 the focus is on the believing remnant.

This important introductory passage to the remnant concept provides us with a pen-picture of what it means to be a faithful believer in God's promises in such times of trial. Distinctiveness and separation are the key ideas, grounded in godly fear, for the Lord who is a sanctuary to the believer is equally a stumbling stone, a trap and snare to the faithless (8:11-15). Note how this imagery is developed further in 1 Peter 2:4-10, quoting Isaiah in verse 8. Also significant here is the relationship of faith to the revealed word of God. The godly remnant is prepared to go on believing God's promises as they actively wait for the Lord to fulfil them, and as such their faith is in itself a sign that God is with them (8:16-18). Any alternative source of so-called 'revelation' is totally rejected since it leads only to frustration, cursing and 'utter darkness'. Isaiah's watchword for God's faithful people is clear – 'To the law and to the testimony!' Without this, there can be 'no light of dawn' (8:19-22). The contemporary parallels for faithful believers in a time of widespread apostasy and unbelief are urgent and persuasive.

The section then ends with the proclamation of hope in 9:1-7. Zebulun and Naphtali are the northern tribal areas in the Galilee region, which bore the brunt of the invading armies, hence 'Galilee of the Gentiles,' so this is where the darkness and the shadow of death were at their deepest. But in this very area the great light shines (cf. Luke 2:9-14; John 1:5) as defeat is turned to victory and as oppression and war give way to liberty and peace. This will be a direct divine intervention, just as was Gideon's victory over the Midianites (cf. Judg. 7). The Immanuel prophecies of chapter 7 and 8 are now filled out, as the focus of God's intervention is shown to be the child who is to be born. That he is, in person, the divine intervention and agent is further stressed by the combination of the human with the divine in each of the four titles given to the child (9:6-7). Each title contains both elements. The unique nature of this divine solution is underlined by reference to the constant expansion and eternal authority of this child's rule. David's kingdom is now at last the righteous and faithful city, described for us in Revelation 21. And if it all seems too wonderful to believe, the guarantee lies in the all-powerful, covenant-keeping Lord, whose zeal (passion, urgency) will certainly carry it through.

Preaching and Teaching the Text
Title   **Waiting for the Lord**
Text   **Isaiah 8:11–9:7**
Structure: Background of Ahaz, who embraced Assyria rather than God
1.   Following the crowd – why God is not trusted

'the way of this people' (8:11)
  – fearing everything rather than God's power (vv. 12-15)
  – believing anything rather than God's word (vv. 19-20)
  Results in distress, hunger, restlessness, anger (vv. 21-22)
2. Waiting for the Lord – Why God should be trusted
  – God reveals and confirms his plans (8:16-18)
  – God shines his light in darkness (9:1-2)
  Results in joy, deliverance, peace (9:3-5)
3. Meeting Immanuel – how God can be trusted
  – Jesus, the man who is God (9:6)
  – Jesus, the everlasting king (9:7)

Leading a Bible Study

1.   7:1-9 What crisis is Ahaz facing and how does God meet him at this point of need?

2.   7:10-17 What does God's offer of 'a sign' and Ahaz's refusal indicate about them both? What is the major message of the sign which God does give?

3.   7:18–8:8 How does the name of Isaiah's son (8:3) expound the detailed judgements depicted either side of 8:1-3?

4.   8:9-10 How does this sudden change of perspective give content to the Immanuel concept (7:14; 8:8b)?

5.   8:11-22 As God's rescue now focuses on a godly remnant, what do these verses teach about how such faithful people should live, both positively (vv. 12-18) and negatively (vv. 19-22), under the judgement?

6.   9:1-7 Explain the nature of the hope contained in these verses. Analyse the details which describe the coming of the Immanuel figure.

Application: Beyond the inevitable judgement of the faithless city, God has great purposes of rescue, but for a righteous remnant, characterised by their devotion to his word. The birth of the divine-human king (9:6-7) is the means by which this new dawn will rise. Work out how faithful believers today should respond to the apostasy around them as they wait for Immanuel's return.

6. God's discipline – threat and promise (9:8–10:34)

As noted earlier, clear structural parallels link this section and the preceding passage. Once again, there is a moment of critical decision, but now the focus is on Israel, also called Ephraim. How will the northern kingdom respond in the light of God's declared judgements? There are also parallels to the 'woes' of chapter 5, as God exposes the sins and the spiritual rebellion against him which they indicate, both to justify his actions and also to wake Israel up at the very last minute.

The root of their problem is their self-confidence, which sees no need of God's deliverance (9:8-12). But such appetites can never be satisfied and the descent into civil war, predicted at 9:21, is the outworking of God's wrath, as he refuses to intervene to protect his rebellious people from the effects of their disastrous choices. There is a striking similarity to Paul's argument in Romans 1:18-32. Those who have abused justice in the courts are now in God's court and there are no human escape routes left (10:1-4).

However, Assyria herself is not immune from God's judgement and in 10:5-19 she becomes the focus of God's wrathful predictions. This introduces the idea, developed in chapters 13-23, that all the nations are governed by Yahweh and subject to his control. It also demonstrates very powerfully to Ahaz why it is so foolish to run to Assyria for support against Israel and Syria, rather than to the Lord. The Assyrian emperor is not the inviolable world ruler he imagines himself to be. 'The light of Israel will become a fire' to burn and consume him and his works 'in a single day' (10:7 cf. 37:36-38). What will remain is not Assyria's glory, but 'the remnant of Israel' (10:20-34), who 'will truly rely on the LORD', although they will be few in number. It must be remembered that the Assyrian invasion is God's anger and wrath, but that when his purposes are complete they will be directed on the invader. The end of chapter 10 with its images of God cutting down the mighty forests (symbolic of Assyria) is juxtaposed with 11:1, the apparently insignificant shoot from Jesse's stump, whose kingly rule will bring universal and eternal righteousness and peace.

Leading a Bible Study

1. 9:8-12 What is the root of Samaria's crisis and what are its consequences?

2. 9:13-21 Why must God's judgement fall on Israel and how will he allow the sins themselves to precipitate this?

3. 10:1-4 In this short lament, what ingredients are designed to motivate Israel to turn back to God, even at this last moment?

4. 10:5-19 What does God's future judgement of Assyria indicate about his nature and character, which Israel has forgotten?

5. 10:20-27 What characteristics should be generated in the faithful remnant by the revelation of these verses?

6. 10:28-34 How do verses 28-32 convey the horror of the Assyrian invasion? What should Judah's reaction be (vv. 33-34)?

Application: This parallel section to 7:1–9:7 focuses on the northern kingdom (Ephraim). Note how threat and promise oscillate according to one's attitude to the Lord's word. How can we encourage one another to take God's discipline seriously? How does the passage help us to walk in humility and obedience with the Lord?

7. *Cosmic Hope (11:1-12:6)*

Just when it seems that David's line is finished, a fresh shoot or branch appears. Clearly, we are now back in the Immanuel territory of chapters 8 and 9, as the character and person of the divine-human branch are sketched in more detail. The sevenfold permanent endowment of the Spirit of the LORD (11:2) makes us aware that this is God's perfect king. He is perfect in mind (wisdom and understanding), in action (counsel and power) and in heart (knowledge and the fear of Yahweh). He has the ability to execute his decisions in perfect justice, by his word of sovereign authority alone (11:4). If this is the character of the king, 11:6-9 explores the nature of his kingdom, which restores and secures the harmony of Eden, before the fall. Here is not just a faithful city, but the whole earth rejoicing in God's righteous rule. Note the forward look into the long-term future in the repeated introductory phrase 'in that day' (11:10, 11).

There are wonderful fulfilments of these gospel promises in the 'now' of our present Christian experience, living under Christ's lordship, but the grandest fulfilment, even for us, is still future, in the 'not yet'. So, the Root of Jesse has become 'a banner for the peoples' (11:10), providing glorious rest for all who turn to him and trust him. Just as he dried up the Red Sea to bring his people out of Egypt, so he will dry up the river Euphrates, the life blood of the Assyrian people, to liberate his exiled people (11:15-16). The Old Testament language describes the gospel reality that no power can resist God's redemptive purposes. He will bring all his people into the rest of his kingly rule.

As that process develops and moves inexorably to its completion, there is already great rejoicing in the Lord who is his people's strength, song and salvation (12:1-3). Notice how their characteristic is faith ('I will trust') which looks to no one other than the LORD for deliverance ('and not be afraid'), settling the controversy which has been raging in these chapters. Faith not fear, promises not policies, God not man – these were the choices facing Isaiah's hearers then and which still face his readers today. The great benefits of being among those people are to be proclaimed evangelistically to all the nations, as they are invited to share the greatest of all God's blessings – the presence of the Holy One among his people, Immanuel – God with us (12:4-6 cf. Rev. 21:3-4).

Preaching and Teaching the Text

Title: **Cosmic hope**

Text: **Isaiah 11:1–12:6**

Structure: The contrast of the mighty forest God destroys (10:33-34) and the shoot from Jesse's stump (11:1)

1.   The nature of the King (vv. 2-5)
     – character (vv. 1–3a)
     – revealed in activity (vv. 3b–5)
2.   The purpose of his rule (vv. 6-10)
     – reversal of the fall (vv. 6-9)
     – gathering of the nations (v10)
3.   The people of this hope (11:11–12:6)
     – universal peace and reconciliation (11:11-16)
     – universal praise and proclamation (12:1-6)

Leading a Bible Study

1.   11:1 How does this verse make its point in contrast to 10:33-34?

2.   11:2-5 How does this description of the Branch focus the hearer's hope? What are his characteristics and how are they displayed in our Lord Jesus Christ?

3.   11:6-9 What are the features of his kingly rule and how do they reverse the effects of the fall?

4.   11:10-16 What will the 'Root of Jesse' accomplish for his people? Note the Exodus vocabulary. How are these Old Testament pictures fulfilled in the New Testament gospel?

5.   12:1-3 What does this epilogue to the whole unit add to our understanding of God's rescue purposes? (Note that in v. 1 'you' is singular and in v. 3 it is plural.)

6.   12:4-6 What is the heart of the praise song to Yahweh and why does all the earth need to hear it?

Application: Once again the Messianic hope for the remnant, made righteous through faith in the promises, becomes the future focus of the Lord's grace, beyond the inevitable coming judgement. All this constitutes a great gospel analogy which exalts Christ and stimulates us to wait in faith for its consummation.

Part 3
King of the Nations
Yahweh's universal sovereignty

Isaiah 13–27

'The whole cycle takes the principles, blessings and warnings of chapters 7–11 on to the next stage, in particular seeking to affirm that the Lord is really and truly ruling history and guiding it to his predetermined end.'

Alec Motyer, *The Prophecy of Isaiah*, p134

Introduction

This unit presents the contemporary preacher with a number of challenges which perhaps indicate why it is among the least read, let alone preached, sections of the whole book. This material, however, is essential for an understanding of Isaiah's prophecy, and merely to pass over it could seriously distort our perception of his message. On the other hand, I would not advocate a ten-week Sunday preaching series in which each oracle was the focus of one sermon. Their variety in length and difficulty of language, combined with their historical distance from us, all leave the expositor in a dilemma.

The 'big picture' relevance to Isaiah's teaching is that all the nations are equally under the sovereign control of the 'Holy One of Israel'. It is therefore useless to look to policies of alliance to deliver God's people from their enemies, rather than to rely on the promises of God. It is equally unnecessary to be afraid of their power, since it is totally dependent on Yahweh's will, and he will always govern the world for the outworking of his plans in the deliverance and protection of his people, as they trust him and obey him. The knowledge of chapters 13–27 is what will turn an unbelieving Ahaz into a prayerfully dependent Hezekiah (ch. 37).

It is knowledge that we need as God's people today. Our worldview needs to be shaped by the conviction that God is governing the history of our planet for the outworking of his eternal kingdom purposes, through the faith of his New Covenant people, the worldwide church. The detail of these oracles can be used to illustrate the similarity of the opportunities and challenges we face, and to strengthen our convictions about God's sovereign grace and power, so that we also come to trust and obey him more.

The section needs to be preached, but probably by selecting two or three of the more dominant oracles, such as Babylon (13:1–14:2), Egypt (19:1–20:6) and Jerusalem (22:1-5) as a representative of the whole. Suggestions for this approach can be found at the end of this chapter.

1. Context and Structure

This unit is probably the least-read and preached section of the whole book of Isaiah. Even experienced commentators refer to its 'tantalizing obscurity'.[1] But there is a basic structure to this part of Isaiah's book and it is not difficult to identify each oracle from its title, or introduction. They are not arranged in chronological order, but grouped together according to other criteria. Motyer argues convincingly that the ten oracles (or 'burdens') between chapters 13 and 23 can be divided into two groups of five, of which the first set is more specific and the second more generalised.[2]

What we observe is that these oracles concern the nations of the ancient Near East, as follows: (1) Babylon (13:1–14:27) concluding with a brief prophecy against Assyria, the super power of Isaiah's day; (2) Philistia (14:28-32); (3) Moab (15:1–16:14); (4) Damascus and Ephraim (17:1–18:7) referring to the current opponents of Judah in Isaiah's time – Syria and Israel; (5) Egypt (19:1–20:6). The argument for the second cycle rests partly on the reappearance of Babylon at 21:1. The sequence then runs: (6) Babylon (21:1-10); (7) Edom (21:11-12); (8) Arabia (21:13-17); (9) Jerusalem (22:1-25); (10) Tyre (23:1-18). Chapters 24–27 can then be regarded as a third cycle although it is a continuous whole, not a selection of oracles.

1. William J. Dumbrell, *The Faith of Israel* (Leicester, UK: Apollos 1988) p105. This comment was removed from later editions.
2. Alec Motyer, *The Prophecy of Isaiah*, p131-132.

In it, the world's civilisation (city), doomed to be destroyed by God's righteous judgement, is contrasted with the strong city, inhabited by God's redeemed people, which is destined to fill the world, as his fruitful vineyard (27:2 cf. 5:1-6) and as the fulfilment of the vision of 2:1-4.

The positioning of this material here in the book is deliberate and instructive. Chapters 1–5 dealt mainly with the threat of judgement and 6–12 with the promise of rescue through the Immanuel figure. This taught us that the promises God made to David concerning his eternal dynasty will be kept, and will reach their fruition in the coming of the great king, described in 11:1-5. While it looks as though Assyria will destroy God's people, we have already learned that Assyria is merely a rod in God's hands and will herself be judged and destroyed for her atrocities. Israel will suffer exile at her hands, but although Judah will be 'up to the neck' in the swirling floods, God will preserve Jerusalem and the danger will be turned away. However, by chapter 39 we learn that it is Babylon which Judah should fear, because that is the nation which will overthrow Zion and exile God's people. Although Isaiah does not disclose this in detail until 39:1-8, it explains why he chooses to begin each of his twin cycles with Babylon – Judah's enemy in chief. If even this great power is totally under Yahweh's sovereign control, then no human agency is able to stop him fulfil his purposes.

2. Preaching Notes

At first sight, this stretch of Isaiah's prophecy can appear to be quite uninviting for the contemporary preacher. The issues seem to belong to history long past. Some of the meanings are opaque, if not obscure. Much of the material can appear to be unremittingly doom-laden, with the repetitive theme of judgement all but exterminating the light of hope. It is hardly surprising that most contemporary Christians will never have heard a sermon from this part of Isaiah's book.

'At first sight'...but take another look! The way to do that is to root these chapters firmly in their original purpose and to cut with the grain of the text, in order to expose its unchanging message and expound its implications for us today. Start with the Bible, not with the demands of your congregation.

Isaiah's work is to be a faith-builder, albeit for a comparatively small remnant, who will rally to God's word, trust his promises and obey his commands. The life of faith is always the life of obedience. Throughout the Bible, when God's people obey his commands it is because they believe his promises, and God gives his promises in order to strengthen faith and encourage their obedience. Promise and command belong together in Scripture and our present-day discipleship equally. These chapters are faith-builders, both as they reveal how God is working in his world, and also as they expose the human rebellion and resistance endemic in man's response to God's sovereignty. They reveal the nature, character and purposes of the creator, while at the same time exposing the folly of human antagonism to God in his world and where that must inevitably lead. Now we are beginning to hear Isaiah as an urgent message for today.

We need these chapters to teach us lessons of which the church today is in desperate need. So, teach the character of God and the ongoing sweep of his purposes from creation to the new creation, from Eden to the New Covenant, from these great texts. In our media-saturated society, even we

Christians don't really believe that God reigns and that everything that happens in our world is under his control and orchestrated towards the fulfilment of his eternal plan. The proof of that lies in our dependence on 'the nations', on human abilities and resources, to see us through.

We can substitute the New Testament's 'the world' for Isaiah's 'the nations' and it all comes alive. Often in the church we are virtually indistinguishable from the culture around us. We have the same priorities and methodologies, the same confidences in man-made plans and resources, the same idols of the heart, though ours often wear religious clothing. So the church (like Judah) is too often weak and vulnerable, oppressed and ridiculed, compromised and defeated. We need the refreshing and humbling perspective of 'the Holy One of Israel' to accept and learn the revelation of the Lord's true character which is the major contribution of these chapters of Isaiah to the sum total of Scripture.

These chapters will also help us to teach the overview of God's great eternal purposes. As we look back on the fulfilment of these prophecies in history, we are convinced that God's purposes will most certainly come to fruition. The timeline may not always be clear, but the theological significance is unarguable. Like the remnant, we are to be patient and remain faithful. These chapters assure us that God is active now, in renewing his people and working towards the final coming of the kingdom, but that this 'now' is a day of grace, when the prophetic warnings can be heeded, through repentance and faith, and when those of every people and nation are being gathered to him. The glory of the Lord will fill the whole earth (11:9), just as it did the temple (6:3), and the light of his presence will outshine the sun and the moon. At a time when God's church is routinely rubbished and his name blasphemed, we need the health-giving instruction of his revealed word, not just to comfort, but also to nerve and put courage into us, as the redeemed of the Lord.

One further very clear benefit of these chapters is their relentless exposure of those attitudes of heart and mind and patterns of behaviour by which the world seeks to squeeze believers into its mould. We need the message that all of earth's proud empires pass away, because as John Oswalt comments, 'It is all too easy to be blown away by the glory of the world…and we think, 'Ah, there is reality'. But that is not where glory resides.'[3]

We too need to be challenged not to put our trust in men (cf. 2:22), whether it is in our western democratic structures, our personal experience and abilities, or even our church programme and its leadership. They are all human in composition and therefore temporary and passing. But, to quote Oswalt again, 'If we put our trust in God and give our lives to finding out his nature and purposes, that will endure whatever crashes time may bring on us.'[4] We need Isaiah's lessons about human pride, with its over-developed self-confidence and its inherent tendency to refuse to submit to God's authority in the deepest recesses of our hearts. We need the exhortation not to trust in what we see, because it is only the unseen realities which are eternal (cf. 2 Cor. 4:16-18). We need to look for our allies not in big business or information technology or communication science; we need to look to God alone.

---

3. John N. Oswalt, *Isaiah: The NIV Application Commentary*, p202
4. *IBID.* p203

Before looking at possible outlines for this section it is important to consider it as a whole from a preaching point of view. It may not be the best plan to work through the ten oracles, one by one, week by week. It is, of course, possible to adopt that approach and biblically justifiable, insofar as we can draw out the reasons why Isaiah has collected these oracles from different periods of his ministry and arranged them in this order. But for most congregations it will probably be better to take some representative passages, since the time for teaching is limited, as is the appetite of many hearers for historical detail. One might select, for example, chapter 13 dealing with Babylon, representative of human pride and glory under God's judgement, and balance that with Tyre in chapter 23 as typical of human wealth and its trust in material prosperity rather than God. Other representative passages could include Egypt (ch.19) and Jerusalem (ch.22), with their contrasting relationship to God, as those outside and within the covenant. Chapters 25 and 26 might then form one exposition, set against the background of the judgement of the whole world (ch. 24) and the expansion and renewal of God's covenant people (ch. 27).

3. Working Through the Text
We shall divide 13–23 into the ten constituent oracles and then explore 24–27 as a continuous entity.

1. First Oracle – Babylon (13:1–14:27)
The oracle (13:1-22) is followed by a taunt (14:3-23), and they are separated by a contrasting announcement of salvation for God's people (14:1-2).[5] These prophecies are primarily designed for God's people to hear, to kindle their

---

5. Barry Webb, *The Message of Isaiah*, p80

faith in God's sovereignty and to prevent them from putting their confidence anywhere other than in Yahweh. We should not imagine Isaiah on a middle-eastern preaching tour, so much as instructing Judah and Jerusalem about God's perspective, which they should share, of his governance of history, in which they are living.

Babylon is, of course, symbolic in Scripture of human defiance and rebellion against God from the tower of Babel (Gen. 11:1-9) onwards. Jeremiah 51 is a particularly powerful Old Testament example of this. The continuance and culmination of this biblical symbolism into the New Testament (see especially Rev. 14:8; 16:19; 17:5; 18:2, 10), with God's ultimate victory over evil, will provide some fruitful connections for the details of this oracle as we apply it to our own contemporary context.

Isaiah's declaration here has a great deal to do with this symbolic significance of Babylon. The major challenge is to discern the two intertwining strands of historical Babylon and symbolic Babylon as the details of Babylon's historical downfall merge with God's final judgement of all rebellious human arrogance and defiance. In 13:2-5, 'the LORD Almighty is mustering an army for war', but is it the Babylonians who are his agents, or are they the target of this divinely generated attack? Because the armies are summoned from the 'ends of the heavens', as well as the earth, and are set 'to destroy the whole world' (13:5 – see same wording at 14:26) it seems that God's historical judgement on Babylon, which is clearly prophesied in 13:17ff., is to be regarded as a prototype of the ultimate execution of his wrath, on the last day, the day of the Lord (13:6, 9). As the two reference points merge, the emphasis is on the fact that such horrors are the initiative of the LORD

Almighty, which is both why the terror is so great (13:6-8) and why any hope of escape is impossible (13:14-16). The historical invasion may be attributable to the Medes, who with the Persians under Cyrus conquered Babylon, but the true agent, as with the ultimate eschatological judgement, is God himself (13:19).

Even more significant, however, is the reason for this action, which is the focus of the unit at 14:1-2. In Scripture, judgement and salvation are the two sides of one coin because the justice and mercy of God are two aspects of his unchanging character. So while God's judgement must fall on all ungodliness, these verses teach us that his ultimate purpose in defeating and destroying the forces of evil is the settlement and security of his people, who in keeping with the eschatological context are now revealed as a universal community.

Such confidence generates the taunt song of 14:3-23, which is a satirical poem describing and deriding the fall and death of a world ruler (14:3-6), which spells a degree of peace for the beleaguered world (14:7-8). Imagining this proud tyrant's arrival in Sheol, his complete lack of power and imminent decomposition are the subject of the writer's exaltation (14:9-11).

We are probably to see in this defeated dictator a powerful symbol of all human rebellion against God, though many preachers and commentators have taken their cue from 14:12, where he is described as the 'morning star', or Lucifer, to see in this figure a picture of the devil and his eviction from heaven (cf. Luke 10:18; Rev. 12:7-9).

It is equally true of the countless tyrants who have briefly exercised power in earthly kingdoms and who were determined to exterminate the knowledge of God along with his people, his promises and his plans. Such arrogance is typical of the devil, the archetypal rebel, so the dividing line is hard to draw and not of great importance. 14:16-21 return to the earthly context where this dead tyrant has no decent burial and where his offspring are slaughtered. The summary verses, 14:22-23, form a fitting and chilling conclusion to the oracle. But before moving elsewhere, Isaiah stops to apply the same principles to Assyria (14:24-27), assuring God's people that the mightiest power in their present cannot for one moment thwart God's purposes, and that no power (such as Babylon) which may succeed them in the future will be able to do so either.

Preaching and Teaching the Text
Title: **The end of human pride**
Text: **Isaiah 13:1–14:2**
Structure:

    1. The inescapable judgement is coming (vv. 1-8)
    2. The explanation of its terrors (vv. 9-22)
    3. The salvation which is the other side of the coin (14:1-2)

Leading a Bible Study
1.   13:1-5 What is happening in the text, as the oracle begins?
2.   13:6-8 What do these vivid pictures tell us about the coming day of the LORD?
3.   13:9-13 What is the explanation of these terrifying events? Work through God's diagnosis of the reasons.
4.   13:14-16 How do these verses reinforce the solemnity of Isaiah's message? How can this whole section help us to understand and teach the realities of God's wrath?

5.   13:17-22 Identify the ingredients that make up the fall of Babylon. How do these help us to understand what is going on in our world too?

6.   14:1-2 What is God's contrasting reaction to his people? How does this help to explain the universal judgement which chapter 13 prefigures?

Application: The fall of Babylon merges with (and is therefore symbolic of) the day of judgement for the whole rebellious world. The passage unlocks not just the fact (why the terrifying detail?) but also the reasons behind it and the purpose of salvation and renewal for God's people which lie beyond it (14:1-2). If we take these as representative of the coming last judgement, what warnings and encouragements should we draw from this study?

2. Second Oracle – Philistia (14:28-32)

See Motyer[6] for a detailed and helpful reconstruction of the historical circumstances generated by the death of Ahaz in 715 BC (14:28) and the subsequent appeal to Hezekiah his son to join an anti-Assyrian alliance, probably with Egypt as well as the Philistines. The broken rod is not Ahaz but the Assyrian emperor, Shalmaneser, who had died. This is confirmed by v31b where the 'smoke out of the north' is the darting venomous serpent of v29 and clearly refers to the Assyrians. The empire was not about to collapse, but to become even stronger under his successor, Sargon (14:29). While Judah will be protected by the Lord (14:30a cf. 14:25), Philistia is doomed to disaster (14:30b-31) and was in fact overrun by the Assyrians during the decade 711–701 BC. The oracle's purpose is theological (14:32). Hezekiah is to refuse human politicking and put his

---

6. Alec Motyer, The Prophecy of Isaiah, p.147

confidence in the faithfulness and power of Yahweh to keep his Zion promises in the defence of his suffering people. It is the same exhortation as to Ahaz – promises not policies.

3. Third Oracle – Moab (15:1–16:14)

This oracle is in the form of a lament, characterised by weeping (15:3, 5, 8) because of Moab's destruction, which mops up alike those who flee and those who remain (15:9). The evacuation is southwards because the enemy, Assyria, comes from the north. At 16:1, the Moabites are in such a state of despair that they contemplate appealing to Judah for help, in the terms of 16:3-4a. The response follows in 16:4b-5, offering even to Moab, who had opposed so often and for so long, the blessings of righteous Davidic kingship. This surely points forward to the universal nature of the Messianic kingdom. But the blessings of 16:5 cannot be received by Moab because of her attitude (16:6). The wailing and mourning will therefore continue (16:7-11) and all her prayers are 'to no avail' (16:12), for there is only one prayer-answering God, whom she has chosen to reject. Her fall now appears to be inescapable (16:13-14).

4. Fourth Oracle – Damascus and Ephraim (17:1–18:7)

Aram (Syria) with its capital Damascus and Ephraim (Israel) with its capital Samaria are linked together in 17:1-3 because of their alliance against Ahaz (see chapter 7). Linked in common opposition to the Davidic monarchy in Judah, they are also joined together in the consequences of God's judgement. Both capitals will be destroyed – Damascus in 732 BC and Samaria in 722 BC. All that will remain of the glory of Israel is 'some gleanings,' 'two or three olives' (17:6). The focus turns to Israel (17:7-11), as her idolatry is exposed in all its stunning emptiness along with her rejection of God, so that all her plans to recover are frustrated.

17:12–18:7 follow on here, whatever their original setting, in order to underline the major theme of the unit, that Yahweh rules the world to accomplish his will, and carries out his purposes of saving grace for those who trust him. Though the nations rage (cf. Ps. 2) they will soon be removed by God's rebuke, and so they are not to inspire fear in his people (17:12-14). The oracle about Cush (Ethiopia), the land of flies, can be included in this section, since its message is substantially the same. Instead of their envoys coming to invite Judah to sign up to an anti-Assyrian coalition, they should know that God will act to remove the threat from Assyria, in his own time and way (18:1-6). Mount Zion is the centre of world rule in reality (18:7), and one day Ethiopia will come to acknowledge Zion's Lord. While human policies are always producing death, by contrast, God's promises are life-giving, and his mercy extends far beyond the boundaries of Judah.

5. Fifth Oracle – Egypt (19:1–20:6)

In some ways, this is the most amazing of all the oracles in this unit. Yahweh himself is coming in power and majesty to Egypt, and its people and their idols are terrified (19:1). Internal strife coupled with ineffective leadership will deliver the country 'to the power of a cruel master' (19:2-4). The economic structures will collapse (19:5-10), and all the accumulated godless wisdom is revealed to be empty and useless (19:11-15). All this is the work of Yahweh (19:14a).

At 19:16 the prophecy changes to prose and runs into five paragraphs, each beginning 'in that day' (verses 16, 18,

19, 23, 24). The phrase indicates an unspecified future time, when God will revolutionise Egypt's outlook. After the judgement, comes restoration and healing (19:22). To ally oneself with the country under judgement in 19:1-15 would be folly of the highest order, and Hezekiah needed to know that, as he was being tempted to rely on Egypt (see 30:1-5; 31:1-3). But God wounds in order to heal, and his mercy extends even to Egypt. The vision of reconciliation and unity with Judah, grounded in a common fear of the Lord, a common language, common worship and a common experience of salvation (19:18-22) looks forward to a new world order. Israel's greatest enemies, Egypt and now Assyria (19:23-25), are to be equal partners with the sons of Abraham as God's people, enjoying his blessing.

The curious addition of 20:1-6 now makes perfect sense. The day will come when all the nations will bow the knee to Yahweh, but that is in the future. In Isaiah's time, Egypt and Cush would fall to Assyria's power and be taken stripped and barefoot into captivity – a picture of abject humiliation and shame, a reality prefigured and enacted by Isaiah for three years (20:3). 'Why would you ever trust such a powerless degraded people?' is Isaiah's question (20:6). How could you possibly expect them to be of the slightest help, when they are reduced to nothing? The survey of the nations shows that ultimately only Yahweh rules in the affairs of men, and therefore he is the only one to be trusted (see the use of the concept of trust and reliance in 20:5-6).

Preaching and Teaching the Text

Title: **Beware! God is at work**

Text: **Isaiah 19:1–20:6**

Structure: What happens when God comes to Egypt (v. 1)?

1.   Judgement (19:1-15), which is seen to be working out
     in the structures of the country
     – socially (vv. 2-4)
     – economically (vv. 5-10)
     – politically (vv. 11-15)

2.   Healing (19:16-25), which will be seen in God's future
     blessing
     – reconciliation (vv. 16-19)
     – deliverance (vv. 20-22)
     – unity (vv. 23-26)

3.   Understanding (20:1-6) – because Egypt will fall to
     Assyria don't look to her for help. She needs to look to
     the Lord and one day will.

Leading a Bible Study

1.   19:1-4 As God comes to call Egypt to account, what
     does verse 1 tell us about these two contenders? How
     is God's judgement active in the social structures of
     Egypt?

2.   19:5-10 What are the signs of judgement in Egypt's
     economy?

3.   19:11-15 How is God acting in judgement in the
     political life of the country?

4.   19:16-25 Following the phrase 'in that day' as a marker
     separating out the five prose paragraphs, compile a list
     of ways in which the Lord will heal the land he has
     struck.

5.   19:16-25 What is the significance of these details of
      his healing and what are their continuing implications?
6.   20:1-6 What is Isaiah's enacted sign of shame and
      captivity designed to teach his own countrymen, in the
      light of chapter 19?

Application: As Egypt is a Gentile nation, we can be
sure that these principles are still being worked out with
regard to unbelieving humanity. Work on the parallels to
contemporary cultures in 19:1-15 and then to God's healing
work in the gospel (19:16-25).

6. Sixth Oracle – Babylon (21:1-10)

The 'desert by the sea' is a strange title (21:1) for this oracle,
since it does not seem to be at all applicable to Babylon,
whose fall is clearly the climax of the section (21:9). Perhaps
the sea is the Dead Sea. The whirlwinds around it are a
powerful visual image of the attacks from Elam and Media
(21:2). The staggering news that the watchman receives
seems almost unbelievable – 'Babylon has fallen, has fallen!'
(21:8-9). Once again, the message is not to trust in the
nations, since we know that Hezekiah received emissaries
from Babylon, to whom he showed all the treasures in his
palace. Presumably they came to encourage him to join in
yet another anti-Assyrian alliance (see 39:1-8). But even
though Babylon seems so powerful and is emerging as the
greatest challenge to Assyria in Isaiah's day, Judah needs to
know that if she relies on Babylon, she will be 'crushed on
the threshing-floor' (21:10). Babylon's power, like its gods,
will lie 'shattered on the ground'.

7. *Seventh Oracle – Edom (21:11-12)*

This mysterious oracle concerns 'Dumah',[7] which means 'silence'. While scholars have identified 'an Assyrian oasis... about three hundred miles southeast of Jerusalem' called Dumah, the question Isaiah is asked comes from Seir, which is Edom. Motyer suggests that this corresponds to oracle 2, concerning Philistia, since both feature Gentiles misunderstanding their tumultuous and troubled times and asking, 'Where is everything going?' as greater darkness and uncertainty envelop them.[8] The heart of the enquiry to Isaiah seems to be, 'How much longer will this night last?' (21:11). His somewhat enigmatic reply signals an unspecified time of waiting – silence (21:12). Release will come, but there is yet more darkness to be endured.

8. *Eighth Oracle – Arabia (21:13-17)*

The Arabians living in the desert between Babylon and Judah would look to Tema (21:14) as an oasis where their caravans could find water, food and refreshment. But the caravan routes were insecure and the whole Arabian area suffered unrest throughout this period of Assyrian activity. Even the nomadic tribe of Kedar, descendants of Ishmael's second son (Gen. 25:13), could not escape the Assyrian scourge (21:16).

9. *Ninth Oracle – Jerusalem (22:1-25)*

This is another oracle with a mysterious title. 'The Valley of Vision' (22:1) seems almost a self-contradiction. However, Oswalt suggests it may be a subtle condemnation of Judah's lack of spiritual vision, on Isaiah's part.[9] In any case, it begins with the people on their rooftops and the city 'full

7. John N. Oswalt, Isaiah: The NIV Application Commentary, p.254
8. Alec Motyer, The Prophecy of Isaiah, p.176
9. John N. Oswalt, Isaiah: The NIV Application Commentary, p.261

of commotion' (22:1-2), full of rejoicing and festivity. Isaiah, though, sees that what they celebrate is at best only a short-term deliverance. His vision extends to a future day when revelry will be turned to shame. Here the future picture seems to be of events including a siege (22:2b-3), the fulfilment of which 2 Kings 25:1-4 describes, when Nebuchadnezzar took the city. God is already mourning (22:4) as the city suffers 'a day of battering' under his inescapable righteous judgement (22:5-8a). Yet even in this crisis, they still look to their weapons, to Hezekiah's water tunnel, rather than to the Lord (22:8b-11) and all his pleas to them to repent have fallen on deaf ears (22:12-13), so that there is no possibility of atonement (22:14).

22:15-19 are a denunciation of Shebna, 'You mighty man,' who seems to be the king's right-hand man. He stands here as an example of all that God detests and rejects in Jerusalem, as a self-made man who arrogates to himself pomp and privilege, even planning a tomb worthy of a king (22:16). He has achieved his position by his own works and intends to preserve it now, with his 'splendid chariots' and for posterity with his 'resting place in the rock'. But just as for the nations and the city, God has a day of reckoning for this man of the world, who is an individual example of the national corruption (22:17-19).

By way of contrast, Eliakim secures God's commendation and favour (22:20-24) and is the polar opposite of Shebna. This servant of the Lord will be appointed in Shebna's place and demonstrate godly characteristics as a father to the people, a ruler of faithfulness and dependability, like a firm peg on which others can hang. But he is not the Messiah. One day, the peg will snap and its load will be cut down. No human figure can carry the weight of government because even the best have feet of clay. Jerusalem can only become the faithful city, which God intends her to be, when the divine-human ruler, Immanuel, the prince of righteousness and peace, is revealed.

Preaching and Teaching the Text

Title: **The folly of short-sightedness**

Text: **Isaiah 22:1-25**

Structure: Isaiah outlines a catalogue of Judah's mistakes, brought about by short-term misjudgements caused by lack of dependence on God.

Mistake 1   Rejoicing in a short-term deliverance, but refusing to accept what lies ahead (vv. 1-8a)

Mistake 2   Looking to human plans and resources, but not acknowledging God as their supplier (vv. 8b-11)

Mistake 3   Fatalistic feasting in the face of danger, but not repenting and seeking God's mercy (vv. 12-14)

Mistake 4   (Shebna) Building a name and reputation for oneself, but not recognising one's total dependence on the Lord (vv. 15-19)

Conclusion: Even a good ruler like Eliakim (vv. 20-23) is insufficient to carry the weight of government (vv. 24-25). We are reminded of the necessity that Immanuel should come (9:6-7).

Leading a Bible Study

1.   22:1-4 The chapter context identifies the 'valley of vision' as Jerusalem. What is going on in the city and why is Isaiah's reaction so different from that of the citizens?

2.   22:5-7 Why is the prophet weeping bitter tears? What is the vision of the future he has received?

3. 22:8-11 What accusations do these verses bring against Jerusalem and why?

4. 22:12-14 What is God's perspective on these events and Jerusalem's attitude to them?

5. 22:15-19 We shall meet Shebna, the steward, again, along with Eliakim at 36:3f.; both are high officials in Hezekiah's government. What is God's estimate of Shebna? On what is this based and what will God's reaction be?

6. 22:20-25 By contrast, why is Eliakim commended by God? What warning does God give even about this 'father' of the people?

Application: Remember that this chapter refers to covenant people and therefore has lines of application to the church. Explore the ways in which we too may drift back to the sort of ungodly behaviour exhibited in Jerusalem and typified by Shebna. Consider how even Eliakim is insufficient to carry the weight of David's house and this prefigures the need for a greater ruler, fulfilled in Christ and the gospel. Are there ways we can depend on men's leadership, forgetting our need for Christ's rule?

10. Tenth Oracle – Tyre (23:1-18)

23:1-14 form a unified 'woe' song or lament bracketed by the invocation 'Wail, O ships of Tarshish' (23:1, 14). The reason is clear, but almost incredible, 'Tyre is destroyed' (23:1). This dramatic opening pictures the Phoenician merchant ships putting in at Cyprus on their way home from Tarshish, a Phoenician colony far in the west in Spain, only to be told that there is nothing to go home to. The significance for Judah is explained by the strong trade links, which had developed since the days of united

monarchy. But now the very hub of the Mediterranean
world of commerce has fallen. Just as the first cycle closed
with the oracle against Egypt exposing the folly of putting
confidence in human politics or armies, so the second cycle
warns of the vulnerability of human trade and commerce,
the uncertainty of riches. The opening verses (1-8) reflect
the world's stunned reaction that such an 'impossible' thing
could happen. What can explain it?

23:9 provides the equally stunning answer, 'The LORD
Almighty planned it, to bring low the pride of all glory and
to humble all who are renowned on the earth'. If he can
bring about the subjugation of the Babylonians at the hands
of the Assyrians (23:13) then Phoenicia is not immune
(23:11). But in neither case was their defeat final, and we
already know that Assyria herself will eventually meet the
same doom. So, the last section, 23:15-18, looks beyond a
period of seventy years when 'the LORD will deal with Tyre'
(23:17) in restoration and when she will again become a
centre of world trade. But as Barry Webb comments, 'this
is where history gives way to eschatology',[10] as 'Isaiah's
words…set all that Tyre represents in the light of eternity.
Wealth is the gift of God and it will eventually return to the
giver' (23:18a). That is why the people of God are not to
trust in the riches of their human 'owners', but in the Lord
who is the giver of all good. Once again, the issue of trust
is foremost. Where will Judah's confidence lie – in human
prosperity or in the divine promises?

Chapters 24–27 continue this eschatological theme,
which seems to be a better description of this tightly-
woven unit than 'apocalyptic'. The controlling perspective
is always the far horizon – the 'eschaton' or end, when the

---

10. Barry Webb, *The Message of Isaiah*, p105.

final and eternal judgement and salvation of God will be revealed. But the focus of interest is always the people of God, the city of Jerusalem, both because this is the ultimate location of all God's gracious work for fallen humanity and also because the dominant agenda of the book concerns the transformation of the faithless harlot city into the faithful city of righteousness, as we have noted.

Preaching and Teaching the Text
Title: **The poverty of human wealth**
Text: **Isaiah 23:1-18**
Structure: Human wealth, which does not acknowledge God, is the target of the divine judgement, in the fall of Tyre.
1. The uncertainty of riches (vv. 1-7)
      – the consequence is human disillusionment
2. The sovereign authority of God (vv. 8-14)
      – the consequence is human instability
3. The promise of restoration (vv. 15-18)
      – the consequence is divine glory.

Leading a Bible Study
1.   23:1-3 What has happened in the opening verses of this oracle to the financial capital of the eastern Mediterranean, and why is it so shocking?
2.   23:4-7 What are the emotive reactions of the various peoples in these verses and what do they show about their view of Tyre?
3.   23:8-9 Why did the downfall of Tyre (human wealth) occur?
4.   23:10-14 What are the consequences for the other nations of Tyre's demise? What is the effect of the mention of Assyria in verse 13?

5.   23:15-18 Why is this not the end of the story for Tyre?
      What will God do for her in the future and for what
      reasons?

Application: Just as human pride was the target of God's
wrath in chapter 13, so here it is human wealth that
imagines it does not need God and can live independently
of him. Explore the parallels in the contemporary world
and the subtle ways they invade the church and seek to
conform Christians to their image. But note too the way in
which Tyre will be used for God's glory in restoration, just
as his sovereign authority was demonstrated by his wrath.
Compare how the same pattern is predicted at the end of
time (see Rev. 21:24-27).

11. *The earth is judged (24:1-23)*

As if to sum up and pull together all the individual nations
referred to in chapters 13–23, the whole earth now becomes
the focus of our attention (24:1). The opening statement of
devastating judgement on the planet (24:1-3) emphasises
individual inescapability (v. 2) in a punishment which is
seen to be total (v. 3). This is followed by one of the most
chilling passages in the whole of the Bible (24:4-13) where
everything that makes human life sustainable and enjoyable
is systematically destroyed – 'a curse consumes the earth.'
This recalls Genesis 3:17ff. where the curse follows sin,
and that same connection is established here in 24:5. The
'everlasting covenant' in this verse is probably referring to
the covenant with Noah (Gen. 9:16f.) which provided a
secure environment on earth for human life. 'In essence,
the annulling of the covenant was the refusal to live in the
fellowship which God opened.'[11]

---

11. Alec Motyer, *The Prophecy of Isaiah*, p199

However, even in the context of such total judgement, there are rays of hope. 'Very few are left' (24:6b) but not all are destroyed. There are 'gleanings…left after the grape harvest' (24:13). This explains the sudden and startling contrast of 24:14-16, where in the place of lament we hear shouts of joy, acclaiming the Lord's majesty and singing 'Glory to the Righteous One.' There will be a righteous remnant, brought through the judgement as trophies of God's grace, celebrating his great salvation, as the next chapters will expand. But here, it is all too short-lived and 24:16b-23 returns us to the theme of awesome judgement with images of treachery and snares, flood and earthquake, so that even the heavenly bodies are involved. They were, of course, the objects of worship in the pagan religion of Assyria and Babylon. Yet they are only created things, over which Yahweh reigns in total sovereignty. The surprise at the end of the chapter is that this glorious reign is to be exercised 'on Mount Zion and in Jerusalem, and before its elders' (24:23b).

12. *The Lord is praised (25:1–26:21)*
26:1 makes it clear that there are two songs of praise in sequence here. The second (26:1-21) is a future song for Judah, celebrating her personal security grounded in Yahweh's preserving care. The first (25:1-12) is perhaps the song of Zion's elders (24:23), picking up the celebration of glory to the Righteous One from earlier in that chapter. In both chapters the Lord himself is the focus of praise since who he is and what he does prompt the adoration which is due to him alone.

26:1-5 praise him for his mighty deeds, which reveal and confirm the steadfastness of his unchanging character.

He makes and keeps his promises. The verses review how Yahweh has carried out his personal plans (v. 1), brought down all his opponents (v. 2), secured the recognition of his sovereignty in his government of the nations (v. 3) and demonstrated his special care for the helpless (v. 4). No wonder the section begins with a reflection on what it means to be Yahweh's people and affirms, in personal trust, 'O LORD, you are my God; I will exalt you...' (25:1).

25:6-8 extends the praise to his glorious provision for all his people, symbolised by a magnificent royal banquet, spread by the Lord as his free gift. It is the best of everything, available 'for all peoples' (v. 6). This theme begins in Exodus 24 where the covenant is sealed as Moses and the elders of Israel eat with God. It develops in chapter 55 of Isaiah where the invitation to attend the banquet is the climax of the benefits which flow from the Servant's work. It is used several times in the gospels as an image of life in the eternal kingdom. But not only does God provide rich provision for life, he also removes death (25:7-8), which is the curse imposed as a result of sin. Everything necessary for eternal life, in all its fulfilment, is made available by this generous Lord to all who put their faith in him.

The last section, 25:9-12, celebrates the simple but profound theological reality which undergirds all God's blessings. The verbs of 25:9 are very instructive: 'We trusted...he saved...let us rejoice...' But note too how the Lord himself is the object of his people's praise – 'This is our God...This is the LORD'. But if the Lord's hand rests on his people, his enemies are trampled under his feet (25:10). The mention of Moab takes us back to chapter 16, where Moab's pride prevented her from seeking the Lord.

Here, that same pride excludes her from the blessings of the messianic banquet (25:11).

In chapter 26, the Zion motif is very strong, as the redeemed city celebrates its security, as a safe stronghold (26:1-6). This is its intrinsic identity because its walls are not of human construction, but are the salvation God affords to his people (v. 1). This is contrasted in 26:5-6 with the lofty city of men's making, which we know will be cast 'down to the dust'. In-between, 26:2-4 teaches us the difference between the two cities. The gates of God's city are open to the righteous (v. 2), who are such because they trust in the LORD and so experience his 'perfect peace' (vv. 3-4). This is justification by faith, with its fruit of peace (cf. Rom. 5:1), embracing those from every nation who turn in faith to the Lord.

But then at 26:7, there is a sudden change of tone from confident affirmation to reflection and meditation. Though the paths of God's people are level and smooth (v. 7), this implies that they will lead straight to their destination, not that they will always be easy and pleasant. Here we seem to be in the waiting time, when God's name does not appear to be vindicated, when the wicked seem to continue unchecked and when his people can only plead for his zeal to be revealed (26:8-11).

Two prayers follow, each addressed directly to the Lord. The first (26:12-15) looks back on what is already being enjoyed and recognises this peace, referred to earlier at 26:3, as entirely Yahweh's work. He delivered his people from adversity, from their many oppressors, who are now forgotten. He has brought increase to the nation, multiplying its people and extending the land, as he promised to Abraham (Gen. 12:1-3). Here is the faithfulness of God.

But the second prayer (26:16-18) remembers the faith of his people, as they turned to him, often in great weakness and such distress that prayer could hardly be articulated. They had no ability to save themselves, so they cast themselves upon the God who had so often been their deliverer. This is justification by faith, as a lifestyle, and it brings God's word of peace.

26:19-21 ends the section on a great note of encouragement. There is life beyond the dust of death, as 25:6-9 promised, and not just in the abolition of death, but in the resurrection of the body and the life everlasting. Perhaps nowhere else in the Old Testament is this doctrine taught as clearly as it is here. In the meantime, the waiting time (26:8), God's people must go on believing that he will vindicate his name, fulfil his promises and punish wickedness. So, they must live by faith, as they quietly observe his prototypical judgements in their present history, which foreshadow the certainty of his ultimate fulfilment time (26:20-21).

Preaching and Teaching the Text
Title: **Something to shout about**
Text: **Isaiah 25:1–26:21**
Structure: Set in the context of the terrifying last judgement of chapter 24. Yet in the middle of it all, faithful people are heard praising Yahweh (24:14-16a). This is the substance of the songs of praise.
1. Praise God for his mighty deeds (25:1-5)
      – as destroyer (vv. 2-3)
      – as refuge (vv. 4-5)
2. Praise God for his gracious rescue (25:6-9)
      – from poverty (v. 6)

– from death itself (vv. 7-9)

3. Praise God for his total victory (25:10-12)

    – over all resistance to his will (vv. 10-11a)

    – over all human pride (vv. 11b-12)

4. Praise God for his safe stronghold (26:1-6)

    – security through salvation (vv. 1, 5-6)

    – righteousness through faith (vv. 2-4)

5. Praise God for his personal care (26:7-21)

    – while evil thrives (vv. 7-15)

    – when judgement falls (vv. 16-21)

Conclusion: Those who praise him are those who trust him.

Leading a Bible Study

1. 25:1-5 In the light of the terrifying judgements of chapter 24, what actions of God move his people to praise him? How do they reveal his character?

2. 25:6-9 What does the Lord promise 'for all peoples'? What do these verses imply and how were they fulfilled?

3. 25:10-12 Contrast being under the Lord's hand and under his feet (v. 10). What are the outcomes for the latter and why does God do this?

4. 26:1-6 Who are the citizens of this 'strong city' and why are they praising God?

5. 26:7-15 As God's people wait for his eternal kingdom to be revealed, what characteristics of God and his activity should encourage them to trust him?

6. 26:16-21 What is God covenanted to do for his people, both in the waiting time and beyond this world?

Application: These two songs of rejoicing need to be set against the sombre background of God's final and universal judgement (24:1-23) and the next chapter (27:1-13) with its promise of the renewal and restoration of her people. Most of this section is about the end of time, so there is much to be learned and applied from it about how those who trust in the Lord should live now in the light of eternity. What will this mean for our priorities of life regarding our time, our money and our energies? How should it affect our attitudes towards the faith challenges we currently face?

13. Israel will be renewed (27:1-13)

This closing chapter brings together a mosaic of themes and ideas already touched on by Isaiah. For detailed study of 'this heterogeneous collection' Motyer provides a valuable guide.[12] The chapter begins and ends with Yahweh's great victories – over Leviathan, 'the gliding serpent' (27:1), and over his human enemies (27:12-13). His total sovereignty over everything which would oppose his purposes issues in the victorious imposition of his will on everything in creation.

The fruit of this is highlighted in 27:2-6, where God's renewed people become 'a fruitful vineyard', in obvious contrast to 5:1-7. Indeed, what God will do for this vineyard is described in direct reversal of the destruction detail of chapter 5. An addition is the understanding that even God's enemies can make peace, find refuge and become part of his fruit-bearing people. 27:6 shows that the fulfilment of this concept will be worldwide and no longer restricted to ethnic Israel.

However, this reference to the nations prompts the reflection, in 27:7-11, on the contrast between the judgement of God on the nations and on the covenant-community. This point is made by the rhetorical questions of verse 7. Isaiah's answer begins to trail for us ideas of a

12. Alec Motyer, *The Prophecy of Isaiah*, p220

better day beyond the judgement, which will be developed increasingly as the book proceeds. War and exile will be God's 'fierce blast' against Judah, but such covenant discipline will lead to new spiritual understanding and the removal of sin – to renewal (27:7-9).

So, the motifs of threat and promise are once more revisited. In 27:9b-11, we are back in chapter 1 with the inevitability of God's destructive judgement, due to the idolatry of God's covenant people, who have deserted their maker and creator. But in 27:12-13, we are beyond the exile as God's people are gathered back to him, sharing his victory, summoned by his trumpet and restored to the holy mountain and the now faithful city. These are promises pointing forward to the gospel and its universal proclamation. Only Yahweh will be victorious. Only he will reign and only he will be eternally glorified by his redeemed people from all over his world.

Part 4

TRUST AND OBEDIENCE
IN HEZEKIAH'S REIGN

Isaiah 28–39

'The Sinai covenant shows that living according to the standards
of truth, integrity, love and faithfulness is not simply a utilitarian
choice but is an act of glad submission to the Creator...
doing it for the sake of the love of God.'

John N. Oswalt,
Isaiah: The NIV Application Commentary, p326

Introduction

For the practical preacher there are several attractions towards a preaching series in chapters 28-39. We have moved from the reign of Ahaz, with its unremitting gloom, to that of his much more godly son, Hezekiah, whose heart is set on seeking the Lord. The issues remain the same, but the note of hope and expectation that God's promises will be fulfilled is much stronger. Hezekiah is still drawn to political alliances rather than a deep trust and dependence. As the chapters unfold it is easy to identify with him, to see our problems as a reflection of his and to learn from Scripture the lessons he had to learn in life.

The section is also a celebration of God's power at work on behalf of his people, in deliverance from both temporal adversaries and eternal loss. It builds our faith, not just in a didactic way, but by revealing more of the character of God. This faith is not an intellectual position merely, but a heart trust and a life of obedience at the most practical levels of everyday experience. Its message is both readily accessible to careful study and greatly needed in the midst of our current perplexities and frequent compromises.

1. Context and Structure

It is important to remember that although Isaiah's finished book has been put together thematically, there is nevertheless a chronological time-sequence running through its sections. The individual oracles are not necessarily presented in any historical order, but the history of the Lord's actual intervention in the world, and especially in the lives of his people, is never far from Isaiah's concern. This explains why successive commentators have clearly identified the (mainly) prose passages of chapters 36-39 as the centrepiece of the prophecy, as in Barry Webb's description, 'the pivot on which the book turns...designed to act as a bridge between its two halves'.[1]

This third part of Isaiah's book, chapters 28-39, consists then of two major sections, the first of which (chs.28–35) is clearly rooted in Hezekiah's reign by the historical detail of the second (chs.36–39). We have already heard God's warning of the Assyrian invasion sweeping like a flood-tide across Judah (8:7-8), and this is now fulfilled in the conquest of the fortified cities and the imminent siege of Jerusalem under Sennacherib (36:1), dated as 701 BC. Much of the content of chapters 28–35 is preparatory to this great historical moment, which threatens the very existence of Judah. It deals with the immediate causes, exposing the folly of Hezekiah's political alliances, but at a deeper level it explores the theological issues which lie behind these unwise choices. We should not be surprised to find that once again the conflict between promises and policies and the issues of where trust should be placed and where lasting confidence can be secured dominate the picture. This is home ground for Isaiah's faith-building enterprise.

Because of the rooting of the theological message in the historical detail, it is important, both in our study and in our preaching, to give adequate attention to these real events. Historically, the Assyrian invasion was a punitive response to a revolt by Hezekiah. In this he was encouraged by the promise of Egyptian military support, to throw off the yoke of tribute exacted by the Assyrians since his father, Ahaz, had fled to them for help, in the face of the Syrian-Ephraimite coalition forces (see chapter 7

---

1. Barry Webb, *The Message of Isaiah*, p147

and 2 Kings 16:5-9). However, the Egyptians were quickly defeated by the Assyrians and chapter 36 finds Hezekiah totally defenceless and exposed to the violent anger of the world's most ruthless and powerful war machine. It is important for the seriousness of this situation to grip our own understanding if we are to give the appropriate spiritual weight to the challenge and counsel which God brings to the Davidic king through his inspired prophet.

More detailed examination of the text of chapters 28-35 reveals that six times the Hebrew exclamation 'ho' is used to introduce a new section in the unit. This is reflected by the translation 'Woe to...' in our English Bibles and also by the chapter divisions. The six references are 28:1; 29:1; 29:15; 30:1; 31:1 and 33:1. Of these, the first is a lament for Samaria, capital of the northern kingdom (Ephraim), which fell to the Assyrians in 722 BC, a date before Hezekiah's accession. Clearly, that had not yet happened when the oracle was spoken. However, at 28:14 the focus is turned on 'you scoffers, who rule this people in Jerusalem', and from then onwards Judah is the subject of the prophet's laments. The next four 'woe' oracles expose the reasons why Judah is equally ripe for God's judgement and what that will involve. The sixth oracle (33:1ff.), however, concerns 'the destroyer', Assyria. God's people are pleading with God to bring about the destruction he has foretold and receiving assurances from him that this is indeed what he will do. '"Now will I arise," says the LORD... "You will see those arrogant people no more"' (33:10, 19).

Beyond this, chapters 34 and 35 form a short unit which can be separated out from the flow. The subject matter contrasts the devastation which God's judgement will produce as it turns the fruitful land into a desert, with the garden-land of restoration and new life when God restores his people to Zion. Chapter 34 (the desert) echoes chapter 24, as all the nations and the whole earth are exposed to God's wrath, while chapter 35 (the garden) will itself be echoed in chapter 55 as the blessings of the servant's work are celebrated and offered freely to all the nations. Some commentators suggest that the two chapters face Judah with a choice. There really are only two ways to live, and each produces predictable, even inescapable, consequences. Others suggest that chapter 35 lies temporally beyond chapter 34. It reveals the blessings that God will bring through his refining, disciplining acts of judgement, and in that sense it begins to move us towards the universal hope contained in the gospel of the suffering servant, which will be the dominant content of chapters 40-55.

Another analysis is provided by Alec Motyer, who sees in chapters 28-35 one of Isaiah's 'doublets', which he identifies as three principles (28:1-29; 29:1-14 and 29:15-24) followed by three matching applications (30:1-33; 31:1–32:20 and 33:1–35:10)[2].

One further comment on structure relates to the composition of chapters 36–39. The threat to Jerusalem posed by Sennacherib's army is clearly a self-contained narrative from 36:1–37:38. But what of Hezekiah's illness in 38:1-22 and the visit of the Babylonian envoys from Merodach-Baladan (39:1-8) – how do they fit in? The internal evidence of the chapters indicates that 'In those days' (38:1) must refer to the period before the invasion, so that, chronologically, chapters 38–39 precede 36–37. The extension of Hezekiah's life by fifteen years leads on to

2. See Alec Motyer, *The Prophecy of Isaiah*, p228ff – for the intriguing and helpful details of this approach

the promise to defend Jerusalem from the Assyrians (38:4-6). Similarly, the Babylonian ruler Merodach-Baladan ruled from 721 to 710 BC and the Jerusalem attack was in 701BC. His approach, following Hezekiah's restoration, was probably to raise money and support for his own revolt against Assyria, since we can discern at this time the beginnings of the stirrings of Babylonian independence and strength which would eventually destroy Assyria. The inversion of the chronology must have thematic and theological purposes, for Isaiah, which we will examine later.

2. Preaching Notes

The theological realities rooted in the historical events of these chapters cry out to be preached from our pulpits today. We need to face head-on that to many of our hearers the two amazing miraculous interventions of 37:36 and 38:8 may seem to be unbelievable. But if that is so, it surely reveals how far short of a biblical understanding of the nature of God we are today. Of course, we are not to encourage gullibility and the sort of fantasy religion which imagines God has said and will do things which he has not and will not because they are the product of human imagination. But these are specifically recorded words of the Lord, special revelation, and if we do not think they really happened, we are in effect unbelievers. That will mean that the life of faith is essentially foreign to our everyday experience and we shall slump into the sort of man-driven externalism of religious formalism, which was Judah's problem. It may even look and sound impeccably 'evangelical,' but it is based on policies rather than promises, works not faith.

The whole Bible is God preaching God to us, and so we need to preach these chapters as a declaration of his true character, in order to generate a genuine faith in the real Lord. This will involve teaching the awesome holiness of God, which lies at the heart of the divine being and which makes his sovereign power such a threat of destructive judgement to sinful humanity. That haunting question, asked by those in Zion who are aware of their sin, pulls together a major preaching theme for this whole section – 'Who of us can dwell with the consuming fire? Who of us can dwell with everlasting burning?' (33:14). The immediate answer, 'He who walks righteously', with its explanation following (33:15-16), reminds us of the parallel theme that such justification is possible only by faith, which expresses itself in heartfelt repentance and practical trust.

However, we also need to give due weight to the idea of spiritual purification through God's covenant discipline, with the New Testament equivalents in Hebrews 12, for example. While it is gloriously true that the price is paid and that those who trust God's promises find the righteousness which he provides by grace through faith, nevertheless God loves us too much to let us get away with the consequences of our fickle, double-minded discipleship. He so often schools us, through adversity, in the lessons of trust and obedience. We are all imperfect learners, as was Hezekiah, but covenant faithfulness will not give us up and will not let us go.

Prayer is another of the great lessons to be preached and taught from this unit, especially by way of contrast with the politicking of Hezekiah and his advisory group, which actually revealed where their confidence really lay. The Rabshakeh's challenge at 36:4 would make a great overview text for the whole section. There can be little demur that our generation of Christian believers in the West is not known for its praying, either personally or corporately. Much of what is happening in these chapters shows God fighting for his people, as he works for their ultimate good by frustrating their alliances and bringing them to an end of their prayerless effort in relying on human resources.

The desert of chapter 34 is a fearful reminder of where lack of faith in Yahweh ultimately leads. In the same way, the garden of chapter 35, with its green shoots, newness of life and promise of fruitfulness, is shown to be totally dependent on God and his grace. He alone is the Lord, the giver of life. Only when we really believe that, will prayer be central to our lives in this world; but only then will we be able to claim with any credibility that our faith is real. We too need to hear the Lord's word to the scoffers, who mock God's work by refusing to take it seriously (28:14-22), especially if our reaction is silent and our unbelief privatised. One indication of whether we are spiritually healthy, or not, will be our appetite for, and attitude to, the Word of the Lord, the Scriptures (see 30:8-14). How far are we willing to receive and respond to this very word in these central chapters of Isaiah?

In applying these great truths, the grace of God, in the promises and wonderful invitations spread throughout the unit, is of course the central reality. But we do live in a generation that wants to hear 'pleasant things' and to 'prophesy illusions' (30:10), so we must be prepared to allow these verses to rebuke our self-centred superficiality and to proclaim that message, without compromise, whatever reactions it may produce. Practical applications might well explore how, like Judah, so often both our church life and personal discipleship still retain a nodding acquaintance with God's Word, but will not allow it to be in the drivingseat. When that is the case, we can be certain that worldly strategies and human policies will take over.

For example, when a church turns from the biblical priorities of preaching the Word and prayer, confidence will inevitably be placed in the latest programmes and strategies, which is a sure sign that something is wrong. Human policies will always fill the vacuum when God's promises are no longer trusted, as can be observed in both local congregations and larger denominational connections. Of course, we want to see gospel growth, to plant new churches and to penetrate our resistant culture with the good news of Jesus Christ, but the lesson of Isaiah 28–39 is that we cannot do it. Only God can bring spiritual life to birth and if we are to see that happen we have to trust (pray) and obey (proclaim by life and lip).

If multiplication-methodologies take us over, if building our own little 'Christian' empires becomes our raison d'être, we may not be without our achievements, but they will be like their creators: transient, mortal, with very obvious feet of clay. We may produce great entrepreneurs, able communicators, first-class Christian management consultants. They may organise attractive, life-coaching churches whose members are encouraged to look to a 'great God', whose main purpose is to help them to fulfil their potential, to make them even more beautiful, healthy, wealthy and wise than they already are; but, in the end, shall we not discover that we have signed up with 'Rahab, the Do-Nothing' (30:7)?

In the midst of all this human activity, which, in eternal terms may prove to be comparatively insignificant,

Isaiah reminds our generation, as he did his own, that 'In repentance and rest is your salvation, in quietness and trust is your strength' (30:15). The ultimate priority is always to see the king in his beauty (33:17), the king who reigns in righteousness, and while in this thirsty land, to live in the shadow of that mighty rock (32:1-2). So, preach Isaiah!

In the outlines in this section, I have taken some representative passages, which are on the longer side. For preaching purposes, they will mean less time on detail, but more time on the principles being taught and their theological connections. The sermon outlines deal with three of the 'woe' oracles, chapters 29, 30 and 33, bring 34 and 35 together and then treat Sennacherib's siege (chs. 36–37) as one unit, ending with a transition sermon on 38–39.

3. Working Through the Text

We will subdivide chapters 28–33, according to the six 'woe' oracles, treat chapters 34 and 35 as contrasting each other, and then deal with 36–37 and 38–39 as distinct, though connected, units.

1. The first 'woe' (28:1-29)

28:1-13 The oracle against the northern kingdom (Ephraim) and its capital Samaria, which is the hill city like a crown or garland decorating its head (28:1), appears to pre-date its collapse, although the image of the 'fading flower' indicates that its glory days have long gone and its end is imminent. The same idea is conveyed by the image of the ripe fig' (28:4). But as Ephraim's crown is trodden underfoot and the kingdom is destroyed, another crown appears. The Lord of hosts will be a crown of righteousness and glory 'for the remnant of his people' (28:5). This judgement, destruction at the Lord's hand (28:2), is due to the drunkenness of Ephraim (28:1, 7-8), which renders its religious leaders incapable of being the channels of revelation or of making right decisions in any areas of the national life. These come from Yahweh in 28:6, but cannot exist where God's word is ridiculed and rejected (28:9-10).

In many ways this is a 'chicken and egg' situation. The dissolute behaviour leads to spiritual incompetence, but the rejection of God's truth is their spurious legitimisation of such godlessness. It is Isaiah's own ministry which they attack (cf. 6:9-10), and the Hebrew text shows that they dismiss his teaching as mere childish gibberish, at best nursery rhyme stuff. There is nothing they can learn from such a simpleton!

Contemporary parallels are all around us. The irony of 28:11-13 is that in refusing the rest God offered through Isaiah, they ensure that his message will come to them in a language they cannot understand (in the form of the Assyrian invasion). This gibberish, incomprehensible to them, will be the accompaniment of their downfall and captivity.

28:14-22 Scoffing, however, is not the monopoly of Samaria; it thrives in Jerusalem as well. Here too the word of the Lord is rejected in favour of something much more palatable (28:14-15). Isaiah exposes the false confidence in Judah that they will be immune from the Assyrian scourge, because they are God's people in God's city, but we know that the city is a whore (1:21). To imagine that they have an agreement with death, that it cannot touch them because of God's promises to David and to David's city, is foolish arrogance which the Assyrian flood will sweep away (28:17-18). For God's plumb line of measurement is righteousness, by which standard every human being falls short. Only those who trust in his king of righteousness, the true cornerstone in Zion, and not in any externals such as the city or the temple or their outward conformity to religious norms (cf. 1:10-20), 'will never be dismayed' (28:16-17). The ultimate Messianic fulfilment of these words is drawn out in 1 Peter 2:4-8, especially verse 6.

All complacency and false confidence is ruthlessly swept away in 28:18-22. Day after day the invaders will plunder and destroy relentlessly and no refuge will prove adequate (28:20). The major thrust is the comparison between this judgement and God's interventions in previous Old Testament history. At Mount Perazim, David attributes his great victory over the Philistines to Yahweh's direct intervention, 'The LORD has broken out against my enemies before me' (2 Sam. 5:17-21). In the valley of Gibeon, the LORD threw the Amorites into confusion and hurled large hailstones down on them, so that the account of Joshua's great victory concludes that 'more of them died from the hailstones than were killed by the swords of the Israelites' (Josh. 10:7-11). In both cases, divine intervention secured victory for God's people. But here the tragedy is that in his 'strange work' and 'alien task', all of the divine power is turned against his covenant people. Mocking the messenger is the last way to respond to this devastating decree of destruction (28:21-22).

28:23-29 might seem at first something of an anti-climax, but Isaiah is reasoning with his hearers, underlining the logic of what he is saying and pleading with them to take seriously what 'the LORD Almighty, has told me' (28:22). He chooses two examples or parables from the world of farming, no doubt familiar to many of his hearers in Judah. They are simple arguments which might appear unsophisticated, even childish (cf. 28:9), but that is the test as to whether they are willing to humble themselves under God's revelation.

Firstly, no farmer goes on ploughing and breaking up the soil indefinitely. Its purpose is to enable him to sow his different seeds so that he can later harvest his crops. This is God's way and there is no avoiding it (28:23-26). Next, when the crops are gathered they have to be treated in different ways, so that the harvest is preserved and not destroyed. This is the way God has structured his creation, and every wise farmer knows he must operate within these constraints (28:27-29). Is it likely to be different in the realm of spiritual reality? God dictates the terms, and those who are wise hear and respond. There may also be a ray of future hope here in the images of a harvest beyond the ploughing and of grain for bread beyond the threshing.

Leading a Bible Study

1. 28:1-6 Contrast the fading flower of Samaria (Ephraim's crown) with the unfading crown of glory who is the Lord (v. 5). What are the causes of Ephraim's collapse (vv. 1-4)? How is God's blessing for the 'remnant' shown (vv. 5-6)?

2. 28:7-10 Contrast the current situation which is precipitating the judgement. In verses 9-10 the sinners ridicule Isaiah (the 'teacher') and accuse him of speaking childish twaddle. What does this say about their attitude to God?

3. 28:11-13 And what is God's response?

4. 28:14-17 The focus shifts to Jerusalem. What wrong thinking does God expose in verse 15 and what is his

surprising remedy in verse 16? (cf. Gen. 49:24; Deut. 32:4; Isa. 8:14; Rom. 9:33; 1 Pet. 2:6)

5. 28:18-22 God addresses the scoffers. What is their future? (See 2 Sam. 5:18-21 for Mt. Perazim and Joshua 10:6-11 for the Valley of Gibeon.) What are we to learn from these comparisons? What is 'alien' about this?

6. 28:23-29 These extensive agricultural metaphors are used to reinforce the message. What aspects of the chapter do they particularly emphasise? What would be a right response?

Application: How are we pressured by our society and by our own sin to view God's Word as childish and irrelevant, as in verses 7-10? What will the consequences be for the church if we give in to this pressure?

2. Woe to Ariel (29:1-24)

29:1-14 The word translated 'woe' is not only a word of emotion and sympathy, but also of summons, as Motyer reminds us, suggesting that each of the six woes in this part of Isaiah may possibly be a summons to the bar of judgement[3]. Ariel (Jerusalem) is summoned from the seemingly endless round of annual religious festivals to hear God's sentence that she will be besieged and become like an ariel (a play on words) – that is, an altar hearth, the location where God's righteous anger is experienced in the consuming of the sacrifice (29:1-2). Just as in chapter 28, the siege is now identified as God's work against his people, his strange and alien work, and it looks like the end for Jerusalem (29:3-4).

---

3. Alec Motyer, *The Prophecy of Isaiah*, p.229

However, at this very point there is a sudden change of tone and focus. Now it is Judah's enemies who are reduced to dust because all the forces of the Lord are employed against them. This is surely prophetic of Sennacherib's defeat when God's power was demonstrated in the silent removal of that overwhelming threat overnight (29:5-8). Yet this amazing and gracious deliverance in no way minimises the continuing spiritual bankruptcy of the southern kingdom. For many, this dream-like deliverance is an ironic confirmation that they are indeed spiritually asleep and this is in itself part of the Lord's judgement. The authentic gift of prophetic insight is hardly exercised, and when it is, as with Isaiah, the reaction is as though it cannot be read – it is incomprehensible; it does not make any sense (29:9-12). Spiritual things have to be spiritually discerned, and whenever God's Word is proclaimed, hearts are either humbled or hardened. There is no neutrality.

In the light of these powerful realities, 29:13-14 provide an explanation of key significance, as the root cause of Judah's predicament is made abundantly plain. Their external 'devotion', in religious orthodoxy and human rules,masks a substitute for a heart that truly draws near to God. Instead of living for him in obedience to his word, they are given over to formalism and human traditions. Man-made legalism will always be attractive because it is self-justifying, depends on works and has no need to humble itself under God's mighty hand. But God will yet break in on such hypocrisy. Such self-referential, man-made wisdom and intelligence, which seems to many to be such a satisfactory substitute for God, will vanish like a puff of smoke (29:13-14). It is no wonder that Paul uses these verses to challenge the Corinthians in their false confidence in human wisdom and power displays, rather than in the gospel of Christ crucified (see 1 Cor. 1:18–2:5).

29:15-24 introduces us to the third woe, which underlines the need for a spiritual solution to Judah's problems, since this is the root of the matter. The political and social upheavals are only symptomatic of a much deeper disease in the hearts of covenant people, who refuse to walk humbly with God in trust and obedience, and who, on the contrary, are seeking to avoid him and hide from him. How can such a life-threatening disease be remedied?

First, there has to be a recognition of their true condition, and the 'woe' that summons God's people into his court also issues the charges against them. They imagine that God does not see or know about their sinful rebellion (29:15), that they can actually hide from him. They imagine that they are wiser than God, and so although in reality they are only clay pots formed by the potter, they despise their creator (29:16). But if they think they can turn things upside down and make their own rules in God's world, as so many do today, 29:17 points out that God will soon turn their cosy world of rebellion upside down. Then his word will no longer be a closed book. Its values will prevail and all the normalities of the present day will be turned on their heads. The pride and self-sufficiency of rebellious man will be removed, and the humble and needy will rejoice in God's deliverance (29:17-23). Through the Lord's presence and the teaching of his Word the fickle will find stability while the stubbornly defiant will submit to the authority of God's truth (29:24). Only Yahweh can bring about such a necessary spiritual transformation.

Preaching and Teaching the Text

Title: **Understanding God's perspective**

Text: **Isaiah 29:1-24**

Structure: Draw out the 'woe' ideas of sorrow and summons.

1. See God at work in his city (vv. 1-8)
   - to humble her pride (vv. 1-4)
   - to deliver by his power (vv. 5-8)
2. Accept God's diagnosis of his people (vv. 9-16)
   - he knows the hardened hearts (vv. 9-13)
   - he sees the hidden rebellion (vv. 14-16)
3. Embrace God's promises for the future (vv. 17-24)
   - the world will be renewed (vv. 17-21)
   - the city will be holy (vv. 22-24)

Conclusion: Such prophecies find their fulfilment in Christ (Mark 7:6-7).

Leading a Bible Study

1.   29:1-8 What are the main points being made about Jerusalem (Ariel) in these verses? How and why will God change the situation?
2.   29:9-12 Compare these verses with 6:9-10. How do they confirm what God told Isaiah at his call?
3.   29:13-14 Here again God stresses cause and effect. What will he do, and why?
4.   29:15-19 What evidences of the foolishness of trying to outwit God do you see in verses 15-16? How will God reverse this situation (vv. 17-19)?
5.   29:20-21 What impact will God's intervention have on the social climate of the city? Why are these examples the focus of the current hypocrisy (cf. v. 13)?
6.   29:22-24 Examine the marks of God's future blessing on the true spiritual children of Abraham. What do

they teach us about how God would have his believing people live in the present?

Application: Read 9:13-14 in the light of 1 Corinthians 1:18-25. How are we tempted in our Christian lives and in our churches to depend on man's wisdom, and not on God's? What does this passage show us of the way God helps us depend on him instead?

3. Woe to the Obstinate (30:1-33)

We are halfway through the sequence of six oracles. We move now in the second part from the general to the specific as the principles are rooted in and applied to the details of Hezekiah's reign. This is seen especially in the historical context of the fluctuating, triangular relationship between Judah, Egypt and Assyria. Remember that the central issues, as ever, concern trust in God's promises and obedience to his commands. The contrasting ways which Isaiah continually underlines are made more vivid in this chapter, where the same basic verb (to trust, or put confidence in) is used of Judah's reliance on Egypt ('deceit' 30:12) and in Isaiah's exhortation to trust in the Holy One of Israel for salvation (30:15). That is the heart of the issue being pursued in chapter 30.

30:1-17 outlines the current political situation in which Hezekiah has been pursuing an alliance with Egypt to assist him in his struggles to throw off the Assyrian yoke of tribute. These are not God's plans; he has not been consulted (30:1-2). Although it all looks very impressive with Hebrew government envoys in the land where once their fathers had been slaves, this policy will only lead to shame and disgrace, because help from Egypt is an empty delusion (30:3-5). To add graphic detail, 30:6-7 pictures the dangers and privations endured by the 'top brass' of Judah as they travel to Egypt with their incentives, to solicit her help. Isaiah's name for Egypt says it all. She is 'the Do-Nothing,' 'the Sit-Still'.

Future generations need to learn from this, because looking to Egypt for help is indicative of spiritual rebellion. Only those who have rejected God's word and refuse to listen to his prophets would follow this path. They have no other point of reference and no other source of refuge. Whenever the church looks to the world for its support, we can be sure that the Word of God lies unopened or, if opened, unheard, or if heard disobeyed (30:8-11). But such rejection will precipitate disaster as the images of collapse and shattering demonstrate (30:12-14). Trust in deceit leads to devastation, but trust in the Sovereign LORD will lead to repentance and faith, which in turn produce rest, salvation and strength (30:15). This is what God would have done for his people, but instead they have chosen horses (the latest weaponry and military tactics), which will leave them decimated and destitute (30:16-17). Again, there are many parallels to be drawn between the faithlessness of God's people and his great faithfulness in our own context, and also between our predisposition to rely on human mechanics and methodologies to provide what we long for most, rather than the relationship of trust and obedience, which is the essence of love for God.

30:18-33 produces another turn in the argument, from warning to pleading and from rebuke to invitation, with the introduction of the word 'Yet' (30:18), or better, 'therefore' (KJV). This is a magnificent verse, with its double use of the verb 'wait' or 'long for'. God longs to move in grace and compassion towards his people because of his steadfast covenant love for them, but his righteousness and justice must punish sin. It is as though behind the sentence of his justice being carried out, he waits to break out in grace. This will be the experience of all who wait for him, who hold on in the faith that obeys. Think of the cross of the Lord Jesus, where love and justice meet and beyond which lie the spiritual blessings, such as those outlined by Paul in Ephesians 1:3-14. But perhaps there is more here. It is not just that mercy follows judgement, but that through the judgement that compassionate grace is exercised and experienced.

This would seem to be the focus and encouragement of the majestic prose passage, which is 30:19-26. God will answer prayer. He will teach his truth. He will direct his people through his word. And they will have done with their idols (30:19-22). Then in typical Old Testament land-blessing terms, the benefits of the covenant are revisited and freshly enjoyed in rain and rich harvests, multiplied herds and well-nurtured livestock, days of refreshment in the place of days of slaughter (see the better ESV translation of verse 25), endless light, healing and wholeness (30:23-26).

Finally, 30:27-33 revisits the current realities of the sweeping flood of God's judgement in the Assyrian invasion. This is God's agency of judgement and it is truly terrifying, yet, in the midst of it all (30:29), God's people are rejoicing and celebrating, because the threat from Assyria is non-existent when the Lord punishes that arrogant nation with his rod (30:31-32). Once again we must set this in its historical context, remembering its fulfilment when the Lord delivered Jerusalem and destroyed, by his breath, the army of Sennacherib. 'Little did the Assyrians know that their imperial progress to Zion (10:8-11) was their funeral

procession with the pyre long since laid'.[4] Yahweh made
the fire-pit and his breath will set it ablaze (30:33). What
confidence in his sovereignty this should give us and what
an incentive to trust and obey!

Preaching and Teaching the Text
Title: **The God who waits**
Text: **Isaiah 30:1-33**
Structure: Identify verse 18 as the pivot verse, which moves
us from the woes (vv. 1-17) to the blessings (vv. 19-26).
1. Why is God waiting? (vv. 1-17)
    – misplaced trust (vv. 1-7)
    – rejected revelation (vv. 8-14)
2. What is God wanting? (vv. 18-26)
    – to reverse their present plight (vv. 19-26)
    – for his people to wait for him (vv. 18-19a)
3. Where is God working? (review whole passage)
    – wherever his people repent and believe
    – when they no longer turn to Egypt for help
    – when he shatters their enemies (vv. 27-33)
Conclusion: Verse 18 is a wonderful promise, grounded in
God's nature and still available to his people. Trust and obey.

Leading a Bible Study
1.   30:1-7 What is Hezekiah looking for in Egypt and
    why won't he find it there? What will he find? What
    do these verses teach us about the root of such folly?
2.   30:8-17 Here we get to the roots of the problem. Where
    are they going wrong (vv. 8-12)? What will the outcome
    be (vv. 13-14, 16-17)? What is the remedy (v. 15)?
3.   30:18-26 How do these promises encourage faith?

---

4. Alec Motyer, *The Prophecy of Isaiah*, p253

4. 30:27-33 The perspective widens beyond the immediate. What does God want his people to realise (vv. 31-33)? How should that affect them in the present?
5. Take some time to reflect on how this section highlights the major challenges of the book – human policies or divine promises? Where will Hezekiah and Judah put their trust – in verse 12 or verse 15? And what about us?

Application: When we sin, how does it show a lack of trust in God? How is 'repentance and rest' and 'quietness and trust' the opposite of this? How can the church be tempted to sin this way, turning to 'Egypt' (worldly plans and methods) for success, instead of God's way? What are the consequences of this, and what is the remedy?

4. Woe to reliance on human resources (31:1-32:20)

31:1-9 returns us to the present foolish diplomacy in which king Hezekiah has engaged himself and his country. The 'woe' on turning to Egypt for help is repeated and contrasted with turning for help to the Holy One of Israel, who is covenanted to defend his people (31:1). Here is a telling indictment of Hezekiah's folly. Who would trust men rather than God, or flesh rather than spirit (31:3)? The text reminds its readers that Yahweh is wise, powerful and totally dependable (31:2). Unlike Egypt 'he does not take back his words'. Instead, he compares himself to a hungry lion and a protective bird. Neither will be deterred from their goal (31:4-5). Therefore, he pleads with his people to return (repent), to have done with their idols and to wait in faith for God's deliverance of them from Assyria, not to rely on Egypt's empty posturing (31:6-9).

32:1-8 This section acts as an incentive to respond by faith to Isaiah's God-given prophecy, by reminding his hearers of the glorious future awaiting those who trust.'See, a king...' (32:1) recalls the Messianic figure, Immanuel, in chapters 7, 9 and 11, and underlines the certainty that Yahweh will bring about the spiritual salvation and renewal of his people, through the perfect Davidic king, who will embody all the promises made concerning the eternal kingdom. His righteous rule will be reflected in those who serve under him, unlike Shebna (22:15-19) and the general ineptitude of Hezekiah's administration and his advisers. These ideal leaders will derive their qualities from the king himself, 'the unique, special man'[5] who is, supremely, the shelter, the refuge and the provider of refreshment (water) and protection (shadow) for his people (32:1-2).

The descriptions of life in this kingdom (32:3-8) indicate that it is like no earthly realm. The blind will see and the deaf hear. These are two of Isaiah's favourite pictures of spiritual obtuseness, overcome by the disclosure of the king. Folly will be overcome by wisdom and wickedness by nobility. But even though these are the glorious future realities which God promises for his people, it will not do to succumb in the present to a complacency which refuses to listen to, or accept, Isaiah's message, like the women of Jerusalem (32:9-14). A true response would be trembling, repentance and mourning, in place of revelry and ease, because terrible days are certainly coming for them and their children.

But as we have seen, throughout the unit, judgement is not the final word for the covenant people of the Lord. It is through the disciplinary chastening of God that his people

5. Alexander, Smith and Snaith, quoted by Motyer, *IBID*. p257

are schooled in holiness, purged of their compromise and brought into a deeper relationship with him (cf. Heb 12:4-11). Fittingly the last paragraph (32:15-20) is all about newness of life. This is the symbolism of pouring out of the Spirit, the Lord, the giver of life, who brings fertility to the desert, justice and righteousness to the barren land scorched by human arrogance and rebellion. The fruit of this great work of God will be peace, quiet confidence (echoes of 30:15), stability and security. In these realities of the eternal kingdom lie great incentives for us too to trust and obey.

Leading a Bible Study

1. 31:1-3 Why is Egypt such a lost cause? Why is the Lord the answer to his people's needs?
2. 31:4-5 What is God's essential revelation to Isaiah? How does this address the people's attitudes?
3. 31:6-9 Analyse the message which Isaiah now preaches to Judah. What implications does this have for their idolatry?
4. 32:1-8 What are the unique characteristics of this righteous king? How does this present the divine answer to the current problems of Judah?
5. 32:9-14 So how should Isaiah's hearers respond now to the message of coming judgement, and why don't they?
6. 32:15-20 How will God change the situation? Why does God keep telling Judah these things?

Application: What are the parallels between our situations and problems and those of Judah? How does the king of 32:1-5 provide the answer for us as well as for them? How does Isaiah's vision of the future give us confidence to keep on trusting God and his king?

5. Woe to the destroyer (33:1-24)

'There is much in chapter 33 which reflects the last-minute turning to the LORD which took place in Jerusalem, led by Hezekiah, when Sennacherib's envoys were at the gates.'[6] This final 'woe' is directed towards the Assyrians, because God's people, led by the Davidic king, have at last learned their lesson and cast themselves on Yahweh's mercy. At 33:2, we hear the voice, at least of the believing remnant, as they ask and wait for the promised grace (cf. 30:18) which is the only possible means of their rescue. So they affirm, albeit belatedly, their faith in his sovereign power (33:3-4). Their growing confidence is articulated in 33:5-6, either as a word from the Lord directly to the situation, through Isaiah, or perhaps as the renewed convictions of Hezekiah and the believing remnant.

33:7-13 forms a subsection in which the reality of the present situation across the Middle East, and especially in Judah, is described in all its sober realism. Diplomacy has failed (33:7-8) and the whole land is becoming, as it were, scorched earth, under Assyria's iron fist (33:9). Yet it is precisely at that moment of critical intensity that God acts. Note the threefold use and emphasis of 'now' in 33:10. When there are no human solutions, God's power is displayed and has to be acknowledged by all who hear of his mighty deliverance (33:11-13).

We must not miss the spiritual nature of the awakening of at least some of Jerusalem's citizens, described in 33:14, in the midst of all their physical terror. To see God's consuming fire in the Assyrian invasion is terrifying enough, but who could ever dwell with this God of holiness, 'a consuming fire' (cf. Heb. 12:29)? The answer lies in the moral perfection

6. Barry Webb, *The Message of Isaiah*,p139

of 33:15-16, from which the dwellers in Jerusalem realise that they fall far short, as do we all. The need for mercy and forgiveness, grace and compassion is obvious, and with that sense of need immediately in 33:17 the word of promise is given. Here is the king again in all his beauty, whose rule over his extensive kingdom is the only spiritual answer to the fallen nature of the whole human race.

The rest of the chapter reflects on what that liberating rule will mean (33:18-24), what we would rightly call the blessings of the gospel. The oppressing invaders have disappeared forever, now just a dim memory. Jerusalem is a city of peace and permanent security, never to be moved again. Immune from all invasion, the ruling presence of the Lord as lawgiver and king will guarantee the salvation of his trusting and obedient people. But Isaiah warns that this can only happen as a work of God, without whom Judah is like a ship without sails. The prosperity, wealth and health of the eternal kingdom find their greatest expression in the greatest of the benefits of God's grace – 'those who dwell there will be forgiven'.

Preaching and Teaching the Text

Title: **Our God is a consuming fire**

Text: **Isaiah 33:1-24**

Structure: Identify verse 14 as the central issue posed by the chapter and explored through the unit.

1. God's fire destroys his enemies, so trust in him (vv. 1-6)
    – depend upon his rescue (vv. 2-4)
    – glory in his resources (vv. 5-6)
2. God's fire consumes all evil, so walk with him (vv. 7-16)
    – the withered land is purged (vv. 7-12)

    – the righteous (who trust and obey) are protected (vv. 13-16)

3. God's fire secures his city, so wait for him (vv. 17-24)
    – the king's sovereignty (vv. 17-19)
    – the city's prosperity/security (vv. 20-24)

Leading a Bible Study

1.   33:1-6 The destroyer of verse 1 looks all-powerful, but how does God's revelation change the whole picture?

2.   33:7-12 Summarise the situation caused by the Assyrian ascendancy (vv. 7-9). What will God do about it?

3.   33:13-16 Trace the steps by which God's people are brought back into a right relationship with him, through these verses. How is this related to justification by faith and not by works?

4.   33:17-19 How does the vision of the king encourage faith?

5.   33:20-22 How should the vision of the king's city motivate present action?

6.   33:23-24 What is the contrast between the human wreck (v. 23a) and the forgiven sinner (v. 24b) designed to teach?

Application: What do verses 12-16 say about relationships between God and man? How should this shape our emotional response to God? Does justification by faith change this, and if so, how? How do verses 22-23 help us understand the relationship between this and forgiveness?

6. Which way? (34:1–35:10)

Chapter 34 reiterates Isaiah's persistent message that all the proud kingdoms which oppose themselves to Yahweh are going to perish. Echoing chapter 24, 34:1-4 picture the destruction which the wrath of God will bring on all the nations, extending beyond planet earth to involve even the heavens. The imagery of the rolled-up scroll (v. 4) signifies the end of the story, so that clearly what is in view here is the final climactic judgement, which we have come to call the end of the world.

Edom, with its capital Bozrah, is cited as the archetypical opponent of God and his purposes (34:5-7). This stretches back to its origins in Esau and his opposition to God's purposes for Jacob. But from Numbers 20:14ff. onwards, when Edom resisted Israel's progress to the Promised Land, throughout the united monarchy period and even on to the future fall of Jerusalem in 586 BC, Edom is the Lord's enemy. See the prophecy of Obadiah for the eventual outcome, where Edom's destruction becomes prototypical of the eschatological day of the Lord (Obad. 15).

The following section, 34:8-17, presents a terrifying picture of God's righteous wrath, in terms which recall the destruction of Sodom and Gomorrah (Gen. 19:24). The eternal consequences seen in the devastation and desolation of the land speak of a world from which human life has disappeared and where only wild birds and animals can find a home or places of rest (v. 14). The last two verses underline the certainty the reader should have that these things will happen, because God has spoken. What he decrees by his word, his Spirit will implement in his sovereign power. Note the emphasis on the written record of the spoken word (34:16 cf. 8:16, 20).

Chapter 35 continues in an eschatological context, but with a totally different future in view. The purpose of God's judgement in all its manifestations through human history and supremely in its climax on the last day involves the rescue and vindication of his trusting, believing people, as this chapter will emphasise (vv. 8-10). But it is even more significantly the vindication of God himself. 'It is God acting to claim at last the honour that is due to him as creator and ruler of the world.'[7] Like the Bible itself, Isaiah's book will end with this ultimate reality (66:22-24); but the everlasting consequences of judgement are as much an indispensable ingredient of the future eternity as are the certainties of everlasting joy and eternal life. They are two aspects of the same reality, which is why these two chapters belong together.

The eternal future is not without human participants, even if the old earth has been destroyed. Shouts of gladness and joy are heard as the desolate desert begins to blossom and bloom. New life is bursting out, like the crocus heralding the spring (35:1-2). The pictures are all of fertility and abundant growth, which will be witnessed by an undefined 'They' (v. 2b), who see in this amazing renewal the glory and splendour of Yahweh. Eventually, in 35:10, we learn that 'they' are 'the ransomed of the LORD'. It is through the fires of judgement that the new world is born, through the destruction of his enemies that God's people are secured in a renewed Zion (the holy city of Revelation 21:2, the New Covenant). Now at last the faithless city has been transformed into God's faithful city, where he will dwell among his people forever. That is why 35:3-4 exhort the people of God to persevere in faith and not to succumb to fear. If the terrors of the judgement are so inevitable, so is the salvation which issues from it. The glory of the resurrection lay on the other side of the sacrificial suffering

7. Barry Webb, *The Message of Isaiah*, p144

of the cross. Indeed, it was only through the propitiation achieved in that sacrifice, as Christ hung in the sinner's place bearing the Father's righteous wrath, that the way to eternal life was opened up. We should, therefore, go on trusting and obeying as we follow in Jesus' footsteps, through our present sufferings, to the glories of our homeland in heaven.

35:5-7 describes the nature of this change, in vivid Old Testament terms, which Alec Motyer sees as the 'background to the New Testament doctrine of the redemption of the body'.[8] The healing miracles of the Lord Jesus, during his earthly ministry, in this way prefigured the fullness of the kingdom he had come to inaugurate, with its ultimate completion in the resurrection of the body and the life everlasting. Moreover, we have his own authority for seeing, in these miraculous signs, the in-breaking of the Messianic kingdom and with it the start of all that to which Isaiah is looking forward here (see Matt. 11:4ff., 15:29-31). The specific references to the burning sand, the thirsty ground and the haunts of jackals deliberately underline the contrast and remedy which God's coming brings to the desolation of chapter 34 (35:7).

The final paragraph, 35:8-10, reveals a holy highway home to Zion, which can be relied upon to deliver its travellers safe to their destination, because of its guaranteed securities. The unclean, wicked fools and ferocious beasts are all excluded, but the redeemed will walk their way to Zion, entering the eternal city with great and lasting joy. This chapter is a wonderful text from which to preach the gospel, the New Testament links being obvious and strong (see above). Set against the darkest of backgrounds in the inescapability of final judgement, the joy of God's

8. Alec Motyer, *The Prophecy of Isaiah*, p274

redeeming work of ransom and renewal, for those who trust his promises and seek to live in obedience to his commands, is guaranteed and totally secure.

For us, the promise, 'your God will come' (35:4), is fulfilled, since 'The Word became flesh and made his dwelling (pitched his tent) among us. We have seen his glory, the glory of the One and Only, who came from the Father, full of grace and truth' (John 1:14). This Christ, who came once to die on the cross for the rescue of his people, will most certainly come again to bring each one of his believing people home to his eternal glory. Preach Isaiah!

Preaching and Teaching the Text

Title: **Which way?**

Text: **Isaiah 34:1–35:10**

Structure: Develop the contrast between the two chapters as a choice facing every human being, but also as God's means of salvation, as chapter 35 stands the other side of chapter 34 (e.g. the cross precedes the resurrection).

1. The wrath of God revealed (34:1-17)
   – the nature of God (vv. 2,8)
   – the horrors of judgement (vv. 2-10)
   – the emptiness of desolation (vv. 11-17)
2. The gospel of grace declared (35:1-10)
   – the promise of new creation (vv. 1-2)
   – the experience of salvation (vv. 3-7)
   – the security of God's people (vv. 8-10)

Leading a Bible Study

1. 34:1-7 What causes this scene of international and universal destruction?

2. 34:8-10 What is the connection between Zion and the desolate world?

3. 34:11-17 How do these verses help to bring home the enormity of God's judgement to those who might make light of it?

4. 35:1-4 What are the contrasts with chapter 34 and why have they happened?

5. 35:5-7 What is the substance of these promises and how should they stimulate trust and obedience? How are they fulfilled in the New Testament gospel?

6. 35:8-10 What are the ingredients of this pilgrim lifestyle and what guarantees are provided to underline its value?

Application: How should the stark choice presented in these two chapters – between judgement and salvation as part of God's people – affect our daily lives? How will it affect the way we tell the gospel to those close to us? And how do they reassure us in the face of the evil and suffering we see in our world?

Chapters 36–39 *Trusting and Obeying in Practice*

The style and mood changes at the opening of chapter 36 are striking indeed. From the glories of the eternal kingdom of the heavens, we arrive abruptly back in the hard realities of the earthly Jerusalem in 701 BC. Sennacherib's huge army is at the gates, about to besiege the city until it capitulates. As noted earlier, the subject matter falls into two parts, which we shall examine in the order of the text, though this is not chronological.

7. *Where is your confidence?* (36:1–37:38)

These chapters are the supreme Old Testament case study of what happens when the Davidic king believes God's promises and acts upon them (cf. 28:16). It is made even more powerful by the obvious contrast between Hezekiah, the believer and the behaviour of his godless father, Ahaz (7:1-25). In the face of life-threatening opposition, Hezekiah's reaction could hardly be more different. We know we are intended to make these connections because of the way in which 36:2 specifically echoes 7:3. What follows is an impressive piece of propaganda, as the Rabshakeh, Sennacherib's chief of staff, publicly ridicules Hezekiah's refusal to submit (36:4-10). The speech is full of its own irony as the field commander poses the very question God has been asking the people, through Isaiah, all through the prophecies, 'On what are you basing this confidence of yours?' (36:4). He dismisses any possible confidence in military strength or Egyptian assistance, just as Isaiah has done (vv. 5-6). But the irony consists in his equally confident rejection of trust in Yahweh (v. 7). With all the ignorant self-assurance of a man who has no knowledge of God, he brashly informs them that Hezekiah's centralisation of worship to the temple (as God had always instructed) must be displeasing to Yahweh, and so will certainly deprive them of his protection (v. 7). Surrender is the only way out and terms can be arranged (vv. 8-9). But the greatest unconscious irony is his assertion on behalf of Sennacherib in 36:10 that the Lord has told him to destroy Judah and will enable him to do it. Assyria is indeed the rod of God's anger (10:5), but that chapter continues with the assertion that he will punish the speech of his arrogant heart and direct his anger to Assyria's destruction (10:12-25).

This message is then repeated, in Hebrew, to the crowds gathered at a well to view the spectacle. The people are incited to revolt against Hezekiah, who has put his confidence in God's promise of deliverance given through Isaiah and clearly passed that promise on to the populace. But there will be no rescue, the Rabshakeh asserts. None of the gods of the other conquered peoples have been able to stand against Assyria's advance, 'How then can the LORD deliver Jerusalem from my hand?' (36:11-20). When Hezekiah receives the report of this meeting from his delegation, he responds in two ways. Putting on sackcloth as a sign of repentance, he seeks the Lord in his temple; he also sends a delegation to Isaiah to seek a word from God. Will Yahweh not rebuke the ridicule that has been poured upon him (36:21–37:4)?

Just as he gave a direct word to Ahaz, so the Lord responds directly through Isaiah to Hezekiah's anxiety. Deliverance will certainly come (37:5-7). But meanwhile, with news breaking of the Egyptian force marching out to engage them, the Assyrians, repeating their arguments, increase the pressure on the king to submit, by means of a letter personally delivered (37:8-13). It is this letter which drives Hezekiah back to the temple, to 'spread it out before the LORD' and to appeal to him, as God of all the earth, to hear and judge the blasphemous ridicule of the Assyrians, which have reduced the one and only living God to the same level as man-made idols (37:14-19). Hezekiah's concern is, of course, for the deliverance of the city, but even more so for the glory of God. Such a mighty rescue when all seems lost will exalt Yahweh as utterly distinct, 'so that all kingdoms on earth may know that you alone, O LORD, are God' (37:20).

A much more detailed prophetic oracle is then despatched from Isaiah to the king, in which the Lord rebukes the arrogance of Sennacherib and promises his imminent downfall. All his vaunted successes are attributable only to the will of Yahweh and not to the power of Assyria (37:21-29). Just as Ahaz received a sign, so does Hezekiah, that in the third year the land will be restored to its fruitfulness and that a remnant out of Judah will exhibit a renewed spiritual fruitfulness, in response to God's defence and rescue of his city (37:30-35). It is significant that Hezekiah's motivation (the glory of God) is the same as that of the Lord's response. He will save Jerusalem 'for my sake and for the sake of David my servant!' (v. 35). God always keeps the promises he makes.

The last few verses (37:36-38) are devastating in their understated simplicity, but jaw-dropping in their effect. This is the end of the Assyrian war machine and of its arrogant leader, Sennacherib. It is the climax of the first half of Isaiah's book, because it is the incontrovertible demonstration of Yahweh's power. This defeat is not due to superior human forces. It is without a battle, during one night, by the direct intervention of divine sovereignty, that the breath given to the men of this vast army is removed, according to God's promise and as a demonstration of God's power.

Here is evidence beyond all question that what God says, he can, and will, do. The implications for those who hear his message, through Isaiah, should change their whole perspective on time and eternity and therefore their behaviour and lifestyle, firstly in their relationship to this awesome covenant Lord and then towards one another. Why would one look anywhere else for one's ground of confidence, in this world or the next, than to the unchanging promises of the Holy One of Israel, the only true and living God?

Preaching and Teaching the Text
Title: **Where is your confidence?**
Text: **Isaiah 36:1–37:38**
Structure: This long passage needs a well-crafted summary of the narrative, relating it to the Isaianic historical background, before identifying and applying its theological teaching.

1. Round one: challenge and response (36:1–37:7)
    (a) Assyria's challenge (36:1-20)
      – the truth of the facts
      – the blindness of pride
    (b) Hezekiah's response (36:21–37:7)
      – dependence on the Lord
      – promise of deliverance
2. Round two: challenge and response (37:8-38)
    (a) The challenge is renewed (37:8-13)
    (b) Hezekiah returns to the Lord (37:14-20)
    (c) God intervenes (37:21-38)
    – explanation (37:21-29)
    – promise (37:30-35)
    – action (37:36-38)

Leading a Bible Study
1.   36:1-3 Jerusalem stands exposed to the Assyrian war machine. For background see 2 Kings 18:1ff., especially verses 5-7, also verses 13-16, which Isaiah omits. In spite of a relatively godly king, Judah is under God's judgement. What bells ring in verse 2 (see 7:3)? The same issue – twenty years later.

2. 36:4-12 Draw out the irony of the pagan's taunt in verse 4 (cf. 7:9b and 26:3-4; 30:15; etc). Where is the field commander right and where is he wrong? (Don't miss v. 10).

3. 36:13-22 Identify the fatal error in the argument (vv. 18-20).

4. 37:1-7 In what ways does Hezekiah model a godly king's response to this terrifying threat? Why is verse 6 really the turning point?

5. 37:8-13 Libnah is c.15 miles from Jerusalem. Sennacherib does not want to have to fight the Egyptians as well as besiege Jerusalem, so this second approach is designed to hasten Hezekiah's surrender. What can we learn of enemy tactics from this?

6. 37:14-20 And what can we learn about how to counteract them? Trace the ingredients of Hezekiah's prayer which are grounded in Old Testament revelation.

7. 37:21-35 In answer to the king's prayer, what does the Lord promise? Why does he promise these things? What deductions are to be made from these facts?

8. 37:36-38 Why the economy of words? Note the irony of verse 38!

Application: What does this passage teach us about the prayers that God answers (see vv. 4, 17, 20, 35)? How should this shape our prayers? Are our churches known for their prayerfulness? If not, why not? How can the lessons of this passage help change that?

8. To be, or not to be..? (38:1–39:8)

The end these chapters give this unit seems to be an anti-climax after this amazing deliverance. We have already

noted that their subject matter historically precedes the
attack of 701BC. The death of Hezekiah was in 687, so
fifteen years earlier (v5) brings us to 702, a year before the
siege, and the promise of verse 6 also seems to indicate that
the attack, though imminent, has not yet materialised.[9] So,
their positioning here must have a strategic significance in
the final form of Isaiah's book, as we have it. The link seems
to lie in the gracious answers God gives to Hezekiah, whose
response to crisis is to pray. Whether it is the imminent
destruction of the kingdom, or, as here, his own death
which is threatened (38:1), the godly king who is truly in
the line of his father David turns to Yahweh in prayer. This
is of course what the life of justification by faith is all about.
It is not only the privilege of the believing remnant 'to carry
everything to God in prayer', it is an absolute necessity if
they (and we) are to be able to persevere.

It is as though Hezekiah goes through the trauma
of facing death in his own life and finding Yahweh to be
a gracious prayer-answering God, so that when the crisis
comes in the next year to the nation, the Davidic king is
already personally convinced of the goodness and grace of
the Lord's promising word.

38:1-8 is a simple prose account, from Isaiah's perspective,
of the event, which is totally governed by two words from
Yahweh (38:1, 4). Hezekiah's prayer may have been wrong-
footed in its focus on his personal integrity. He had done
much spiritual good to the kingdom (see the extensive
record in 2 Chron. 29-31), but we know that he was also
courting the Egyptians and chapter 39 will show how easily
he was influenced by the Babylonians. The content may
have had the wrong focus, but the direction of the prayer

9. Alec Motyer, *The Prophecy of Isaiah*, p291

and the trust it expressed were entirely right. God responds not only to the immediate personal situation of the king, but with a promise for the future to a ruler who is learning to trust (38:5-6).

The sign, in 38:7-8, given freely by God, recalls his earlier offer to the unbelieving Ahaz (7:11ff.) and confirms the truth and reliability of God's promises. A more detailed narrative is found at 2 Kings 20:1-11, where Isaiah's intercession is shown to be crucial in the giving of the sign and where 'a poultice of figs' is the immediate agent of Hezekiah's healing (see also 38:21).

The extraordinary nature of the sign may test the credulity of some contemporary congregations schooled in the scientific materialism of their generation. But as Motyer comments, 'It would be as improper for us to be dogmatic about how this was done as to deny what is plainly stated. Scripture presents the creator God as the sovereign master of his creation, and the believing mind accepts that he could at will add ten units of time to that day'.[10] Equally, he can add fifteen years to the king's life.

38:9-20 consists of Hezekiah's meditation poem on his experience, beginning with a moving account of the trauma he underwent upon hearing that he would not recover (38:9-14). Recognising the whole experience to have been governed by God for Hezekiah's benefit, he acknowledges God's gracious restoration and resolves to use his remaining years to walk humbly, to testify to the next generation and to worship the Lord on a daily basis. The cure is applied (38:21) and the outcome is the renewed daily access to God in temple prayer, which was so vital in the crisis, soon to come, with Sennacherib's attack.

---

10. Alec Motyer, *The Prophecy of Isaiah*, p292

39:1-8 deals with the Babylonian approach to Hezekiah to sign him up as an ally in their anti-Assyrian alliance. The king's recovery presents a useful occasion, but is probably not the underlying cause of the Babylonian embassy (39:1). His display of all his resources is probably designed to be a positive response to Babylon's flattering overtures. This is what little Judah can offer. But there is no seeking the Lord, no dependence on God. It seems as though chapter 38 might as well not have happened. Isaiah, who was obviously not consulted, uncovers the sad story (39:3-4) to follow it with a devastating revelation from the Lord (39:5-7). Everything the Babylonians saw will become theirs. Assyria will not conquer Judah, but Babylon will, and all Hezekiah's treasures will be removed. Not only that, but 39:7 could well be understood as predicting the end of the Davidic monarchy. The king's response seems inordinately self-centred. This is the last we hear of this good king in Isaiah's book.

So why do chapters 36-37 not conclude this unit? Surely, it is because Babylon now fills the horizon and the book needs to develop the lessons of trust in Yahweh's promises in a context where deliverance is not experienced. The best of human kings, such as Hezekiah, have been shown to be mortal (ch. 38) and fallible (ch. 39) – there is no ultimate solution in a merely human son of David. But in the face of far greater pressures and tragedies than chapters 1–39 recount, chapters 40–66 will show us why and how God is to be trusted and what are his greater universal and eternal purposes, beyond the Babylonian exile. 'Isaiah is showing that there is no final salvation in a human being, no matter how good he might be. Our hope is not in the perfectibility of humanity. The Messiah we look for is better than that.'[11]

11. John N. Oswalt, *Isaiah: The NIV Application Commentary*, p437

Preaching and Teaching the Text

Title: **To be, or not to be…?**

Text: **Isaiah 38:1–39:8**

Structure:

1. Dealing with a personal crisis (38:1-8)

     – a desperate need brought to God (38:1-3)

     – a gracious answer miraculously confirmed (38:4-8)

2. Celebrating an amazing deliverance (38:9-22)

     – realism about the need (38:9-14)

     – resolve about the future (38:15-22)

3. Compromising the key principle (39:1-8)

     – flattery subverts faith (39:1-2)

     – judgement removes blessing (39:3-8)

Conclusion: Though Hezekiah wanted to be the man of 38:15, when Babylon came to call, his pride overcame his faith. Exile for Judah must come because the nation reflects the king's unwillingness to trust in God alone. A greater king is needed – and will be revealed (chapters 40–55).

Leading a Bible Study

Note: Chapters 38–39 are effectively a flashback to the period before 701 BC, because of the future tenses of 38:6 and because the Babylonian envoys were part of Hezekiah's anti-Assyrian policy initiative (alliance with Egypt) which precipitated the invasion.

1.   38:1-3 This personal crisis is every bit as challenging for Hezekiah as the later invasion. How does the godly king deal with it?

2.   38:4-6 What is God's magnificent response? Has he changed his mind?

3.   38:7-8 What is the implicit contrast with Ahaz (cf. 7:11-14)? See also verse 22.

4.   38:9-20 These psalm-like verses are Hezekiah's reflection on the whole experience. Trace the development of his emotional reaction in verses 10-14. How might that help us? What lessons did Hezekiah learn (vv.15-20)? Would a New Testament Christian want to express things differently in any way?

5.   38:21-22 What is the blend of divine and human in the healing?

6.   39:1-2 Why did this seem such a good idea at the time?

7.   39:3-7 How does the judgement pronounced match the folly of Hezekiah's actions? Underline the importance of the prediction of the Babylonian exile.

Reflection: Issues in focus, but unresolved, at the half-way point in Isaiah's book: what are the implications for the Davidic dynasty? For God's covenant promises and purposes? Who rules? Is trust in the Lord still an active possibility?

Application: Hezekiah displays great trust in the crisis of chapter 35, but he struggles to continue with a lifestyle of trust in chapter 39. In what ways are we too tempted to place trust in God in emergencies, but not as an ongoing lifestyle? How do the lessons of this chapter help to change that?

Part 5

THE SERVANT KING
A NEW EXODUS
AND THE RESTORATION OF ZION

Isaiah 40–55

'a veritable OT biblical theology in itself. It might well be called the "Old Testament book of Romans"'

Walter Kaiser, *Towards an Old Testament Theology*, (Grand Rapids, USA: Zondervan, 1991) p.205

Introduction

There is little disagreement that the major division in the book of Isaiah is between chapters 39 and 40. With the chilling revelation that the ultimate fate of the Davidic kingdom of Judah will be exile in Babylon (39:6-7), the focus of the book abruptly changes from eighth-century Jerusalem to that much more distant future. As we follow its themes, we are taken beyond the exile to the eventual destruction of mighty Babylon, the return of God's people to their land and on into an unspecified future time. Then, the fallen and faithless city will become truly faithful, and God's universal and eternal kingdom will draw men and women from every tribe, kindred and nation into relationships of peace with God and so with one another. The canvas could hardly be wider, or the future pitch more expansive and all-embracing.

It is this extraordinary future sweep in all its detail, as for example, Cyrus the Mede (44:28) or the fall of Babylon (46:1-2; 48:20-22), which has produced so much critical disquiet. How could Isaiah know such historical details so far ahead of his time? How could he predict in such detail the suffering servant's death and resurrection (53:4-12)? The answer must be either that they are divinely revealed by a sovereign God who knows the end from the beginning and orders all things according to his perfect will, or that we are reading material of a much later date than Isaiah. But even that could not account for the detailed description of the cross and resurrection. For my own part, I am persuaded of the unity of the book, which I will assume throughout this section. More detailed arguments for this can be found in the appendix, 'One Isaiah, or more?' (p. 297)

It will be important to bear in mind in approaching these chapters that such questions will be in some of our hearers' minds and that if this material is to do its faith-building work, we need to furnish them with answers to the prevailing contemporary scepticism.

Perhaps it is not surprising that this magnificent section has been under such sustained attack, since it is one of the mountain ranges of the Old Testament in its glorious proclamation of God's sovereign plan and Christ's finished work. To read and believe these chapters means that we have a God who is working out his great salvation purposes in human history, whose word can be trusted and whose kingdom will know no end.

This section is probably the best-known and most often preached part of Isaiah's book, because of its gospel content and the theme of the suffering servant threading through its chapters, which finds its fulfilment in our Lord Jesus Christ. But there is much more even than these peaks of revelation to explore here. The other side of its faith-building ability is its devastating exposure of the follies of idolatry and of all confidence in men. Idols are delusions simply because they are the product of human imagination and manufacture, but it is only when their hollow mockery is revealed that the magnificent contrast of faith in Yahweh and his unbreakable promises shines out in its full splendour. These are truths and convictions which are both sadly lacking and greatly needed among contemporary Christians, so preach Isaiah!

1. Context and Structure

Before we look at the detailed content of these chapters, we need to get a bird's-eye view of the unit's structure and also to set it in the context of the whole book. We saw that the great challenge of the opening sections of the book was whether Judah would be found trusting in God's promises in the face of the multiple Assyrian threats, or relying on her own policies and diplomatic alliances with unbelieving pagan nations. Ahaz and Hezekiah represent the two positions, with God's own faithful covenant-love and trustworthiness being wonderfully confirmed and gloriously vindicated in the climax of his supernatural deliverance of Jerusalem from the besieging armies of Sennacherib (chs. 36–37), as Hezekiah fulfils his role as the Davidic king and puts all his trust in Yahweh.

However, the unit ends, as we have seen, with the prediction of the Babylonian exile and with the larger problem posed back in chapter 1 unresolved. How is the faithless city to become a faithful city? How are God's people to be persuaded to trust in him and his words as their consistent lifestyle? It will not be enough to deal merely with the symptoms of their rebellion politically or socially. The returning exiles will have the same fallen, sinful nature, because, in the familiar phrase, 'the heart of the human problem is the problem of the human heart'. The real issue is whether that can ever be remedied and, if so, how God can do it, for it will certainly require divine intervention.

These questions would be particularly acute at the time of the exile, during the Babylonian captivity and even more so when the generation of returnees was faced with the enormous challenges of rebuilding the city and the temple. So, we can see why God gave this message to Isaiah, so many decades before it all began to happen, to prepare his people for the inevitable, so that they could come to the right spiritual understanding of the conquest when it happened.

But he also intended to sustain his people, through the seventy years of exile and on their return, with the knowledge that the glorious future of renewal and restoration still awaited them and that his promises were to be trusted. He had not been defeated, either by the gods of Babylon or by the idolatry and rebellion of his covenant people. 'Your God reigns!' (52:7) is a dominant message, certainly of great comfort, but also of deep challenge and ultimately of limitless hope. Since these are the realities assured by God's word, why should they give way to fear or be diverted into foolish and fruitless idolatry?

In subdividing the unit, we should note that chapters 40–41 form something of a bridge between the book's two halves, so that some commentators have suggested that the second part might more properly be seen to begin at 42:1, with the monumentally important words, 'Here is my servant'. While recognising that this is indeed a key moment in the progressive structure of the whole book, it seems better to make the division at chapter 40, so that the Babylonian identification is the climax of the first half and then the double imperative 'Comfort' (40:1) introduces the developed message of what lies ahead, in the exile and beyond. Chapters 40–41 therefore look both ways, back to the unresolved issues of the first three sections of the book, but forward to the redemptive work of the servant and the coming of the heavenly city through the work of the anointed conqueror (chapters 56-66).

In some ways, chapters 40 and 41 follow Isaiah's favourite methodology of the 'doublet', where the same truths are taught twice, first with regard to his covenant people (ch. 40) and then with regard to the pagan nations (ch. 41). Together, they pose the ongoing, and yet unresolved, problem of human alienation from God the creator, but begin to point to a new divine initiative. Both rebellious Judah and the Gentile nations will be rescued: Judah from her suffering, and the Gentiles from their hopeless idolatry. Hence, 'Here is my servant' (42:1).

Chapters 42–48 expound how God will meet with his people and deal with their desperate condition, which is seen to be both political (the exile) and spiritual (idolatry). At the very beginning, the servant is introduced as God's agent, by whom deliverance will come, since he will be both 'a covenant for the people' (Judah) and 'a light for the Gentiles' (42:6). We might have expected this agency to be fulfilled by the covenant community itself, since the responsibility of testifying to God's grace before the nations had belonged to Israel from the very inception of her national life (see Deut. 4:5-8), but the original 'servant' is disqualified for the task, being 'deaf and blind' (42:18-19, cf. 6:9-10). If the covenant nation is unable to carry the light of Yahweh to the nations because of its apostasy, clearly God must deal with that issue first. In the long section, 42:18–43:21, God exposes the causes of Judah's political bondage, reveals the uselessness of idols, as of all merely human solutions, but declares himself to be both able and willing to rescue his people. He is the only Saviour and he will bring about a new exodus for his people.

An equally detailed section, 43:22–44:23, parallels this revelation almost exactly, but with its focus on the spiritual needs of God's people. The same realities are affirmed, and a spiritual deliverance is promised. It is no wonder that the two sections end with the whole creation rejoicing in the Lord's demonstration of his glory as he redeems his people (44:23). There are helpful sections in Motyer's *The Prophecy of Isaiah* which establish this overall reading of chapters 42–44. This is followed by a shorter section, 44:24–45:7, in which the means of this political deliverance is revealed. God will raise up a Gentile ruler, Cyrus by name, whom he designates as 'my shepherd' (44:28) and even 'his anointed' (45:1).

Because God's hand is so powerfully with Cyrus, all that Yahweh purposes will be fulfilled through him. This is in keeping with Isaiah's understanding that God raises up pagan kingdoms and rulers, Assyria, Babylon and now the Medo-Persian empire, to accomplish his sovereign purposes in the government of the nations, since he is the creator and sustainer of all, the only potentate, who is King of kings and Lord of lords (see 1 Tim. 6:15-16). All this provides further nails in the coffins of the idols. This also explains why God's people have no right to quarrel with his purposes. They do not have him on a string, which is of course the attraction of idolatry. Rather, Yahweh majestically affirms, 'there is no God apart from me...for I am God, and there is no other' (45:21-22). The whole section, 45:8-25, reaffirms the purposes of God: to reach the whole Gentile world with his salvation, and to bring all humanity to bow before him.

Chapters 46 and 47 seem particularly designed to hearten God's people as they faced the reality of the exile, though their foundational truths are timeless in their relevance. God reminds his people of his dependable faithfulness and covenant commitment, in spite of all their faithless rebellion (46:3-7). He proclaims his incomparability – both in his uniqueness ('there is none like me' 46:9) and in the execution of his purposes (46:8-13). This is further reinforced by Isaiah's very vivid pictures of the utter futility of the idols of Babylon in the face of the conquest of Cyrus

(46:1-2; 47:1-15). When Yahweh moves against her, even mighty Babylon is powerless, which is what his people must keep believing as the exile begins, if they are not to capitulate to the apparent power of Bel and Nebo and all the other 'deities' who seem to have defeated Yahweh. The fall of Babylon is as certain as the exile itself.

The first part of the section is rounded off by chapter 48, which stands alone as a summary and reiteration of the thought-content of the whole unit thus far. God reminds his people of the issues which have precipitated his judgement, and how his prediction demonstrates his own existence, reliability and wisdom, in contrast to their inert idols. Yahweh, the only true and living God, speaks, and he does what he says he will do. He promises and he fulfils. He predicts and he delivers. Indeed, the coming deliverance in the new exodus from Babylon (48:20-21) will be still further proof of his divine power.

Chapters 49–55 contain the last three of the four 'servant songs', or poetic oracles, which detail how God's work of eternal redemption will actually be accomplished. 49:1-6 provides the text of the second song, in which the servant's work is expounded, again with a double emphasis on the restoration of Israel (v. 3) and 'that you may bring my salvation to the ends of the earth' (v. 6). This is followed by a prolonged dialogue between God and his people (49:8–52:12), which is itself divided into two by the third of the servant songs (50:4-9).

As the Lord promises to restore his people to the land (49:8-13), he is met by Zion's accusation that he has forsaken and forgotten her (49:14). Yahweh's response is to affirm not only the return, but the future blessing of his people in expanded numbers and prosperity (49:15-21), which Zion stubbornly refuses to believe (49:24). However, the Lord continues graciously to explain that the exile is not divorce, but discipline (50:1-3). At this point, the servant is reintroduced as a contrasting example of one who listens to God's word and lives in obedience to it, even though that proves costly in terms of physical suffering (50:4-11).

The dialogue continues as the Lord twice summons his people to listen to his promises of restoration and righteousness (51:1-8). And for the first time there seems to be at least the germ of a believing response in their prayer, 'Awake, awake…O arm of the LORD' (51:9-11). In a deeply pastoral passage (51:12-16), God shows that they fear their enemies only because they have forgotten his power. He then uses their own appeal, 'Awake, awake…' turning back on to his people the responsibility to be ready for their promised deliverance (51:17-23) followed by the redemption and renewal of Jerusalem, as the new exodus brings them home from Babylon (52:1-12).

This is the cue for the final and greatest of the servant songs (52:13–53:12) in which the servant's saving work is expounded and explained, in terms of his substitutionary sacrifice, followed by his vindication in life beyond death. The last two chapters of the unit describe the results of this amazing ministry of the servant, firstly, with reference to the sons of Abraham, as the covenant family is enlarged (54:1-10) and the covenant city delivered from her afflictions and beautified by righteousness (54:11-17).

Then the scene expands to the whole of humanity, as membership of God's covenant community is offered to all who will turn to him and trust in his powerful and effective word (55:1-13). Because the spiritual benefits secured by the servant's obedience are indestructible and eternal, the chapter echoes Isaiah's now familiar theme of the whole creation rejoicing in the Lord and in his great purposes at its close (55:12-13). The restoration of the earthly Jerusalem is therefore only a pale foreshadowing of the foundation and permanence of the New Covenant, the faithful city, which is eternal in its duration and universal in its scope and which is the supreme outcome of the servant's life and work.

2. Preaching Notes

This part of Isaiah is the one in which New Testament Christians are most likely to feel at home. The apostles use the songs of the suffering servant extensively to speak of Christ and the gospel. Indeed, the Lord Jesus himself did the same. For example, in Luke's treatment of the betrayal and arrest, it is Jesus himself who insists that in the coming hours the prophecies of Isaiah 53 will be fulfilled in him. 'It is written: "And he was numbered with the transgressors"; and I tell you that this must be fulfilled in me. Yes, what is written about me is reaching its fulfilment' (Luke 22:37). So we need have no qualms about preaching Christ from the servant songs and expounding them as wonderful prophecies of the gospel realities, traced out in their detail in the pages of the New Testament.

In preaching prophecy we need always to have in mind that the same text will have three points of relevance, each of which is to be found at a different point along the timeline of God's chronological development of salvation-history. As with all biblical work, the preacher must firstly set the text in its original context, exploring the significance of the prophecy for its first hearers through the ministry of Isaiah. If we fail to understand what it meant to them then, we shall be unlikely to interpret its message correctly for us now. Often, this is regarded as purely historical, in the sense of informing our hearers about the characters and events to which the prophecy alludes, or to the setting in which it was given. But I want to suggest that it has more value to the preacher than simple historical accuracy, important though that is.

We need to delve deeper into the spiritual condition exposed in the hearers, and to realise that this was not restricted to them, but shows us unchanging human nature, as evident today as it was then. This will help us to draw parallels from the covenant community then, to ourselves as God's people today.

So this section uncovers attitudes of compromise and unbelief found in all our hearts and congregations. Themes here – reasons for idolatry, the spiritual states that lead to fear of men and doubting of God's promises, the way in which Judah misread her privilege of covenant with Yahweh as justifying her lack of concern for the pagan world – do not merely tell us about ancient Judah. They show us problems that are common to our fallen humanity.

However, we must not fall into the trap of thinking that we are in exactly the same position as old covenant Israel. Two other events move us on: firstly, Christ has come in his incarnation to inaugurate the kingdom; and secondly, he will return in glory, as the kingdom reaches its consummation in eternity. We stand between these two points, looking back through the lens of Christ's life, death, resurrection and ascension to the content of this book, unable to interpret it rightly in any other way than through Jesus and his finished work.

But we are also looking forward to the final fulfilment of all that is promised in the heavenly city. We are only too painfully aware, in a fallen world, of how far short our present experience must be of the glories that await us in the eternal kingdom. We are God's covenant people now, on the same basis of his grace and with the same requirements of faith and obedience as were demanded of Israel. But Christ has come. The work of redemption is complete. The Lord Jesus is enthroned, far above all. He has poured out his Spirit on his church, and he lives within us, changing us into his likeness from the inside out. The blessing promised to Abraham has come to the Gentiles through Christ Jesus, 'so that by faith we might receive the promise of the Spirit' (Gal. 3:14).

It is very important for us to keep these realities in view when we are preaching Isaiah, so that we do not drift into the position of automatically equating the church with rebellious Judah under God's sentence of judgement, just because there are parallels between God's Old and New Covenant communities. Of course, God disciplines his New Covenant people as he did the Old, and a passage like Hebrews 12:4-13 is an extremely important reference point for this spiritual reality. But the emphasis is entirely positive. It is 'for our good, that we may share in his holiness' (Heb. 12:10). It is not a punishment for sin but a means of grace to prepare us for glory.

We must not lose sight of the gospel perspective that 'there is now no condemnation for those who are in Christ Jesus' (Rom. 8:1). The servant's work is complete; the price is paid. Without this perspective, we shall find ourselves using the rebuke passages in Isaiah like a big stick trying to beat our congregations into godliness. But godliness never came through the law and its works. This book is the prophecy of justification by faith, and faith is totally dependent on grace.

We are not to be legalistic in our approach and preach that we are effectively justified by our sanctification. We must all fight our natural tendency to works-religion. We are not to equate ourselves with pre-exilic Judah under sentence of wrath, nor is the church in exile because of her sin. The apostle Peter refers to life in this world as 'the time of your exile' (1 Pet. 1:17 ESV), but this is because we are not yet in the enjoyment of the fullness of the gospel and its blessings in the heavenly city. Our citizenship is in heaven (Phil. 3:20), and we are pilgrim people on our way home to the New Covenant. The promises of Isaiah 40–55 have been fulfilled, and we are to live in the enjoyment of them while we wait in hope and anticipation for their completion in the heavenly, faithful city.

The great value of these chapters to the church is to generate and deepen faith. They draw us to Christ: to come as thirsty people to the waters and to come as guilty sinners to the servant, our substitute, the sacrifice for the sins of the world. They generate saving faith and then encourage us to realise that the way into the Christian life is also the way on. It is in every way a life of faith, believing the promises and obeying the commands. But neither are separable from the Lord who speaks them. They reveal his wonderful nature and character – his sovereign rule and authority, his limitless power, his brilliant righteousness and glory, his tender compassion, his boundless grace, his unchanging faithfulness and his unique person.

These are great chapters to extend our vision of God, to bring us in repentance and faith to the cross and to help us live in dependence and submission, as the redeemed of the Lord. The opening declaration, 'Here is your God' (40:9), expounded throughout the unit, is met with the resounding assurance near its close, 'Your God reigns' (52:7). That restoration of the throne of God, in our hearts and in the whole created order, is the purpose of the servant's work, the glory of his accomplishment and the joy of our hearts both here and hereafter.

The sermon outlines which follow attempt to pick up the major ideas we have observed in the structure and contents of chapters 40–55. They present them with a view to the contemporary congregation and to practical application, though that can only be hinted at, as each preacher will need to make particular applications to his own congregational context.

Group Bible Study Questions
In this series of outlines, I have put together longer units so that the leader can decide how much detail to concentrate on. It is possible either to take an overview of the passage by moving through the series of questions looking for the major ideas, or to divide an individual study into one, two or even more units so as to give more time to the detail. The consecutive nature of the material enables choices of this sort to be made depending on the capabilities of individual groups. The leader will need to read the section on 'Working Through the Text' for background to the questions.

3. Working Through the Text
1. Here is your God (40:1-31)
This is one of the best-known and most well-loved chapters of the Old Testament, especially familiar to all devotees of the Authorised (King James) version of the Bible or of Handel's *Messiah*. But what is well known in language is often not understood in its own context, so that its effect

is even diminished by its familiarity. The challenge for the preacher is to dig deep enough to uncover its powerful message with fresh force and compelling relevance for our hearers.

To do this, we need to remember Isaiah's central theological purpose for his own hearers, which is to look beyond the coming judgement to encourage faith in the unchanging promises and purposes of God for his people. He wants those who read the prophecy to be assured of the dependability of God's steadfast word, so that whether they are in Judah or Babylon, they will learn to trust his promises and so obey his commands. In this way, Isaiah purposes to gather a faithful remnant, in his own and succeeding generations, in which present obedience (godliness) is motivated by a sure and certain future hope. Our own generation is certainly no exception to this need.

The chapter is best divided into two sections, verses 1-11 and 12-31. The opening section presents God himself, returning with his people from the exile (vv. 3-5), which is the comfort verse 1 promises. Just as the announcement of the Babylonian exile is the climax of chapters 1–39, with their predominant note of judgement, so this chapter, which serves as the overture to the whole of the second half of Isaiah's book, climaxes in the proclamation to Jerusalem and Judah, 'Here is your God! See, the Sovereign LORD comes…' (vv. 9-10). God is the answer to his people's needs and problems, and he does not merely send his blessings; he brings them.

The 'comfort' of verse 1 is not a life of ease but the breathing of new life and strength into a defeated and demoralised community: the exile is ending; its punishment is complete and matches (as the two halves of a 'doubled'

– folded – sheet of paper exactly match each other) the dimensions of the offences.[1] This 'comfort' is God himself visiting his people, stepping into history to rescue and restore, which he does in three spectacular and comforting ways. He reveals his glory in bringing his exiled people home (vv. 3-5). He demonstrates his faithfulness by fulfilling his promised word (vv. 6-8). He shepherds his flock, as he exercises on their behalf both his sovereign power and his detailed personal care (vv. 9-11). The shepherd-king who powers his way through the trackless desert, so that nothing can resist his advance, is the one who 'gathers the lambs in his arms and carries them close to his heart' (v. 11).

This magnificent opening serves as an introduction to the swelling themes of God's universal salvation with which the section will close in chapter 55. But as so often in Isaiah's ministry, the people of God are less than convinced by what they hear. This was what God had predicted in 6:9-10. So, the rest of the chapter deals with the two major objections which Isaiah encounters, which can be summed up in the form of two related questions. Does God really have the power to do this (vv. 12-26) and equally, does he really have the will (vv. 27-31)? Put in their simplest terms: can God rescue and does he care? Verse 27 sums up these complaints. God's answers are presented in a series of wonderfully powerful poetic pictures, which expound the declaration of verse 9, 'Here is your God!', as they stretch and expand our inadequate, pocket-sized concepts of his deity.

In preaching, it is worthwhile stopping on verse 12, for example, in order to unpack the nuances of Isaiah's detail. This is one of the reasons why Isaiah's message is never

1. For the detailed language of the opening verses, see Motyer's illuminating comments: Alec Motyer, *Tyndale Old Testament Commentary on Isaiah*, (Nottingham, UK: Inter-Varsity Press 1999) p243

stale or boringly repetitive, even though the same issues and themes are frequently revisited. The genius lies in the variety of the detail. So, in verse 12, we are given four human measures to consider – the hollow of the hand, its span from thumb to little finger, a basket and a pair of scales. They are comparatively small everyday measurements, but see what God encompasses in his equivalents – the oceans, the heavens, the dust of the earth, the mountains and the hills. It is meant to blow our minds, to force us to stop and think about the sheer incomprehensibility of the vastness and power of our God.

Does God really have the power? Verses 12-17 hammer home the message that his power in creation and in sustaining life on planet earth is beyond all human measurement. It is off the scale of all our reckoning. Similarly, verses 18-24 indicate that God is beyond all our human comparisons. These sections pointedly underline the stupidity of trusting in man and trusting in idols, which chapters 1-39 have already ruthlessly exposed. The prophet's method here is more than irony; it is ridicule. He is a God beyond all rivals as verses 25-26 eloquently testify, 'the Holy One'. When God's people are tempted to join the idolatry of Babylon in worshipping the stars, they need to recall 'Who created all these' and know that the starry hosts only exist 'Because of his great power and mighty strength'.

Does God really know about his people and does he care? These are the great questions in verses 27-31. This complaint is shown to be wrong and unfounded on both the counts of theology and experience. The theology is re-stated in verse 28, which is the basis for the experience of verses 29-31. The most foolish behaviour is to judge by what we see or think we understand, given that we are dealing with a God of limitless power and incomparable love. The sovereign's authority and ability are exercised for the well being of his flock (vv. 10-11). Indeed, as God's people our very weaknesses constitute our position of strength because they drive us to put our trust in God. In verse 30, it is the young and strong who tire and stumble. Only God has limitless strength, which he shares with those who hope in him. So it is the weary and the weak who prevail, because they 'exchange' (literally) their weakness for God's power. The effects are wonderful – strength to soar, stamina to run and perseverance to keep walking – and all are supernaturally provided. The supply is assured to those who patiently wait, as a demonstration of their restful trust. 'Here is your God!' (v. 9).

This is a great chapter which cries out to be preached and whose powerful relevance is only increased when we take the time to set it not only in its historical context in Isaiah's day, but also in its theological context in the whole of biblical revelation. For ourselves, as we look back on Isaiah's words from our point on the chronological time-line of God's salvation-history, we can and must understand them through the lens of Christ's coming, of his incarnation, atoning death and subsequent resurrection. If we are asked when these prophecies were fulfilled, doubtless we could rightly point to some level of fulfilment when the first band of exiles returned to Jerusalem as a result of the decree of Cyrus the liberator. But the real exile and its spiritual issues remained unresolved down nearly five centuries, until a voice was heard crying in the desert, 'Prepare the way for the Lord…' and John the Baptist 'went into all the country around the Jordan, preaching a baptism of repentance for the forgiveness of sins' (Luke 3:3-6).

It is in Christ, the shepherd-king, that these promises find their ultimate fulfilment, and as we preach the realities of God's sovereign power and shepherd care, we must show them to be perfectly displayed in the glories of our Saviour. All the great Isaianic themes are here in this chapter, culminating in Christ's person and work. Our twenty-first-century congregations desperately need both the nourishment and the practical challenge which this chapter so uniquely brings.

Preaching and Teaching the Text
Title: **Here is your God!**
Text: **Isaiah 40:1-31**
Structure: Set the text in the context of the exile to Babylon prediction (39:6-7) and how it looks beyond the exile to restoration.
1. God's message of comfort (vv. 1-11)
    – he will reveal his glory (vv. 3-5)
    – he will keep his word (vv. 6-8)
    – he will shepherd his flock (vv. 9-11)
2. But does he really have the power (vv. 12-26)
    – beyond all measure (vv. 12-17)
    – beyond all comparison (vv. 18-24)
    – beyond all rivals (vv. 25-26)
3. But does he really have the will (vv. 27-31)
    – yes, because of his faithfulness (vv. 27-28)
    – yes, because of his power (v. 29)
    – yes, because of his compassion (vv. 30-31)
Conclusion: Here is your God! Trust him.
This sermon could equally well be divided into two, verses 1-11 and verses 12-31, in which case more attention could be paid to the vivid details of the text.

Leading a Bible Study

1. 40:1-2 Noting that 'comfort' means 'revive', or 'breathe new life into', what is (a) the nature and (b) the cause of the good news in these verses? NB 'double for all her sins' (v. 2) signifies 'total' in the sense of 'exactly matching' (a doublet).

2. 40:3-5 The 'comfort' begins to be explained in detail. What are the physical pictures and what do they symbolise? In the light of Matthew 3:3 and Mark 1:3 what does the New Testament teach us about the end of the exile and the fulfilment of these promises?

3. 40:6-8 How do the ideas of this paragraph strengthen the faith of Isaiah's hearers that the promises of the last few verses will really happen?

4. 40:9-11 What are the physical pictures here and why are they significant? What do these verses teach us about the rescuing God who comes? Note that the sovereign (v. 10) and shepherd (v. 11) images control the rest of the chapter. Reflect on how we see these in Jesus' ministry.

5. 40:12-20 Does God really have the power to achieve this rescue? How do these verses answer the sceptic? Take time to unpack the vivid imagery of verses 12, 15, etc. and reflect on its implications. In the light of all this, how does Isaiah emphasise the futility of idols (vv. 18-20)?

6. 40:21-31 Does God really care enough for his people to achieve this rescue? How do these verses answer that question? Look for the themes: God is beyond all human comparison (vv. 21-24), beyond all rivals (vv. 25-26), and beyond all weakness or inability (vv. 27-31).

Application: In this chapter, God's people are given hope for their transformation and rescue by an awesome God.

How does it give us, also, hope for our own transformation and rescue? How does this picture of God's greatness change our perspective on life and on history?

2. Glory in the Holy One of Israel (41:1-29)

The connection to chapter 40 is made clear in verse 1, where the nations are summoned to 'renew their strength', which echoes the promise of 40:31 made by Yahweh that 'those who hope in the LORD will renew their strength'. Clearly, the Lord is the source of the strength of the believing remnant of his people; but what about the nations who are not in covenant relationship with him and who have only their futile idols on which to depend? This is the issue which verse 1 summons the whole earth to contest at the bar of Yahweh's court. And it is urgent, because verses 2-3 describe a hugely successful conqueror who is sweeping across the world in victory, to the consternation of the nations. 'Why is this happening?' is the presenting question, but God's more penetrating enquiry is 'Who has done this and carried it through' (v. 4a), which serves to reveal the creator's hand in all the changing scenes of human politics, 'I, the LORD...I am he' (v. 4b). Although the figure may well be intended to be Cyrus, at this stage he is anonymous.

The opening summons from God meets with two contrasting reactions. The idolatrous nations are driven into a panic, which reveals the futility of their religion (vv. 5-7). If you rely on idols, you have only yourself, because you are the creator of your 'gods', rather than having a God who created you. The battle is as old as the history of the fallen human race and needs to be exposed in our preaching in all its contemporary disguises.

However, God turns to 'Israel, my servant' (v. 8), a term which will become increasingly significant as the unit progresses and which always carries with it reference to a special relationship with God and commissioning from him. Though Israel is described as a worm (v. 14) and 'poor and needy' (v. 17), God's presence and covenant grace transform each situation of human helplessness (see verses 10, 14-15 and 17b-20). This is what marks Israel out as distinct from all the nations. The people of the world create their own idols and are sunk in futility. By contrast, Israel has been created, as a unique people, by her God, who is himself the source of all that she needs to survive and prosper.

In the final section, verses 21-29, we are back in court as the issues are summarised and the contrast ruthlessly exposed. Idols can do nothing because they are 'less than nothing' (v. 24). They have no ability to influence the present or the future. So when Yahweh stirs up the unstoppable conqueror, they have no answer. Their plight is hopeless. 'Their images are but wind and confusion' (v. 29b). The difference lies in what you worship. As Psalm 115:8 reminds us about idols and idolatry, 'Those who make them will be like them, and so will all who trust in them.' The question we are left with at the end of chapter 41 is whether their creator is content to leave the majority of his human creation to stew in this hopeless condition. We can hardly believe that the God revealed in Scripture would be willing to do so, in the light of his promise to Abraham in Genesis 12:3, that all the peoples of the earth will be blessed through his seed. The opening words of chapter 42 immediately reassure us that this is so. 'Here is my servant', who will prove to be the salvation of the Gentile world.

Preaching and Teaching the Text

Title: **Glory in the Holy One of Israel (41:16)**

Text: **Isaiah 41:1-29**

Structure: Relate the theme of the chapter to the prevailing issues in Isaiah. In whom will you trust – the gods or God, policies or promises?

1. A great claim (vv. 1-4)
   – the whole world 'in the dock' (v. 1)
   – God's evidence, which demands a verdict (vv. 2-4)
2. Great confidence (vv. 5-20)
   – not human idols, but God's faithfulness (vv. 5-10)
   – not human opposition, but God's help (vv. 11-16)
   – not human resources, but God's refreshment (vv. 17-20)
3. A greater proof (vv. 21-29)
   – idols cannot explain and cannot predict (vv. 21-24)
   – only God predicts and delivers (vv. 25-29)

Leading a Bible Study

1. 41:1-4 We now shift to the practical corollary of this amazing revelation of Yahweh in chapter 40. The nations are summoned (v. 1) to meet with God and answer the questions of verses 2-4. What does the world need to know about God?

2. 41:5-7 And what is humanity's typical reaction? Draw out the savage irony of idolatrous stupidity.

3. 41:8-20 Pull out the three uncomplimentary images used to refer to 'Israel, my servant' in verses 9, 14 and 17. What is the common thread? How will each situation be transformed? See verses 10, 14-15 and 17b-20. What is stressed about why and how this will occur?

4. 41:21-29 We are brought into a law court where the pagan nations are on trial, before God, for their

idolatry. List all the arguments against idolatry in these verses. How do they help us to follow the exhortation of 1 John 5:21?

Application: While Old Testament idolatry may seem very distant to us, the New Testament makes it clear that idolatry can look very different – for instance, speaking of '...greed, which is idolatry' (Col. 3:5). What do we depend on or use in the same way people in the Old Testament depended on idols? What does this chapter have to say to this? How do the arguments against idolatry in verses 21-29 apply to us?

3. A light for the Gentiles (42:1-17)

It is striking that as soon as the servant is introduced, his ministry is immediately related to the nations (v. 1b), to whom he will bring justice, or righteousness, an emphasis which is repeated in verses 6b-7. The NIV translation obscures the connection between 42:1 and 41:29 in the word 'hēn', which is common to both and better translated 'see' or 'behold'. First you see the terrible situation of the nations, and now you see the wonderful solution from the Lord.

The servant 'song' is verses 1-4, introduced almost out of the blue, as it were, and full of mystery. The 'servant' is not named. Nothing is said about his origin. He seems already present although his mission clearly lies in the future. What is clear, however, is the nature of his God-given task, which is stated three times: to bring forth or establish justice (vv. 1, 3, 4). This can easily be misunderstood if we do not give proper attention to the noun used, which is 'mispat'. The verb behind the noun (sapat) means 'to give judgement', the authoritative pronouncement of king or judge.[2] This approximates to our use of the phrase 'in my judgement...',

---

2. Alec Motyer, Tyndale Old Testament Commentary on Isaiah, p.259

though in the servant's case this decision is infallible because of his divine enabling. He brings an authoritative word of God to the nations.

At this stage in God's plan, he does not execute justice in the sense of passing sentence on evil and carrying out its destruction. That awaits a future time (see 63:1-6). For now, the servant's ministry is declaratory; but that is a preparation for his eventual establishment of a universal kingdom of justice and truth, where wrongs will be righted and 'mispat' prevails.

Chosen and upheld by God and endowed with his Spirit (v. 1), he will be God's channel of self-revelation to the Gentile nations. All over the world, people will come to know the nature of God and what is pleasing to him, through the work of this servant. Perhaps a good contemporary illustration might be the decisive clarity of 'the third umpire' in a cricket or rugby match, where the replay of a video recording, often in slow motion, provides the vital evidence needed to make a decision based on truth, on reality. It is righteous and just, because the decision is made on the basis of how things really are.

Verses 2-4 contain seven negatives which contrast vividly with the normal methods by which human leaders impose their 'mispat': by rabble-rousing or breaking people's wills through a relentless use of force. This is not going to be a human conquest by propaganda or force. But he will not be stopped (v. 4a). Instead, the servant will win minds and hearts throughout the world by the consistent, faithful penetration of his truth and compassion. You have only to read the pages of the New Testament Gospels to see the fulfilment of the prophecy.

This first song is entirely task-oriented, but it is a feature of all four servant poems that each is followed by a divinely given commentary to explain either how such apparently impossible predictions will actually be fulfilled, or to expound the results that will flow from the servant's work. Verses 5-9 form that commentary here, with the focus on verse 6b. God's covenant will be extended to all the nations through the servant's work, as he becomes the light of God to the Gentile world. The blind will see; the captives will be set free (v. 7), which is God's answer to the paralysing idolatry of the nations. These are the 'new things' proclaimed in verse 9, which prompt the ends of the earth to erupt in a song of universal praise to Yahweh, the mighty warrior (vv. 10-13). The darkness of idolatry will at last be eclipsed by the light of the Lord, and the whole world will be turned upside down by the new life and transforming power of God, the mighty rescuer (vv. 14-17). Like his servant, God will not be deterred. 'These are the things I will do,' he declares (v. 16b), and he has.

Preaching and Teaching the Text
Title: **A Light for the Gentiles**
Text: **Isaiah 42:1-17**
Structure: Establish the nature of the servant songs and their explanations and introduce the passage as God's answer to the plight of the pagan world, sunk in its hopeless idolatry.
1. The servant's task (vv. 1-4)
     – to bring forth justice
     – to transform the nations
2. The servant's confidence (vv. 5-9)
     – the Lord's commitment to the servant

– the Lord's assurance about his ministry

3. The world's reaction (vv. 10-17)
    – rejoicing in the Lord's victory
    – trusting in the Lord's faithfulness

Leading a Bible Study

1. 42:1-4 Link to 41:28-29. The servant is the answer to the plight of the nations, but the first song is quite enigmatic. Note the repeated 'justice' (Heb: mispat), verses 1, 3, 4. This is a royal word. The ruler is making authoritative decisions.

    What do we learn from these verses about the person of 'my servant' and his mission or task. What is unusual about him?

    The song is quoted in detail in Matthew 12:18-21. Why does Matthew use it and what clues does this provide to help our understanding?

2. 42:5-9 What more does the Lord's address to the servant teach us about the nature of his task and the likelihood of its completion? Verse 6b is especially relevant in the light of the New Covenant.

3. 42:10-12 Who is doing the singing, and why? What does this teach us about God's salvation purposes?

4. 42:13-17 What is God promising to do? For whom? And what is the outcome for the rest?

Application: God's servant declares justice quietly and humbly. When we see injustice at work – whether at work, at home or on the world stage – are we tempted to do things differently? If so, what does this show us of the difference between God and us? What is God being praised for in verses 10-12, and how should we join in this praise?

4. The God who makes things new (42:18–43:21)

The introduction of the 'servant' imagery in this section would automatically point Isaiah's original hearers towards themselves, as those who do Yahweh's will, his servants. But the startling reality, proclaimed by the Lord in verse 19, is that Israel's spiritual blindness and deafness disqualify her for the task. 42:18-25 contain many echoes from the first half of the book, as their demoralised and defeated condition (v. 22) is directly attributed to their unwillingness to pay attention to the law and to the prophets. Still they have not learned the lesson that the devastation of the land, at the hand of the Assyrians, is the outpouring of God's burning anger against their persistent sin (vv. 24-25). How can Israel speak for God or demonstrate his glory when they themselves are deaf and blind to the spiritual realities of his word? The exposure of sin and its root causes are always God's first steps towards the spiritual renewal of his people.

That renewal provides the wonderful contrast of 43:1-7. 'But now' at the start of verse 1 is as glorious an intervention of God as Paul's 'But God' in Ephesians 2:4. Twice the creator who is their redeemer (v. 1) instructs his people not to be afraid (vv. 1, 5). Again there is a strong chapter link here between the flames of 42:25b and 43:2b. Under God's judgement the flames did burn and destroy, but no longer will this be so. Beyond the judgement, whether the exile or the bearing of God's wrath for our sins by the servant on the cross, God's purposes are for deliverance and renewal. What is expressed in terms of the end of the Babylonian exile in verses 5-7 is fulfilled in the spiritual blessings experienced by the universal church through the servant's completed work. It is especially instructive here to see how

God describes himself in verses 1 and 3 and to realise that rescue and renewal only become possible because of who God is. His essential nature itself guarantees his saving intervention.

Such a declaration of God's redemptive purposes prompts another insistent application in 43:8-13 of the utter futility of idolatry. For Isaiah, as for the author of Psalm 115, idols are characterised by their total lifelessness. Their unseeing eyes and unhearing ears are a graphic demonstration of the spiritual lifelessness of their adherents. So verse 8 refers not only to the nations and their idols, but also to faithless Israel in her dalliances with their false religion. The tragedy is that God's people have failed to fulfil their servant task of witnessing to the world that there is only one true and living God, and therefore only one Saviour (vv. 10-11). These are great verses revealing the unique character of the God of the Bible (vv. 11-12) and well repay exposition to the contemporary church, as we too are called to be his witnesses to a largely unbelieving world.

The final and logical development of the unit in 43:14-21 is to demonstrate how God will deliver his people, so that they turn from any of the spurious attractions of idolatry and put their faith in him alone. Babylon is mentioned for the first time since chapter 39 in verse 14 and now in terms of her ultimate fall and evacuation. Such an apparently incredible deliverance is possible with God. His people have only to consider their amazing exodus from Egypt to know that (vv. 16-17). But the prophet's burden is to look back, only in order to gain strength in faith to look forward to the deliverance of the nation from its Babylonian exile, as God covenants to bring them, through the inhospitable waste places, home to the land. The 'new thing' of verse 9 is the new exodus, which of course links up with our previous observation that the exile only fully ended with the coming of Christ the Messiah and his completed work, which secures the exodus of his New Covenant people from God's righteous wrath and judgement. Having redeemed the church out of bondage to sin and false religion, he will most certainly bring his people home to the glories of the eternal kingdom and the heavenly Jerusalem.

Preaching and Teaching the Text
Title: **The God who makes things new**
Text: **Isaiah 42:18–43:21**
Structure: The disqualification of Israel as God's servant leads God to proclaim his plans of renewal for a faithful remnant.
1. Why is renewal needed? (42:18-25)
     – the explanation of Israel's state. They are careless about God's works and words (vv. 20-22), disobedient (vv. 23-24) and therefore under judgement (vv. 24-25).
2. How will renewal come? (43:1-7)
     – by a sovereign work of the covenant Lord, who creates (v. 1), redeems (v. 1), preserves (v. 2), purchases (v. 3), loves (v. 4), gathers (v. 5) and rescues (vv. 6-7) his people.
3. What will renewal mean? (43:8-21)
     – God vindicated (vv. 8-13)
     – evil overthrown (vv. 14-15)
     – a new exodus (vv. 16-21)

Leading a Bible Study
1.   42:18-25 Why can these promises about the ministry of the servant not refer to national Israel? List the

faults which disqualify Israel from fulfilling her original 'servant' role.

2. 43:1-7 Remembering that chapter 42 ended with Israel's disqualification as God's servant to the nations, these verses disclose his remedy. List the things that God promises he will do. What will he do for his people in their trials (vv. 2-4)? What will be the eventual outcome (vv. 5-7)? What are the parallels for us as New Testament believers?

3. 43:8-13 Why are the idols reintroduced at this point? God directly addresses his people at verse 10, in the context of pagan idolatry. What are its implications for the exile and beyond?

4. 43:14-21 What is the relationship between 'the former things' and 'the new thing'? How should the one inform the other?

Application: In 42:18-25, we see why Israel is disqualified from her role as God's servant by her faults. What effect do similar faults and weaknesses have on our own service of God? God declares his people's disqualification and sin before promising to renew and change them. What does this pattern tell us about the way he renews and changes us also?

5. The God who redeems (43:22–44:23)

Motyer's observation that this section is a matching 'doublet' to the previous one provides a very helpful handle on these central chapters, which by virtue of their length can sometimes seem to be confusingly repetitive and complex. He writes of the two sections running on twin tracks, developing two themes in parallel; 'Captivity will be ended by national liberation (42:18–43:21), and sin dealt with by spiritual redemption (43:22–44:23)'[3] . We might relate this to the parallel themes of the political/social and the spiritual experience of the people of Judah, with which we have become increasingly familiar since chapter 1.

As already indicated, the physical experience of exile from the land and subsequent restoration have parallels to the spiritual experiences of God's New Covenant people through the gospel, but we need to keep the corporate focus clear in our preaching of the material. It is very easy to individualise the plurals of these verses to an over-personalised set of promises. While the glorious assurances of these sections can be applied to the individual believer, this is because each individual believer is a part of the church, to which the assurances are given. The major focus of application is corporate, and we must be careful not to underplay this in our preaching. These chapters have real significance for the life of a local congregation, for the church in a particular community or area or indeed in the nation and across the world.

In this section, the spiritual applications are, by the very nature of the material, more obvious and ready-made for contemporary church contexts. 43:22-24 provides a parallel diagnosis of the problem of God's people to that already noted in 42:18-25. At first sight it might appear that Judah has no religious life, but we know from 1:11, for example, that the opposite is the case. God rebukes them for the multitude of their meaningless sacrifices and rituals. The original text has the pronoun 'me' in the emphatic position. The recurring problem was that the outward form was not matched by the inward reality of repentance. It was all a wearisome burden (vv. 22b, 23b), just going through the

3. Alec Motyer, *Tyndale Old Testament Commentary on Isaiah*, p264.

motions. None of it was in fact true worship of Yahweh. Instead ritual had become a substitute for repentance and heart-devotion. The parallels in contemporary evangelicalism are not difficult to identify – keeping up appearances, empty attendance at church meetings, closed Bibles, prayerless lives, no heart for the lost. The dead end of empty formality is present in every generation.

43:25–44:5 shows God breaking into this otherwise hopeless situation. Affirming himself to be the God of forgiveness (v. 25), he nevertheless prosecutes his case against his people (vv. 26-28), revealing their sin and justifying his punishments. But the dominant message is one of spiritual renewal (44:2b-3) and subsequent expansion and growth (vv. 4-5). Israel is still 'my servant' (v. 1a); Yahweh still is their creator (v. 2a). They are not to be afraid (v. 2b cf. 43:1, 5) for they will experience the refreshment of God's Spirit and not just the restoration of the nation, but its expansion to include those who had previously been outsiders (v. 5). This underlines a theme that has pervaded this section: God's saving mercies will be extended even to the Gentiles.

But again, the other side of God's faithful deliverance is the total rejection of all false gods, the abandonment of idolatry. 44:6-20 provides a superb and highly memorable passage on this great Isaianic theme, in parallel with 43:8-13, but here much more extended as it is applied to the root spiritual needs of Judah. The genius of the oracle is that it does not merely expose the sin of idolatry or rail against it, but underlines the controlling motivations and subtle, but empty, magnetism of what we might call 'designer religion'. Its attraction is at the same time its inherent destruction: we can make our gods. Isaiah never allows us to forget that this is the nonsense which lies at the heart of idolatry.

As in the previous sections of confrontation with the idols, God begins with irrefutable statements about his own uniqueness and incomparability (vv. 6-8). Since idols are shaped by human minds and hands, they cannot be greater than their creators, who are nothing but mortals. Their attraction is that we can make them what we want them to be, but the pictures of the exhausted blacksmith (v. 12) and the careful carpenter (v. 13) only serve to illustrate how fatuous and shameful the whole process really is. All you have at the end is 'the form of man…in all his glory' (v. 13). The irony is immense, as Isaiah follows through the whole process with ruthless, deconstructive sarcasm (vv. 14-17). This cries out to be preached! Can human beings, made in God's image, really be so blind and stupid to imagine that they could create a 'god' in theirs (vv. 18-20)? We cannot give life to our creations. How could any god-substitute be anything other than inferior to its maker? Is that the sort of 'god' we want to have to rely on?

In preaching this material, we may well expose the contemporary idols of our culture – health, wealth, status, popularity, image, sex, power. These are all bottom-line substitutes for the true God. But it would also be helpful to examine our 'Christian' idols: church programmes, numbers, booming budgets, celebrities, mega events – all of which can subtly move us away from humble submission to the Lord, towards this self-worship and idolatry.

The unit closes with 44:21-23, where the focus is on the Lord as the creator and redeemer of his people, in direct antithesis to the hollow sham and empty shame of the idols. No wonder all creation bursts into praise in celebration of the only true God, the redeemer of his people!

Preaching and Teaching the Text

Title: **The God who redeems**

Text: **Isaiah 43:22–44:23**

Structure: Establish the parallel nature of the passage to the one before, but here the emphasis is on the spiritual rather than political situation. Throughout this sermon the parallels of entry into the New Covenant and life within the New Covenant community will need to be drawn.

1. The dead ends of delusion
    – empty religious formality (43:22-24)
    – futile idolatry (44:9-20)
2. The crossroads of confrontation
    – forgiveness in the context of rebellion (43:25-28)
    – new life in the place of fear and deprivation (44:1-5)
    – certainty in the face of the future (44:6-8)
    – which will you choose?
3. The highway to fulfilment
    – remember your relationship (44:21)
    – return to your redeemer (44:22)
    – rejoice in your rescue (44:23)

Leading a Bible Study

1.   43:22-24 What is the nature of Israel's spiritual state and what light does this throw on the necessity of the exile?

2.   43:25–44:5 The nature of the remedy explains why only Yahweh can produce it. What is the connection? What is God promising to do in these verses and where do we look for their fulfilment?

3.   44:6-20 This is one of the greatest Old Testament passages about the futility of idolatry. It needs to be savoured to be effective in converting us all from the

stupidity of idolatry. What are the characteristics of
idols and how are they reflected in their worshippers?

4.   44:21-23 The rejoicing is built on the two imperatives
     'remember' (v. 21) and 'return' (v. 22). What is the
     content of both and how do they work?

Application: When we examine, in 44:6-20, the
characteristics of idols and the ways they are reflected in
their worshippers, what parallels can we see in our own
lives? Do we put our trust in things, like they did? When
we examine God's appeal to his people to 'remember' and
to 'return' (44:21-22), how does this relate to our own
experience of God's grace in the gospel?

6. The God who rules (44:24–45:25)

We may well find that having received God's amazing
promises of his future redemptive activity in the preceding
sections, we need to take a step back and assimilate the
implications for ourselves and our world. But the insistent
question for Isaiah's original hearers must have been 'how?'
How can such apparently impossible things ever happen
when you look at the undeniable realities of the present? If
Isaiah's faith-building work is to make progress, the 'how'
question has to be dealt with.

As we look back down the centuries and marvel at
the clear fulfilments – in the exile, the fall of Babylon, the
restoration of Judah, the coming of Christ the Messiah,
his death and resurrection, the gift of the Holy Spirit and
the worldwide expansion of the church – we should surely
find our own faith immeasurably strengthened. One of
the great purposes of predictive prophecy is to increase
the confidence in God and his word of those who have
the privilege of witnessing, or reviewing, its fulfilment. In

application, it would be good to explore the areas where we think intervention by God, to change the situation, is unlikely or impossible. We need to know that he has a perfect track record of promise-fulfilment and that human barriers are as nothing to the power of his sovereign will.

These passages are designed to build our confidence in the same faithful, promising God so that we live in confidence that 'His purposes will ripen fast',[4] even though we may puzzle over how this could ever be. When we think about the challenges faced by the church in the Western world, or when we reflect on the promises of Christ's return and the eternal kingdom, the 'how' questions can sometimes loom large for us too, which is when a passage like this is of special value and nourishment to our faith.

44:24-28 form one sentence, one of the longest in the whole Bible. It is carefully constructed to lead us to its climax in verse 28, which is totally unexpected. Throughout the sentence, the emphasis is upon the sovereign authority of the Lord, which consists in his ability to do whatever he wishes in and with the world which he has made. From creation onwards (v. 24), he acts alone to accomplish his will. This note will continue all the way through chapter 45. See, for example, verses 5a, 6b, 14c, 18b, 21b, 22b. Of course, this proclamation of his total sovereignty is designed to demolish all residual confidence in idols, as we have already noted. The theme is reinforced at every opportunity throughout these chapters. In preaching this section we should remember that here God is preaching God to us, so that we draw out the characteristics of his nature, revealed by the verbs describing his actions. However, the clear

---

4. Words: 'God moves in a mysterious way' William Cowper, 1774. Music: Scottish Psalter, 1615.

climax of the sentence is the revelation of the name 'Cyrus' as 'my shepherd [who] will accomplish all that I please' (v. 28). This is God's answer to the 'how' question regarding the restoration of Jerusalem and the rebuilding of the temple.

45:1-7 explain this answer by giving more detail. To call a pagan emperor 'his anointed', a term usually associated with the kings or priests of Israel is, however, not only unusual but potentially offensive to God's people. This gives rise to another 'how' question. How can God call a Gentile king 'Messiah'? The answer is that he has been appointed and equipped by the Lord alone to fulfil a specific task for which the Lord has selected him. This was always the significance of 'anointing' and in biblical terms it comes to its ultimate fulfilment, of course, in Christ who is both priest and king. So, all of the verbs in 45:1-5 have Yahweh as their subject. Everything that Cyrus will achieve he does in and through the agency of the Lord, the unique and only deity. 'so that…men may know there is none besides me…I, the LORD, do all these things' (vv. 6-7). And these things are the victories of God, through Cyrus, by which his people will be delivered and restored.

Clearly there is an objection among God's people to the method which the sovereign Lord has chosen to employ, which he compares with a pot's questioning its potter, or a child its parents (vv. 9-10). Either example illustrates the foolishness and ignorance of human disputes with God. This now becomes the focus issue which God addresses in 45:8-13. As verses 11-13 make clear, man is not in a position to require 'the Holy One of Israel' to justify his ways. And yet how we love to do it! The God who made the stars can raise up a Cyrus, and he will accomplish his plans in his own way and by his own unaided power. There is no seat for human beings on this committee!

The problem at root is that we try to reshape God into our human image. It was so in Isaiah's day, and it is equally so in our own. We fail to see God's hand at work in the affairs of our world. We think we know how things ought to be panning out, forgetting that he is sovereign. We even give him advice, in our public intercessions, about what he should be doing in his world. In J. B. Phillips' memorable rebuke, 'Your God is too small', we cannot believe that he could use people we do not approve of or who would not do things our way. We fail to identify with God's great love for all his world and with his grace, which is constantly working through the gospel to bring blessing to new people.

The rest of the chapter, 45:14-25, contains two distinct messages, each introduced by the prophetic formula, 'This is what the LORD says' (vv. 14,18). They affirm God's sovereignty, countering Israel's grumbling about his using the Gentile Cyrus. At root, the message is that God's people need to change their view of the unreached Gentile world. In verses 14-17, the message is that God's salvation is going to stretch beyond the boundaries of Judah, to embrace the people of upper Egypt, Ethiopia and the Sudan. This is characteristically expressed in Old Testament terms of submission. While these pictures of chains and prostration (v. 14) may offend our political sensitivities, they nevertheless convey the spiritual reality. Total submission to God is a necessary requirement if the blessings of the gospel are to be ours, for the gospel means no longer being your own, having been bought with a price (see 1 Cor. 6:19-20; 1 Pet. 1:18-19 for example). Perhaps verse 15 indicates the somewhat grudging response of those who reluctantly come to admit that while God reveals enough of himself for faith to grasp and prove, enough remains hidden so that the unbeliever is not to be intellectually coerced, but won by his rescuing grace and compassion.

The second proclamation (vv18-25) reminds us that God delights to reveal himself to men and women, both in the general revelation of the creation (v18) and in the special revelation of his word (v19). The chapter ends with a wonderfully compassionate and liberating invitation to the ignorant idolaters of the world to cast off their burdensome false religion and to find in the Lord the only Saviour of the nations (vv. 20-22). As always in Scripture, the final analysis reveals only one choice between only two ways. The alternatives are trust and rebellion, but the only end-point is submission to God (v. 23), either in grudging shame (v. 24) or with exultant joy (v. 25). To know God as Saviour is the only way to be 'found righteous.'

Preaching and Teaching the Text
Title: **The God who rules**
Text: **Isaiah 44:24–45:25**
Structure: God establishes his uniqueness and sovereign authority by predicting what he will do and carrying it through to completion.
1. God's sovereignty in action (44:24–45:8)
        – his total control of his world (44:24-27)
        – his decision to raise up Cyrus (44:28–45:5)
        – his government of all human affairs (45:6-8)
2. God's sovereignty in question (45:9-13)
        – argument has no place (45:9-11)
        – resistance has no effect (45:12-13)
3. God's sovereignty in salvation (45:14-25)

– the end of idolatry (45:14-17)
– the rescue of the nations (45:18-21)
– the gracious invitation (45:22-25)

Leading a Bible Study

1. 44:24-27 How do these verses distinguish the Lord from all man-made idols? In what ways can they be used to encourage our faith today to be in the Lord alone?

2. 44:28–45:7 How do these verses add extra weight to the last section? What does God's use of Cyrus teach us about God? Why did the Babylonian empire fall?

3. 45:8-13 What is Israel's objection against what God has decreed? What arguments does the Lord use to answer and ultimately to dismiss it?

4. 45:14-17 What elements of these verses surprise the reader? How do they illustrate the idea that Yahweh is 'a God who hides himself' (v. 15a)?

5. 45:18-21 What is the Lord promising to do (a) for 'Jacob's descendants' and (b) for ignorant idolaters? How do these actions reveal his character as outlined in these verses?

6. 45:22-25 How can these verses be used to preach the gospel of Christ?

Application: How can looking back at Old Testament prophecies and their fulfilment encourage our faith? What situations around us do we tend to think God cannot change? How can we use this passage, especially 44:24-27, to encourage us to think otherwise? Do we, like Isaiah's hearers, argue with God and give him advice on how to run the world (perhaps in our prayers) as in 45:9-13?

7. What is your bottom line? (46:1–47:15)

As if to remind us of the physical and historical grounding of God's universal salvation purposes in the events of the exile and the return, 46:1-2 bring us back to Babylon, where the city is about to fall and the people are evacuating their homes, carrying their idols on the backs of their beasts or on their own backs. Bel was the chief god of Babylon and Nebo their god of wisdom. In the face of the onslaught of Cyrus ('his anointed' 45:1) they are utterly useless. In fact, they become an encumbrance, wearying their carriers. Immediately, the Lord draws the contrast with himself in his relationship with Judah, 'you whom I have upheld since you were conceived, and have carried since your birth' (v. 3b). What is the point of a 'god' you have to rescue and carry, when there is a true and living God to rescue and carry you?

The structure of 46:3-13 revolves around two commands, each repeated. 'Listen' is the summons of verses 3 and 12, and 'remember' the imperative of verses 8 and 9. The vivid picture of the idols' evacuation gives way to Yahweh's insistent word to his covenant people (vv. 3-5), which is summed up by the statement of his activity as the only means of salvation. 'I have made you and I will carry you; I will sustain you and I will rescue you' (v. 4b). Paul makes exactly the same points in his deconstruction of the gods of Athens in his Areopagus address (Acts 17:24-28). To patronise an idol factory is the height of folly (vv. 6-7).

What God's people hear, they are to remember. The biblical usage of the word means calling truth to mind in order to act upon it. For truth to be foundational in a changed life, it has to be fixed in the mind and taken to heart (v. 8), since it is the only antidote to our human default position, rebellion: not letting God be God in our lives. They are to remember all his past deliverances, which prove that God not only knows the future, but governs it by his sovereign power. He is the only one who is able not just to make promises, but infallibly to keep them. If he says that he will summon Cyrus ('a bird of prey', v. 11) to destroy Babylon's hegemony, then he will. So, although his people are stubbornly resistant, they should 'listen' because the salvation God is promising will be accomplished.

We are back to the challenge Ahaz faced as long ago as chapter 7. What are you trusting? Where is your faith grounded? In the divine promises, or in human policies? The message of Isaiah is that the righteousness and splendour which God offers his people can only be obtained by faith in him. 'The idolater makes a god in his own image; the Lord intends to make his people in his.'[5]

47:1-15 is a powerful example of what is called a 'taunt poem' or song, where one nation or god taunts another in its moment of defeat. It is a song of conquest and victory. In this chapter, Babylon's capitulation and conquest are the subject of the divinely inspired taunt. This means that the whole chapter is historically conditioned, but as we saw earlier in chapters 13 and 21, Babylon has a wider framework in Scripture than the historical city and empire. It looks back to the archetypal human rebellion against God at Babel (Gen. 11:1-9), forward in New Testament context to the pagan Roman empire and its anti-Christian opposition (e.g. 1 Pet. 5:13), and on to the ultimate judgement of God against all the rebellious pride and power of the world in its opposition to its creator (e.g. Rev. 18).

However, as with all Scripture, even a taunt song contains revelatory instruction, and this chapter identifies

---

5. Alec Motyer, *Tyndale Old Testament Commentary on Isaiah*, p296

three major characteristics of idolatrous Babylon which precipitate her downfall: luxury, tyranny and pride. Her luxury will be turned to degradation and the lowest form of slavery (vv. 1-3) at the hand of the Holy One of Israel (v. 4). She has exercised her delegated power in merciless tyranny, without any humanity or concern for those she has abused and oppressed (vv. 5-7). Because of that power, she has developed a pride which imagines itself to be inviolable, a false sense of security which imagines that no one knows the wickedness of her heart (vv. 8-10). Twice, she is shown to apply words to herself which can only be properly used of Yahweh himself. This only highlights how just God is to destroy her. 'I am, and there is none besides me' (vv. 8, 10).

Babylon has become her own god-substitute; she worships herself in the most appalling idolatry, which can only bring disaster and calamity (v. 11). All her pagan worship and occult practices, her sorceries and spells, can make no difference to her fate (v. 10). Her spiritual gurus are powerless, and her gods are carted away. The fire of God is coming, not as warming comfort but as consuming destruction, without the slightest hope of salvation (vv. 14-15). There is, after all, only one God who is able to save and to reject. His righteous rule means that we are inevitably committed to his righteous judgement. For in every generation we need to remember that 'our God is a consuming fire' (Heb. 12:29, citing Deut. 4:24).

Preaching and Teaching the Text
Title: **What is your bottom line?**
Text: **Isaiah 46:1–47:15**
Structure: Our value systems mould our lives and we all become like the gods we worship, so that where we put our

treasure reveals where our hearts really lie. Set in the context
of Babylon's fall. We need to apply these principles to all
the God-substitutes our culture relies on and by which the
church is so often tempted.

1. What sort of God do you worship (46:1-7)
   - idols which have to be made and carried
   - the living God who made and carries us
2. What sort of foundation do you build on (46:8-13)
   - proof from the past
   - faith for the future
3. What sort of future do you face (47:1-15)
   - Babylon's misplaced confidence
   - luxury, power, pride
   - Babylon's utter impotence to save

Conclusion: There is only one God and therefore only one
Saviour. Turn to him (cf. 45:22).

Leading a Bible Study

I have combined this section's study with the next section, as
their common themes naturally make one study. Of course,
the questions could be split up if a separate study is needed.

8. The mystery of mercy (48:1-22)

As we come to the end of the first part of the unit, chapters
40–55, it may be useful for the preacher to summarise some
of its major themes, since the chapter is in itself a reprise
of what we have already heard. The big picture has been
the establishment of Yahweh's sovereignty over the whole
earth. This means that the fact of the forthcoming exile to
Babylon is due not to Yahweh's defeat by their 'gods,' but to
the sinful rebellion of his people against his righteous rule.
The covenant relationship God had established with Israel

carried not only enormous privilege, but also equivalent responsibilities, as he commissioned his people to be 'my servant' in bearing his light to the nations. This task was met with abysmal failure. The situation is therefore that they are politically bound because they are spiritually blind.

Yet God is faithful, remembering his covenant and fulfilling his promises. He will not let his people down, nor will he let them go. Isaiah's message is therefore one of deliverance and salvation. Politically, this will come through 'my servant Cyrus', 'my shepherd' (44:28). Babylon will fall, and the Lord will return his people to the land. But the greater problem, the need for spiritual deliverance and renewal, cannot be met by Cyrus. It will require a mighty intervention of saving grace by God himself to rescue men and women from all the nations and to bring them into his eternal kingdom. This last and greatest rescue mission will be the subject of chapters 49-55. Its urgency is beyond question, because throughout this section the utter futility of all the idolatrous God-substitutes, invented by human minds and shaped by human hands, has been remorselessly exposed.

48:1-11 again summon God's people to listen to God's words (v. 1). The stress is on an outward conformity to their calling which serves to mask an inner unreality. They are none of the things they claim to be (vv. 1-2). In the past, he has often forewarned his people of what he will do in their future and now, looking back, Isaiah's generation can see that they all happened, which shows that God, and not their idols, is in control of the world's government (vv. 3-6a). Secondly, looking to the future, God makes a new appeal, telling his people of what he will do. In this they are entirely dependent on his revelation (v. 7), but their hardened hearts remain unimpressed, even though God delays his wrath in covenant mercy (vv. 7-11). Both examples are designed to prove the authority of the only living God, who will not yield his glory to another (v. 11b).

Now, at 48:12-19, the focus moves to the present, with a fresh command to 'Listen' (v. 12) and face up to their own responsibilities. The pagan world viewed the process of history as a circular movement governed by impersonal laws, which meant that history was relatively unimportant. But for the Hebrew mind, history had a beginning in the activity of the creator and moved chronologically forward with the accomplishment of God's sovereign will. Past, present and future all belong to the God who is the 'I am,' so what he foretells will most certainly occur, which means that Babylon will fall (vv. 14-15).

But the focus is shifting now from the political to the spiritual. The speaker from verse 16 onwards (either Isaiah himself or perhaps even 'the servant,' in anticipation of chapter 49) reminds his hearers that the way of peace is always the path of obedience, the implication being that lessons from the past ('If only you had paid attention,' v. 18a) still apply to the present. The promises to Abraham of God's favour seen in the multiplication of the nation are still available to be claimed and fulfilled for those who are obedient (v. 19). The deliverance from Babylon is as certain as the first exodus from Egypt, and the same covenant God will accompany and sustain a trusting and obedient people in his faithfulness to his promise (vv. 20-21). But the choice remains.

The unit ends on a sobering note, reminding us that the root problem must have a spiritual solution. 'There is ... no peace ... for the wicked' (v. 22) is an unbreakable spiritual principle at the heart of God's government of the world. The problem of fallen human nature and the endemic sinfulness of the control centre of each personality (the heart) remains the biggest issue. Without change in this area, there can be no ultimate solution to the dilemmas which Isaiah so poignantly and powerfully describes. That is why the servant of chapter 49 is so much needed and why we need him to reign in our stubborn hearts too.

Preaching and Teaching the Text
Title: **The mystery of mercy**
Text: **Isaiah 48:1-22**
Structure: Establish as the bridge passage between the focus on historical Judah of chapters 44–48 and the universal spiritual focus of the servant and his work in 49–55.
1. A problem Israel has always posed (vv. 1-11)
     – outward conformity but inner rebellion (vv. 1-2)
     – from the past (vv. 3-6a)
     – in the present (vv. 6b-11)
2. A promise God is always presenting (vv. 12-19)
     – prediction and fulfilment (vv. 12-15)
     – direction and prosperity (vv. 16-19)
3. A purpose God will certainly fulfil (vv. 20-22)
     – deliverance and provision

Leading a Bible Study
1.   46:1-13 Using the contrast between being a Babylonian and being an Israelite, how does God motivate his people to fulfil their potential? What do they need to do?
2.   47:1-15 What is going to happen to Babylon and what are the immediate and ultimate reasons for her fate?
3.   47:1-15 What does this chapter tell us about God's present rulership of his world and about its future as his eternal purposes come to fruition?

4. 48:1-11 In what ways is the 'house of Jacob' just like Babylon? Why will her own fate be different (vv. 9-11)?

5. 48:12-19 In this section the Lord draws the attention of his stubborn people to certain of his own unchanging characteristics. What are they? And what are their implications for Israel both in the present and in the future?

6. 48:20-22 What does the exodus language of verses 20-21 add to the summons to leave Babylon? Why does the section end with verse 22?

Application: This passage shows us the parallels between the Babylonians and the 'house of Jacob'. Do we have similar failings – luxury, tyranny, pride? What are their consequences? What, despite this, do the assurances of God's character in verses 12-19 mean for New Testament believers like us?

9. Good news for everyone (49:1-13)

As was noted in chapter 42, with the first servant song, each of the four poems is followed by a divinely given commentary or explanation of its significance and results in the accomplishment of God's redemptive purposes. We can therefore divide this section into the song itself (vv. 1-16) and the following commentary (vv. 7-13).

49:1-6. Summoning the extremities of the earth to listen to him, the servant appears a second time, unannounced and undescribed, to introduce himself and his work to the whole creation. The formula 'Listen to me' (v. 1) is used in Isaiah elsewhere only to introduce a direct word from God, so the servant is shown at the outset to possess divine authority, yet the reference to his birth (v. 1b) clearly establishes his humanity. Chosen by God before birth, his whole life is governed by God's call to act as his spokesman (v2). Like a sharpened sword or a polished arrow, he is to speak words of penetrating power given by God himself. The Lord prepares and conceals his servant until the moment of revelation arrives.

Suddenly, in verse 3, the servant's name is revealed: 'Israel'. At first sight, it might seem that God is recommissioning the nation in spite of their disqualification in 42:18-19, but when we read on to verse 5 we see that part of the servant's task is to 'gather Israel to himself [the Lord]'. How can Israel gather Israel? Something more profound is happening here, in that the name of Israel seems to be transferred to the servant. He is to fulfil in his mission all that Israel had failed to be, as he faithfully reflects the splendour of Yahweh to the nations (v. 3). However, verse 4 takes a very different turn, in that the servant seems to have failed in his purpose. Has it all been in vain? The answer (v. 4b) lies in the servant's commitment of his work and its outcome into God's hands, because God is faithful and the due reward will be given by him. The climax now follows (vv. 5-6) as the servant's task is redefined in a double role, not only to bring back Jacob (Israel) but God further declares, 'I will also make you a light for the Gentiles, that you may bring my salvation to the ends of the earth' (v. 6).

49:7-13. The first hint of suffering in the servant's work, from verse 4, is now picked up in verse 7 as the commentary begins. His experience will be to be 'despised and abhorred', but this will lead to the submission of earthly rulers before him. So far what this involves is shrouded in mystery, but God promises the help and vindication of his servant, making him 'to be a covenant for the people' (v. 8b) in repetition of the promise in 42:6, following the first song. If the servant is himself to be a New Covenant, then all of

God's commitment to deal with his people in faithful love and fulfilment of his promises must find its focus in him. The result will be liberty for the captives, which is then described in the image of God's flock returning through the desert places to the land of promise (vv. 9-12). As so often in Isaiah, the proclamation of God's great salvation leads to an outburst of praise, from the whole creation, for God's comfort and compassion towards his covenant people (v. 13). The hope which flows from the servant's work extends therefore to the whole world. The fulfilment of these strands in the person and work of the Lord Jesus Christ make this a great gospel passage for the Christian preacher.

Preaching and Teaching the Text
Title: **Good News for everyone**
Text: **Isaiah 49:1-13**
Structure:
1. The servant's testimony (vv. 1-6)
     – his appointment (vv. 1)
     – his ministry (v. 2)
     – his identity (v. 3)
     – his discouragement (v. 4)
     – his victory (vv. 5-6)
2. The Lord's confirmation (vv. 7-13)
     – to the servant – commitment (vv. 7-9a)
     – to his people – restoration (vv. 9b-12)
     – to the whole creation – hope (v. 13)

Leading a Bible Study
I have combined this section's Bible study with the next section to give a better understanding of the overall themes.

The questions can of course be broken up into separate studies if necessary.

10. *Objection over-ruled!* (49:14–50:3)

In the light of these great promises it would be difficult to imagine a greater privilege than to be one of God's people. However, the reaction of Zion (Israel) comes with a sickening thud in 49:14. The world may be singing, but all that God's people seem able to do is to grumble and complain, accusing God of forsaking and forgetting them, with echoes here of 40:27.

Sadly, it is not unusual to find parallels in the contemporary church of a similar stubborn incredulity in the face of God's promises, which may well provide us with a bridge of application from Isaiah's context to our own in preaching this section. The people of God can so quickly forget their privilege of declaring God's salvation to the world and become immersed in their own divisions, bickering and criticising one another and ultimately the Lord himself. So the church turns in on itself and love, joy and peace (the fruit of the gospel through the Holy Spirit) are the casualties.

49:14-23 present us with Israel's complaint in one verse and God's gracious response in the next nine verses. Zion's peevish response to the declaration of the salvation God is preparing for the whole world is that he seems not to care about her state, suffering as she is at the hands of the Assyrians, and will do under the Babylonians. She still stubbornly refuses to recognise that her current situation is not only under God's control but is the outcome of her sinful rebellion. The Lord's response is, however, full of love and tender compassion (vv. 15-16), culminating in the glorious vision of their future return to a land of prosperity and further multiplication of the nation (vv. 17-21). But God will not be limited by the sinful jealousy of Israel or the narrowness of her vision. His purposes include the blessing of the Gentile nations, through their submission to him as Lord and through their inclusion in his New Covenant community. 'The imagery is political subservience, the reality is spiritual indebtedness.'[6]

49:24–50:3 pick up a second quizzical and probably unbelieving comment from God's people (v. 24). If they are plundered and taken into captivity, is there any likelihood that such a situation could be reversed? This is the sort of question which arises whenever God's ability to convert and change people and situations is disputed. Is real change possible in a fallen world? The Lord's response is two-fold. First, he affirms that conquering forces can always be overcome by a superior power, and his power is superior to every human manifestation (vv. 25-26). Secondly, he reminds them that they are misreading, and choosing to misunderstand, the significance of his dealings with them in covenant discipline. Having answered their accusations of negligence and impotence, God now answers the most devastating charge of them all – that of rejection. They are claiming that God has divorced them (50:1).

The Deuteronomic law required a certificate of divorce to be written to make the matter legal (Deut. 24:1-4), but no such certificate exists. The idea of God selling his people to meet his debts is equally preposterous. The discipline of God fell in the exile because they had abandoned him, not vice versa (vv. 1-2a). And it is equally false to imagine that God does not have the power to reverse the situation

6. Alec Motyer, *Tyndale Old Testament Commentary on Isaiah*, p314.

whenever he wishes. Nothing has happened which cannot be retrieved. The God of creation controls what he has made for the accomplishment of his purposes. He can raise up a Cyrus, and he did. He can send a rescuer, and he did. He can bring the Gentile nations into his kingdom, and he has. Zion's accusations are rebuked, and the whole perspective of negative despair and discouragement is shown to be false.

Preaching and Teaching the Text
Title   **Objection over ruled!**
Text   **Isaiah 49:14–50:3**
Structure: Introduce the idea of a dialogue between God and Zion, dealing with his people's objections by expounding his covenant grace and mercy.
1.   Objection: forsaken and forgotten (49:14)
      Reality: loved and remembered (49:15-18)
2.   Objection: bereaved and barren (49:21)
      Reality: multiplied and restored (49:19-23)
3.   Objection: plundered and captive (49:24)
      Reality: rescued and renewed (49:25-26)
4.   Objection: divorced and sold (50:1)
      Reality: disciplined and ransomed (50:2-3)

Leading a Bible Study
1.   49:1-6 Piece together the portrait of the servant and his work in these verses? What is he called to do and how does he accomplish the task?
2.   49:7 What is the LORD's promise to the servant? Why does he make it? How was it fulfilled in Christ? Note that this verse refers to the Gentile nations.
3.   49:8-13 Now the commentary moves to Israel, but with reference to the returning remnant (a prototype

of New Covenant Israel). How does 2 Corinthians 6:2 help us to interpret this section?

What is the spiritual substance to which the metaphors of verses 9-12 refer? What does verse 13 add?

4. 49:14-23 Zion's first reaction is to accuse God of negligence (v. 14). How does God refute this charge? What is he promising to do for his 'afflicted ones'? How should these verses motivate Zion to believe?

5. 49:24-26 What is Zion's second objection, expressed in verse 24? What does God's answer reveal about their spiritual state? Why is he so committed to restoring them?

6. 50:1-3 What is the third objection, contained in verse 1? How does God argue that the exile is not proof of his abandonment? What do they (and we) need to remember about God (vv. 2-3)?

Application: How do verses 1-7 help us to understand Jesus and his mission? How does that help us to trust and worship him? What do we learn of the way God's power works through weakness in verse 4, and how does that change our attitude to the way he uses us? Do we ever grumble in the way Israel does in 49:14; 49:24 or 50:1? How do God's answers to them comfort and rebuke us also?

11. Walking in the fear of the Lord (50:4-11)

The third servant song is presented in verses 4-9, with the usual commentary, in summary form, in verses 10-11. We discover the servant song as an interval in the prolonged debate between God and his people, in which God first defends himself against their baseless accusations (49:14–50:3) and then challenges them to wake up and claim by faith the blessings which he is offering to them (51:1–52:12).

50:4-9 begins by reiterating the theme of the servant's task as word ministry, which we saw in 49:2. The commentary will also begin with a reference to 'the word of his [God's] servant' (v. 10). In the context of chapter 50, this 'word' seems to refer primarily to the new exodus, which God is promising for his people. This is a pointed reminder of the way God accomplished the first exodus from Egypt – by the power of his word: 'By a mere rebuke I dry up the sea' (50:2). If that is the power of God's word, then the servant's privilege to be given an instructed tongue is very great (v. 4).

However, the strongest ingredient of the song and the most significant addition to our understanding of the servant and his work here is the note of obedient suffering which dominates verses 5 and 6. We are not told at whose hands he suffers, or what task he is trying to perform. It is clear that his obedience to the word of the sovereign Lord has brought about the confrontation, but he faces this with great confidence in God's protection and vindication (vv. 7-8).

It seems best to understand the song as partly teaching by contrast and partly as an example of what faithful submission to God's will demands. The contrast is with the complaints and misrepresentations of unbelieving Zion already examined. The servant is all that God's people should be, but refuse to become. They do not listen for God's voice and they are not obedient to his call (50:1-2). The example of true service of Yahweh includes listening to his word with an open, accepting ear (v. 4), obeying his instructions without rebelling or turning back (v. 5), enduring suffering and degradation as a result of that obedience (vv. 6-7), but trusting all the time in God's presence, help and vindication, until his accusers and enemies fade away (vv. 8-9).

The servant's example is one of faith in the words of God's promise, through the experience of terrible suffering, issuing finally in the silencing of all his opponents. Clearly, this model was perfectly fulfilled by the Lord Jesus Christ in his obedience to death on the cross and the horror of his physical suffering and degradation, but also in his resurrection and ascension to glory, by which he is 'declared with power to be the Son of God' (Rom. 1:4).

Later, in Romans 8:31ff., the apostle Paul clearly links that pattern to the Christian life. The questions of 50:8-9 are deliberately echoed for the faith-building of New Testament believers. In obedience to God's word, following in Christ's footsteps, Christians are often surrounded by enemies who mock our faith and deny its reality. Paul identifies them as trouble, distress, persecution, famine, nakedness, danger and death. Can we really be sure that we are loved by God and shielded from his wrath when we live in that sort of context? Paul's resounding 'yes' is built on the servant's conviction that nothing can separate him from the Lord, and so he will never be put to shame. It is a conviction every obedient Christian can share.

50:10-11 not surprisingly calls on the hearers to follow the servant's example. To fear the Lord is to listen to his word through the servant's ministry. It is this word which generates faith that God will keep his promises. Truly to listen, and so to understand, will lead God's people to trust his character (name) and rely on his person (v. 10b), even though their present context is often one of impenetrable darkness. Those who listen and obey do not always walk in unbroken sunshine, any more than Jesus did. Walking in the dark when we cannot see the outcome is the time to trust the word of God and rely on the God of the word.

There is, however, an alternative (v. 11). As we call ourselves and others to faith in God's word, we need to be crystal clear about what the alternative way of dealing with the darkness will inevitably produce. People may have their own light sources, which may flare brightly for awhile, but they cannot save. In fact, to use them is to reject God, the only Saviour, which in the end can only lead to 'torment,' that deep darkness of 8:22 where God is rejected and absent. It is a sobering conclusion to the song, but it still needs to be believed and proclaimed in our twenty-first-century church and culture. In the end, all the substitute lights kindled by men will go out, just as all their idols will be carted away to destruction. Only those who learn to listen and who consequently give themselves to trust and obey will know the help of the sovereign Lord and the 'not guilty' verdict (no condemnation) at the last day, and only through the work of the servant, as we are about to discover.

Preaching and Teaching the Text
Title: **Walking in the fear of the Lord**
Text: **Isaiah 50:4-11**
Structure: The third song takes us more deeply into the inner 'psychology' of the servant and provides an example for us to follow in his steps.
1. The servant's pattern (vv. 4-9)
    – an instructed mind (v. 4)
    – an obedient will (vv. 5-6)
    – a determined trust (v. 7)
    – a victorious confidence (vv. 8-9)
2. The continuing challenge (vv. 10-11)
    – trust and obey (v. 10)
    – reject and perish (v. 11)

Leading a Bible Study

1. 50:4-6 What are (a) the source and (b) the cost of the servant's obedient suffering?

2. 50:7-9 What assurances nerve the servant to persist with his obedience to the Lord's will, whatever the personal cost? Compare this section with Paul's convictions in Romans 8:31-39 and consider what impact both assurances should have on us.

3. 50:10-11 What is involved in the two alternative responses presented here, and what are their outcomes? In what ways might we be tempted to kindle our own fires?

Application: What impact should the assurances of verses 7-9 and the way Paul shows how they can also be ours in Romans 8:31-39 have on our Christian lives? In verses 10-11, what would it mean for us to walk by the light of our own fires, rather than trusting in God?

12. God's wake-up call (51:1–52:12)

It is important to grasp the internal structure of this rich section. There are three imperatives: 'Listen' (51:1, 4) and 'Hear me' (51:7) which introduce short paragraphs of great encouragement, each rooted in God's unchanging character and eternal purposes. These are followed by three 'wake up' calls at 51:9, 17 and 52:1. The first is addressed by God's people to the 'arm of the LORD,' while the other two are spoken by God to Jerusalem/Zion. The link to the servant song commentary in 50:10-11 is intentional and strong. To listen to the voice of the servant is to listen to God, and the way in which obedient faith is strengthened is by holding onto that word in the midst of adversity.

51:1-3 is addressed to the righteous remnant who have not only an appetite for godliness, but also an active pursuit of it, as they give themselves to seeking the Lord. They are encouraged by a word from the past, recalling God's faithfulness to Abraham, who 'believed the LORD and he credited it to him as righteousness' (Gen. 15:6). In Abraham's case, God overruled the most unpromising circumstances (v. 2), and he will do the same as he restores Zion (v. 3). For Abraham, righteousness was credited as he believed the promises and so obeyed the commands. It is never any different in the Christian's pursuit of godliness.

51:4-6 is a more personal appeal from God to the whole covenant community, requiring a more corporate application. This looks forward to what God is going to do as his 'arm' (the servant, 53:1) brings mispat (right decisions) to the nations (cf. 42:1-4). The implications of verses 5-6 are mind-boggling. The Lord is on the march to bring about an eternal rescue, which will satisfy his never-failing righteousness. The two are inseparable and are more enduring than even the physical creation. So the call is to look forward in faith and hope, confident that the new and better world for which we long has already come in the breaking-in of the kingdom of heaven and is yet to come in the fullness of his glory.

51:7-8 is probably directed to the remnant who are seeking to integrate God's instruction into their hearts and lives, exhorting them not to fear men and their transient opposition. In an echo (v8b) of verse 6b, the Lord asserts again the eternal permanence of his righteous salvation.

51:9-11 reveals the first positive response of the people of God in this long dialogue sequence (from 49:14 to 52:12). It is a cry of faith to the 'arm of Yahweh' to do what he is promising, based on obedience to the injunction in 51:1-2 to look back and find encouragement from God's faithfulness in the past. On the grounds of the exodus, 51:11 expresses faith that the glorious future promises for Zion will be fulfilled. The speaker may be Isaiah, but, in context, it seems more likely that these words are the faith-response of the believing remnant, gathered through the prophet's ministry. As always, faith expresses itself in prayer.

The response of God is eager and active as he reinforces his message of future blessing in 51:12-16. This is a key passage in the faith-building intention of this section of Isaiah's book, before the servant's work is revealed. Note the connection between fearing man (v. 12) and forgetting God (v. 13). To live in terror of mortal men who are like grass, insubstantial and transient, always shows forgetfulness of the eternal nature and sovereignty of Yahweh. Such 'forgetting' is the opposite of that active 'remembering' in Scripture, which is calling truth to mind with a determination to act upon it. This failure of memory reveals, at its root, a failure of trust.

That is why the paragraph builds up evidence that increases faith. Yahweh is the creator who has all things under his sovereign control (v. 13). He liberates the captives and feeds the hungry (v. 14). He rules the uncontrollable sea and is the Lord of the hosts of heaven, the 'Almighty' (v. 15). He reveals himself to his people in his word and brings them into personal relationship ('my people') as the expression of his will (v. 16). This God does not need to be woken up (cf. v. 9) because he is already active in accomplishing his sovereign purposes. It is his lethargic people who need to be awakened to recognise the realities and to pursue them in faith and godly obedience.

That is why 51:17-23 turns the tables on the hearers and calls upon Jerusalem (the covenant people) to wake up and to recognise that a new day of restoration is dawning after the long night of God's discipline and punishment. Threading through the paragraph is the theme of the 'cup of wrath.' The fury of God's righteous anger has been 'drunk' in the experience of the exile, but now the same 'cup' is removed and becomes instead the experience of 'your tormentors.' 'Divine wrath reduced Jerusalem to helplessness, but while she slept the cup has been removed: the wrath is over'.[7] This is the reality to which the people of God need to wake up.

52:1-10 is a second wake-up call, following 51:17, not simply to realise the passing of God's anger, but for Zion to assume her new role as 'the holy city' (52:1). This is no easy transition as the first five verses show with persistent emphasis what Barry Webb calls her 'sense of utter worthlessness.' He writes, 'Zion had been defiled (v. 1), enslaved (v. 2), sold (v. 3), oppressed (v. 4), and mocked (v. 5). No wonder she felt worthless. The word "nothing" in verses 3 and 5 captures it exactly – she had been "sold for nothing" and "taken away for nothing".'[8]

Whenever God's people feel the disciplining hand of the Lord there is always a danger of imagining in despair that restoration is impossible; but it is not, not with God. In an echo of 40:9, another messenger appears, whose good news of peace and rescue is grounded in the key statement of reality, around which the whole passage revolves – 'Your God reigns!' (52:7). Because of that single, central reality, God's broken, demoralised people can rejoice. Jerusalem will

7. Alec Motyer, *Tyndale Old Testament Commentary on Isaiah*, p326..
8. Barry Webb, *The Message of Isaiah*, *The Bible Speaks Today*, p206.

be restored and the 'arm of Yahweh' will exercise his sovereign power in saving grace towards all the nations (52:10).

The concluding verses, 52:11-12, with their urgent repeated imperative, 'Depart,' echo the double 'Awake' of 51:17 and 52:1. The blessings of restoration bring with them an entirely new way of living – a departure from Babylon and all its defilements and a pilgrimage home, with the Lord before and behind his people (as in the exodus), bound for the faithful, holy city.

This rich section has many parallels, which the preacher can and should draw both to the individual Christian and to the life of the church in the hostile world, as God's New Covenant community. Look for particular relevance to the contemporary situation in the Western church, where, under God's permissive will, and sometimes surely also as an act of covenant discipline, the hostile opposition of secular atheism is both demoralising and depressing. Like Zion in this section, we need our eyes to be turned exclusively to the Lord's ability and our hearts to be strengthened, so that we return to him and begin again to call upon his promises for deliverance. While it will always be true that we can never save ourselves (there is only one Saviour), God's word has power to raise even the dead to life. As we believe and preach the truth that 'our God reigns,' we will be given strength to claim God's promises in believing prayer and to exchange our despair and apathy for the God-honouring faith and confidence, expressed in our active anticipation that the best is yet to be. It is in that context that Isaiah now unveils the mystery of the suffering servant's person and work.

Preaching and Teaching the Text

Title: **Great expectations**

Text: **Isaiah 51:1-16**

Structure: We resume the dialogue between God and his people, punctuated by the urgent imperatives of the Lord (vv. 1, 4, 7) and their response (v. 9).

1. Great truths to listen to (vv. 1-8)

– 'The LORD will surely comfort Zion' (vv. 1-3)

– 'My salvation will last for ever' (vv. 4-6)

– 'Do not fear the reproach of men' (vv. 7-8)

2. Great encouragements to pray (vv. 9-11)

– look back and see God's faithfulness (vv. 9-10)

– look forward and trust his promises (v.11)

3. Great reasons to remember the Lord (vv. 12-16)

– he is eternal and men are mortal (v. 12)

– he is the maker and we are his creatures (v. 13)

– he is the sovereign and Zion is his people (vv. 14-16)

Preaching and Teaching the Text

Title: **God's Wake-up Call**

Text: **Isaiah 51:17–52:12**

Structure: God picks up the prayer of 51:9 for the arm of the Lord to awake and applies the instruction to his lethargic people (51:17, 52:1).

1. Wake up to your spiritual deliverance (51:17-23)

– the cup has been drunk – the cross (51:17-20)

– the cup has been removed – the curse (51:21-23)

2. Wake up to your restored status (52:1-6)

– holiness and liberty (52:1-2)

– redemption and vindication (52:3-6)

3. Wake up to your assured future (52:7-12)

– your God reigns (v. 7)

– he has redeemed (vv. 8-10)

– he will go before you (vv. 11-12)

Leading a Bible Study

1. 51:1-3 Who are the addressees of verse 1? What are they being told to do? What benefits will listening bring them? What parallels can be drawn for New Testament believers like us?

2. 51:4-6 What is the scope and extent of Yahweh's new initiative for the nations? Why is this so significant (v. 6)? How does this answer the questions still pending from earlier?

3. 51:7-8 What assurances does God provide here for the faithful remnant? How do they meet their current needs?

4. 51:9-11 Verse 11 is an exact repetition of 35:10, which looked forward to the eschatological inhabitants of Zion singing Yahweh's praise. Now the restored remnant are in view and are seen as forerunners of a restored world. How does the language of verses 9-10 serve to build their faith and ours?

5. 51:12-16 Verse 12 is strongly reminiscent of 40:1 ('comfort') and 40:6 ('All men are like grass'). How is verse 13 explained by verse 12? Why should the faithful remnant have confidence in these promises? How should they view the exile in the light of these declarations? What are the practical applications to our own lives as we wait for Jesus' return?

Application: How does this passage encourage us in our faith as we wait for Jesus' return? What does our fear of what other people can do to us say about our faith in God?

Second study

1. 51:17-23 Verse 17 recalls the statement of 40:2. What has God done and why did he do it? But when the cup has been drunk, what will the future hold? Why is this a summons to Jerusalem to wake up?

2. 52:1-6 What further reasons are given here for Jerusalem to rouse herself? How does God's perspective on the events of Israel's history challenge the predominant view expressed in Zion's objections (49:14ff.)?

3. 52:7-10 Verse 7 recalls the strikingly similar earlier passage, 40:9-10. What is happening in this paragraph? Why is it such a cause for joy? Why is it so central to God's greatest purposes?

4. 52:7 Reflect on how Paul uses this great statement in Romans 10:14-15. What clues does the whole verse in Isaiah give us as to what our emphasis should be in proclaiming the New Testament gospel?

5. 52:11-12 The summons is to leave Babylon, which brings us full circle to the return narrative in 40:3-5 again. What characteristics of the return are highlighted here? Why?

Application: What does this passage have to say to us when we feel that the church is ineffective and weak, especially in the context of opposition from secular atheism? What does it have to say to us when we feel unable to answer those who criticise our faith – whether families, friends or colleagues?

13. Salvation accomplished (52:13–53:12)

One of the most famous and well-loved passages of the Bible lies before us in this final and most comprehensive of the servant songs. At the outset, we need to recognise that it is a very carefully crafted poem, a reality often obscured by the unhelpful chapter division. The song divides into five stanzas of gradually increasing length, each occupying three verses in our English translations. The structure of the poem works like this: stanzas 1 and 5 (52:13-15 and 53:10-12) represent the same theme of the servant's victory through his suffering. Stanzas 2 and 4 (53:1-3 and 53:7-9) focus on the factual realities of the servant's suffering and humiliation, culminating in his death and burial. The central third stanza (53:4-6), right in the middle, reveals the heart of the matter as the meaning of the servant's suffering and death is explained. The central concept is located here at the heart of the poem and the mid-point of the mid-point is 53:5, which the structure shows us is the heart of the matter. 'he was pierced for our transgressions, he was crushed for our iniquities; the punishment that brought us peace was upon him, and by his wounds we are healed.' This is the salvation of God, which reaches to the ends of the earth!

The song begins with an echo of 42:1, the first servant song, 'See, my servant...' but the first stanza, 52:13-15, is shrouded in mystery and paradox. The verb translated 'act wisely' is probably better rendered 'prosper' or 'be successful' (cf. Joshua 1:8), and this is given weight by the progression of verse 13. The servant is revealed as risen, ascended and glorified. The paradox is the contrast of 52:14 where this figure of glory is shown to have been disfigured and marred in the most appalling way. How can this be the same person? Yet, clearly, he is because 52:15 swings back to the exaltation theme and illustrates the profound effect he will have on the nations and their rulers. We are witnessing an event like no other in the history of the world.

53:1-3 picks up the idea of awe, even perplexity, with its enquiry, 'Whoever would have thought the arm of the

Lord would be revealed in this way?' It looks all wrong to the unbelieving world. But the description of the servant's person (53:2) and his life or ministry (53:3) confirm that it is indeed the case. He had none of the trappings of majesty or human glory in his origins, his appearance or his relationship with others. Twice we are told 'he was despised,' his life characterised by sorrow and familiarity with suffering. The stanza ends with the all-inclusive 'we,' indicating the common verdict of the human race against the servant.

A dramatic change develops in 53:4-6 as the poem suddenly becomes intensely personal. 'He' and 'we' or 'us' are juxtaposed throughout the stanza. The purpose of his suffering is becoming clear. We are now shown that the infirmities and sorrows of verse 3 are 'ours'. He has lifted this burden on our behalf. It was not wrong to see this as an act of God's judgement. The mistake is to see him as suffering for his own sins, whereas the amazing truth is that it is for our transgressions and iniquities that he suffers, to bring us peace and wholeness. Here is the provision of peace, even for the wicked (cf. 48:22), achieved by the penal suffering of the servant as the substitute for the sinner. 53:6 could not be clearer. The Lord is acting through the servant's suffering to receive foolish, wandering sheep like us. He has literally 'caused to meet upon him,' the one truly substitutionary sacrifice, the iniquity of us all. Could there be a more wonderful summary of the means by which the world's salvation, heralded ever since chapter 40, was at last accomplished?

In 53:7-9 we return to the details of his suffering with the comparison to a sacrificial lamb, as the servant voluntarily accepts his role, perfectly obedient to the Father's will (see

Heb. 10:5-10). The injustice of his condemnation and the violence of his death are stressed in 53:8, but the repeated point is that it was for his people that all this has happened. 53:9 establishes the certainty of his death, confirmed by the reference to his burial.

But the song ends on a totally different note, as 53:10-12 declare the servant's triumph. The beginning of 53:10 establishes the supremely important understanding that all this is Yahweh's plan and will. The servant's life is laid down as a guilt offering, the only means by which guilty sinners can be reconciled to a holy God. Yet, amazingly, that is not the end, for it is equally the will of Yahweh to raise him up to life and to accomplish all his purposes in the salvation of sinners through the servant's death, resurrection and glorious triumph.

'Do you understand what you are reading?' Philip asked the Ethiopian eunuch returning from Jerusalem and puzzling over Isaiah 53:7-8. Who can the prophet be speaking about? 'Then Philip began with that very passage of Scripture and told him the good news about Jesus' (Acts 8:30-38). And can we twenty-first-century preachers of the same good news do anything less? We can use the gospel narratives to fill out the amazingly detailed fulfilment entailed within Isaiah's prophecy, seven hundred years before the event. We can show how the Messiah's work, as spoken of by the song, is the key answer to the questions asked by the whole book of Isaiah: how can the faithless city become the faithful city? How can the sinful rebellion of the human heart be changed into the life of faith and obedience? The answer is here in Isaiah 53 and it came to fulfilment on a Roman cross outside the city wall, on a Friday afternoon, as 'the Son of God, who loved me... gave himself for me' (Gal. 2:20). There can be no more important message for our generation to hear than this, so preach Isaiah!

Preaching and Teaching the Text
Title: **Salvation Accomplished**
Text: **Isaiah 52:13–53:12**
Structure: Clear the ground at the beginning by establishing the New Testament perspective that the servant is the Lord Jesus (e.g. Acts 8:35; Luke 22:37; John 12:41). Use the Gospel passages to fill out our understanding of the text.

    1. Mysterious identity (52:13-15)

    2. Incredible strategy (53:1-3)

    3. Perfect remedy (53:4-6)

    4. Powerful humility (53:7-9)

    5. Total victory (53:10-12)

Leading a Bible Study
1. 52:13-15 Draw out the contrast between (a) the servant's elevation to the position of ultimate authority (v. 13), with the same vocabulary in use as in Isaiah 6:1 (cf. John 12:41), and (b) his appalling disfigurement (v. 14). Why is this so incongruous? How are both these verses brought to fulfilment in the cross, resurrection and ascension of Christ?

2. 53:1-3 Incredulity is the key note of verse 1. 'Whoever would have thought this would be the way God's saving arm would be laid bare?' (cf. 52:10, also 40:10-11). In what ways does that note still affect our gospel proclamation?

53:2-3 Taking the details of these verses, can you relate each part to their fulfilment in Christ – his infancy, ministry, etc.?

What are the dangers he faced, referred to in verse 2a? (cf. 1 Cor. 1:23-29). What events from the last week of Christ's earthly life are prefigured in verse 3?

Note the surprise inclusion of 'we' at the end of verse 3. What is its significance?

3. 53:4-6 What is the common understanding of the cross described in verse 4? Where is it right and where wrong? How does verse 5 teach us what happened to the servant, why it happened and what happens to us, as a result? Relate these specifics to the Gospel account of the crucifixion. How does this verse teach the meaning of Christ's death? The last verb in verse 6 is (literally) 'caused to meet upon him.' What further understanding of ourselves and of our rescue does this verse add?

4. 53:7-9 This paragraph details many of the events surrounding the crucifixion which are faithfully related in the Gospels. Take each statement and work out how it was fulfilled and what its imagery teaches us.

Verse 7 Why the 'lamb' imagery? Why 'oppressed and afflicted'? Why the 'silence'? cf. 1 Pet. 2:21-23)

Verse 8 Why the reference to 'descendants'? What doctrine does the verse teach?

Verse 9 What are the historical references here? Why the emphasis on his innocence?

5. 53:10-12 What is Yahweh's attitude to the servant's death? (Look at each of the three references to 'the LORD'). How does Christ see his offspring (cf. 54:1-3)? Note the recurrence of 'prosper' (cf. the NIV's footnote to 52:13).

Verse 11 How is the resurrection in this verse? Note that the second part can be translated 'by knowledge of him…' What blessings come from knowing the servant in this way? What physical events at the cross and in the temple proved this to be true?

Verse 12 These are all images of triumph and victory. How are they fulfilled in Christ? How does the last sentence underline the major truth that Christ is both priest and offering (cf. Heb. 9:11-14)?

14. *Future perfect (54:1-17)*

This chapter and the next conclude the unit (chs. 40–55) by providing the authoritative commentary on the final servant song. Here in chapter 54 the benefits of Christ's sacrificial conquest on the cross for his people are explored under the symbolism of Zion, the holy city. In chapter 55 the scope of the servant's work is related to the whole world. These are the twin foci of so much of Isaiah's prophecy: the people of God and the Gentile nations, the church and the world.

The imagery of 54:1-3 is of a massive expansion of the numbers of God's people. Exiled Israel is like a childless woman in a state of continual mourning, but with the completion of the servant's work, children are being born, the family is expanding and so must their accommodation. The cross reminds us that God is in the business of saving a multitude of people, and if we are not passionately interested and involved in that we simply shunt ourselves into a siding. One of the greatest glories of the gospel is the expanding family of God (cf. Col. 1:6).

54:4-10 present to us the effects of the servant's work for his people. Fear, shame, disgrace and humiliation are removed and obliterated from the memory (54:4). The creator has become his people's redeemer, calling them back into intimate relationship with himself, like an abandoned wife restored to her marriage (54:5-8). This is seen as an extension of God's covenant mercy: just as God made an unbreakable promise to Noah never to flood the earth again, so his covenant promises of peace and unfailing love, secured by the cross, are unbreakable and certain (54:9-10).

A glorious vision of the heavenly and eternal city dominates 54:11-17 and doubtless provided the foundation materials for the fuller New Testament depiction in Rev. 21:10ff. The beauty of the city is paralleled by its peace and security, and all are rooted in the promise that these are the eternal heritage of the Lord's servants, reconciled to God by the servant's work. The Isaianic context reminds us that the suffering of the earthly Jerusalem was due to God's covenant discipline, not because the 'gods' or armies of Assyria or Babylon were stronger. Chapter 36 and 37 have reminded us that God was completely able to deliver them from the strongest war machine by his miraculous intervention. That is why the heavenly city is secure. It is God's city where he dwells forever with his people with no more sorrow or separation. It is because of the servant's work that we too can live in our generation on earth as citizens of heaven, as a people who know that our future is perfect.

Preaching and Teaching the Text
Title: **Future perfect**
Text: **Isaiah 54:1-17**
Structure: The implications of the servant's work are spelled out for the covenant community (Zion). This leads

us to consider their significance for the New Covenant community and the heavenly Jerusalem.

1. Zion repopulated (vv. 1-3)
    - new life and multiplication
    - the norm of gospel expansion
2. Zion restored (vv. 4-10)
    - experienced in compassionate love (vv. 4-8)
    - guaranteed by covenant promise (vv. 9-10)
3. Zion resplendent (vv. 11-17)
    - the beauty of righteousness (vv. 11-15)
    - the freedom of security (vv. 16-17)

Leading a Bible Study

1. 54:1-3 Identify the two commands in these verses and the reasons for them. What are the supernatural ingredients in verse 1? And what do the Abrahamic echoes add to our understanding? (Remember 51:1-3.)

2. 54:4-8 The marriage analogy shifts us to the covenant at Sinai. How does this section refer to Judah's suffering in the Babylonian exile?

3. 54:9-10 What are the Gospel parallels with Noah? How does this echo and reinforce verses 2-3?

4. 54:11-17 The vision expands to Jerusalem (the afflicted city) which is itself representative of the new universal community of gospel believers who will dwell in the eternal city, the ultimate 'faithful city'. What are the characteristics of the New Covenant, as compared with the city the Babylonians destroyed? How do the 'servants of the LORD' (v. 17) relate to the servant?

Application: Work through the blessings of verses 11-17, and apply it to the blessings we enjoy as the people of God.

What do we enjoy now, and what is still for the future? What kind of confidence are these verses meant to give us?

15. Eternal certainties (55:1-13)

Now the effects of the servant's completed work are surveyed and proclaimed to the entire Gentile world.

55:1-5 offer a series of promises in the form of gracious invitations. At first sight they seem strange – buying 'without money and without cost' – but we soon realise that this is because the price has already been paid. Money may be spent on that which does not satisfy, but the 'richest of fare' for the soul is the gift of God, paid for by the death of the servant (55:2b). Spiritual satisfaction comes through listening to God's invitation, coming to him personally and so being incorporated into the covenant community instituted by God's promise to King David of an everlasting kingdom, ruled over by an eternal king from David's line. This promise is now open to the nations, as they appropriate the benefits of the servant's rescue mission and submit to his sovereign rule and lordship. Just as 54:1-3 pictured a growing family, so 55:5 envisages an ever-expanding kingdom as the Gentile world hastens to bow the knee to God and to greet David's greater Son.

55:6-13 begins with the logical link from these promise invitations to their enjoyment and fulfilment. It happens when individuals seek Yahweh and call on him, which involves repentance, turning from evil, and dependence by faith on God's mercy and pardon (55:6-7). The next verses (55:8-11) indicate why such faith is essential and what its basis is. Faith is the recognition that God's thoughts and ways are far beyond our finite human limitations and that we are therefore totally dependent on his self-revelation in his word if we are to know him and live in fellowship with him.

Like the rain from heaven, God's life-giving word is his free and gracious gift to man, bringing spiritual satisfaction, for which the food at the beginning of the chapter is a physical metaphor. We can have great confidence that it will never fail in its purpose. So the future blessings of 55:12-13 could not be more assured, for they are achieved and guaranteed through the word of the Lord. Freedom instead of slavery, with joy and peace in the place of fear and conflict – these are the blessings of Christ's work, in which the whole created order rejoices. Fruitfulness replaces the barren land, trees of beauty and usefulness, the thorns and briers. These are surely symbolic of the changed lives of those who receive the servant's work. They are the currency of heaven, which nothing can destroy and for which his redeemed people will praise the Father and the Son throughout the ages of eternity. This is the fruit of the servant's work and this is the gospel of Christ, so let us preach Isaiah!

Preaching and Teaching the Text
Title: **Eternal certainties**
Text: **Isaiah 55:1-13**
Structure: The whole world benefits from the servant's completed work as God's invitation to live reaches out to the nations.
1. An everlasting covenant (vv. 1-5)
    – the needy recipients (vv. 1-2) – the price is paid.
    – the ancient promise (vv. 3-5) – the King has come.
2. An ever-present invitation (vv. 6-7)
    – seek, call, forsake, turn
    – mercy and pardon

3. An everlasting sign (vv. 8-13)
   – The rain cycle produces physical bread (vv. 8-10)
   – The word cycle produces spiritual food (v. 11)
   – The grace cycle produces eternal joy (vv. 12-13)

Leading a Bible Study

5. 55:1-2 What is the connection between this great invitation and the preceding verses? Why is this such a wonderful description of gospel grace?

6. 55:3-5 Here we are in the context of the Davidic covenant. What did God promise? How was it fulfilled in the servant's work and the results that flow from it?

7. 55:6-7 Identify the ingredients of an authentic response to the grace revealed in the servant's sacrifice.

8. 55:8-11 These are great promises for gospel evangelists. Why do we need verse 8? What are the confidences and encouragements contained in the extended metaphor of verses 10-11?

9. 55:12-13 What was the immediate relevance of this promise to the exiles? How is it fulfilled in Christ?

Application: What do verses 6-7 tell us about the way our lives should be if we genuinely respond to the grace given through Jesus Christ? How do verses 8-11 encourage us to persevere in gospel proclamation? What encouragements should verses 12-13 give to Christians today?

Part 6

THE SOVEREIGN CONQUEROR
WAITING FOR THE FULFILMENT
OF GOD'S PURPOSES

Isaiah 56–66

'The true servants of God ... so demonstrate
the righteousness of God in their ethical behaviour
that all nations are drawn to him.'

John N. Oswalt, *NICOT: Isaiah*, vol.2 p.463

Introduction

For many commentators, and not a few preachers, this last section of Isaiah's book poses something of a conundrum. In comparison with chapters 40–55, which are bound together by the development of the two inter related themes of the forthcoming deliverance from Babylon and the redemptive work of the suffering servant, these closing chapters seem to many to be a rag bag collection of disconnected prophetic utterances. Critics have found it difficult to discern any single governing purpose in this final unit. This has sometimes been used to justify multiple authorship theories, but is also to some extent the product of those theories, which predispose their proponents not to look in any detail for continuity of theological thought or literary structure, in a book which they have decided cannot be a unity.

However, when we approach the text of chapters 56–66 in the canonical context of the whole book as we have it, we discover that it forms the logical climax of all that has gone before. There are several themes which are developed throughout the unit, giving it coherence and focus and relating it firmly to the earlier chapters. There is also a further portrait of the agent of Yahweh, already portrayed as the branch from the stump of Jesse and as the suffering servant, by whom God's eternal redemptive plan is both accomplished and implemented. Here he is presented as an anointed conqueror, trampling his enemies under his feet in his righteous wrath (59:15-19; 63:1-6).

References such as these encourage us to reprise the earlier agenda of the book, which we have observed, in order to appreciate its ultimate climactic fulfilment. At the beginning we noted that the tale of two cities might be summed up in the question: 'How is the faithless city of 1:21, Jerusalem the "harlot", to become the faithful city of 1:26, "the City of Righteousness"?' By the time we reach 66:19-24, the book's concluding sentences, we find the Lord's servants proclaiming his glory among the nations 'that have not heard of my fame'. They bring a multitude from all the nations 'to my holy mountain in Jerusalem', where 'all mankind will come and bow down before me,' says the LORD'. The city has been transformed and as a result, a new community of 'brothers, from all the nations' (66:20,23) is reconciled to God and brought into relationship with him.

This is not universalism, as the last verse of the book underlines, with Yahweh's reference to 'the dead bodies of those who rebelled against me; their [whose] worm will not die, nor will their fire be quenched...' (66:24). But it is a recognition that the people of God will no longer be ethnically determined by physical relationship to Abraham. Rather, they will be defined by their trust and obedience, deepening and developing their new spiritual relationship with Yahweh, which he has himself initiated. By chapter 66 that transformation has occurred.

This would seem to indicate that we should always be looking for the fulfilment motif in the climax of the book, whether it is viewed historically or theologically. From the historical standpoint, the book which begins with Isaiah's prophetic call 'in the year that King Uzziah died' (6:1), 740BC, traces the ongoing development of Judah's history: from the Assyrian threat in the reigns of Ahaz and Hezekiah, to the Babylonian conquest and exile (still future), and on beyond that, first to the return and restoration after the exile and then to the eschatological fulfilment of the eternal kingdom. The time boundaries between these huge and enormously significant developments of God's plan are sometimes blurred and intertwined, but the certainty of the fulfilment is very clearly stated.

It is our privilege, as we look back through the lens of the cross and see the detailed outworking of prophecies that, for Isaiah, lay far in the future, to recognise the amazing accuracy of the divine predictions and the inevitability of their enactment. That is why this book is such an encouragement to our faith, as we are challenged to keep on trusting and obeying while we wait for Christ's return. In the light of what has already been predicted and fulfilled, we can surely have every confidence that all which is yet to be fulfilled will be accomplished, and so we are heartened to persevere faithfully in the waiting time.

This idea of 'waiting' is central to the whole book and powerfully shapes the unifying purpose of this concluding section. From its early stages, we have found Isaiah's ministry to be geared not to widespread, national spiritual renewal (6:9-10), for which he doubtless longed, but towards the gathering of a comparatively small number of people, who will hear, trust and obey the Lord's word. This 'remnant', gathered and then nurtured by the truth of the prophetic message, is characterised by a faith which waits on God for the fulfilment of all his promises. The demonstration of the reality of that faith, in the meantime, is their obedience to God's already revealed will, both in their belief and their behaviour.

The waiting time is the testing time. If God's judgement is stayed because of his mercy, as before the Babylonian conquest, will the waiting be a time of repentance and renewed commitment? Or, will its characteristic be continuing rebellion and rejection of God's will, on the careless presumption that he is not going to do anything about it? If the suffering servant's ministry has achieved a worldwide salvation on the basis of God's free gift (55:1-7), how will his people live in the waiting time between the servant's work and the eschatological fulfilment of all that he has accomplished? Whether the focus is on the pre-exilic attacks as God warns his people, the experience of the exile when it seemed that Babylon's gods had conquered,the post-exilic return, the coming of the Messiah, or the end of human history at the last judgement, the question is always the same. How must the remnant demonstrate its reality, by living in the waiting time in faith and obedience?

The focus of chapters 56–66 is therefore especially appropriate to us, as contemporary Christians, still waiting for the Lord's return and the culmination of his eternal plan. We shall learn lessons here about how we too should live as God's redeemed people, about the nature of our hope, about the future of Christ's judgement and about the priorities of our witness, by life and lip, to a lost and needy world. We shall learn, in John Oswalt's words, how 'a trusting, redeemed servant Israel becomes the messenger with clean lips, through whom the world can find its Saviour'.[1]

1. Context and Structure

It is generally recognised that the final section of the book is centred on chapters 60–62, immediately preceded (59:15b-21) and followed (63:1-6) by the portrait of the sovereign conqueror, whose task is to don the battle garments of God's anointed warrior and execute his righteous wrath in the just destruction of all his enemies. At the heart of

---

1. John N. Oswalt, *New International Commentary on the Old Testament: Isaiah* vol 2, p11.

this central section, we hear the voice of the Lord's anointed describing his ministry of grace and judgement (61:1-3) and the repercussions which will follow from it (61:4ff.).

If then we assume that 59:15b–63:6 constitutes this central section, we can recognise that the substance of its message is that the Lord will triumph over all his enemies and that he will achieve this through an appointed agent, commissioned with divine authority and anointed with divine power. This is a similar pattern to that of the Immanuel figure in chapters 1–39 and the servant in chapters 40–55, where in both cases divine enabling is granted to a human figure to carry out God's purposes in the face of determined opposition.

This leaves us with the two bordering sections, 56:1–59:15a and 63:7–66:24. Recognising that these divisions are, in one sense, artificial and that chapter 56 flows on directly from chapters 54–55, itself the divinely given commentary on the servant's work in chapter 53, it is helpful to link the subject matter of chapter 56 with the issues which are left unresolved at the end of chapter 55. The promises in that great gospel chapter do not focus only on the gathering of a multitude of new believers into covenant relationship with the Lord, through their repentance and his mercy and pardon. They also speak of the renewal of the whole created order, as God's people are led into a new world, the consummation of God's promises and the restoration of all that was lost in Eden.

This raises the issue of the behaviour appropriate to men and women of faith in the waiting period, as we have seen, but the very beginning of the unit at 56:1 seems at first sight to return us from free grace to a form of works religion. 'This is what the LORD says, "Maintain justice and do what is right…"'. Have we not learned that this is impossible for sinful human beings to fulfil, and so are we not back with the insoluble problems of the start of the book? Isaiah's answers to these questions would be 'yes' and 'no'. Our human inability to extricate ourselves from our sin and its effects will certainly be reiterated in these chapters. But we are in chapter 56 now, and we already know the wonderful solution to the problem of human sinfulness provided by the servant's work. 'The LORD has laid on him the iniquity of us all' (53:6b).

However, the fact that we are to read the demands of chapters 56–59 in the light of the servant's atoning sacrifice is established in the motivation which the Lord explains in 56:1b. 'For my salvation is close at hand and my righteousness will soon be revealed.' It is in the light of the assured consummation of the servant's work, in the eternal kingdom, that we are brought back to the necessity of personal covenant obedience, if covenant blessings are to be personally enjoyed in the present. So these chapters will expose once again the ingrained nature of human rebellion, but alongside it runs the free offer of boundless mercy and covenant relationship to the repentant. Alec Motyer's suggestion is that we have here another of Isaiah's favourite 'doubles', with the same pattern being repeated immediately after its first exposition. This integrates the section and helps us to see its logical line of development, as follows.

If we take the first part of the unit to run from 56:1 to 59:15a, the two fold division works out as 56–57 and 58–59:15a. At the beginning of each half (56:1-8 and 58:1-14) there is a divine exhortation to righteousness, particularly focused on the Old Testament law, in commitment to Sabbath observance (ch. 56) and fasting (ch. 58) which is not merely external but indicative of far-reaching social righteousness.

'Do what is right' is balanced, however, with 'my righteousness will be revealed', since the blessings which accompany covenant faithfulness are numerous and extensive. Outsiders, such as foreigners and eunuchs, can be welcomed into covenant relationship and privilege when they 'bind themselves to the LORD' (56:3-7). Those who delight in covenant obedience will find God's protection and provision, experience his guidance and answers to prayer, and know his joy in restoration (58:7-14). Each passage is then followed by some of Isaiah's most devastating exposure of human failure and rebellion in the light of God's law (56:9–57:13 and 59:1-8). But far from ending in despair, the movement of the text is towards repentance in 57:14-21, which the NIV titles 'comfort for the contrite', and in 59:9-15a, where the penitent no longer pretend that all is well, but accurately acknowledge their pitiful state due to their iniquities. We might represent the structure of the unit in this way:

56:1-8	1 God's righteous demands and gracious promises
56:9–57:13	2 Human inability and sin are exposed
57:14-21	3 Penitence expressed and dependence on God's mercy.
58:1-14	1 God's righteous demands and gracious promises
59:1-8	2 Human inability and sin are exposed
59:9-15a	3 Penitence expressed and dependence on God's mercy.

This provides a template for how the people of God are to live in the waiting time, whether it is for the first or second coming of the Messiah.

We turn now to the third section of this final unit, 63:7–66:24, which forms the conclusion of the whole book. The pattern here is rather different, though the subject matter, with its emphasis on the need of holiness of life and dependence on God's grace and mercy, reflects again the main themes of the section we have just explored. But here the emphasis is on the intercession of the faithful remnant and God's gracious response to their cry. After a reflective survey of the Lord's faithful dealings with Israel, particularly with reference to the days of Moses and the exodus (63:7-14), the plea from those waiting is 'Why not now?' (63:15-19). This then broadens out into one of the most moving and instructive prayers of the Old Testament, expressing penitence, calling on God to have mercy and above all imploring him not to hold back, but to 'rend the heavens and come down'.

There is a direct response from Yahweh in chapter 65, pointing out that he has been continually offering himself ('here am I') – but to a people who were careless and disinterested (65:1-2). A catalogue of iniquity follows (65:3-7), but with the telling recognition that a righteous remnant does exist. This is then used to highlight the life choices and consequences of those who are Yahweh's servants and those who choose not to be (65:8-16). The chapter culminates with a wonderful incentive, the dramatic revelation of the 'new heavens and a new earth', symbolised by the New Covenant, with the limitless blessings which its members will receive (65:17-25). There are strong echoes here of the earlier promises, particularly in chapter 11.

The final chapter again presents the need for holiness of life (66:1-6), with its portrait of the remnant member whom the Lord esteems – 'he who is humble and contrite in spirit, and trembles at my word' (66:2b). Then the focus shifts to the suddenness with which the Lord will eventually complete all his purposes of grace in the birth

of the New Covenant (66:7-13), which is at the same time
the final and total destruction of all his enemies (66:14-17).
The acceptance of many from the nations into covenant
relationship with Yahweh is the glorious prospect of
66:18-21, but the book ends on a note which has often been
sounded through its chapters – a note of division between
those who 'come and bow down' and those who 'rebel'. It is the
difference between everlasting life and everlasting destruction
(66:22-24). The existence and security of the New Covenant,
with all her detractors and foes defeated, is beyond doubt, but
the question Isaiah asks his hearers and readers is whether or
not we shall be found within her walls.

Before we approach the content of the unit in more detail,
it is worth noting that John Oswalt suggests a persuasive
chiastic structure for chapters 56–66, in his two-volume
NICOT commentary. An excellent section[2] explores a
number of possibilities in seeking to discover a coherent
overview of the whole unit. The appearance of the 'outsiders'
within covenant relationship, which begins chapter 56 and
concludes chapter 66, provides the clue to structure, which,
by way of the various passages about human rebellion and
inability and the two portraits of the sovereign conqueror,
lead us to the eschatological vision of chapters 60–62, as
the central point of the section.

But where Oswalt is most helpful is in his ability not
only to see the structure but also to discern its theological
purpose and didactic power. The foreigners and outsiders
will only populate the New Covenant if the grace of God is
appropriated, in order to bring about the penitence which
recognises how far short of the divine requirements we

2 John N. Oswalt, *New International Commentary on the Old Testament: Isaiah*
vol. 2, pp461–465

all fall and that only the initiative of Yahweh himself can ultimately conquer and destroy the forces of evil. This is a major theological lesson to be learned through this unit, which has profound implications for our practical teaching of the Christian life, or in Isaiah's terms, how the remnant are to live righteously in the waiting time. Oswalt comments, 'Righteousness is no more to be achieved by human struggle than deliverance from Babylon was. It is by the grace of God, who alone (59:15b-21, 63:1-6) will defeat the enemy and enable his people to live the righteous lives that he demands. Righteousness is still a requirement, but it is through divine grace that it is to be produced.'[3] So, preach Isaiah!

2. Preaching Notes

If it is true that Isaiah, as a book, is sadly underused and under-preached in the contemporary church, it is even more the case that chapters 56-66 are frequently ignored or put on the back burner, as being too difficult or obscure for today's pulpit. I hope that the preceding, all-too-brief exploration has convinced you otherwise, and that this section will play a significant role in any preaching series on Isaiah you may undertake.

The structural difficulties have largely been dealt with by John Oswalt and Alec Motyer in their respective commentaries, with their emphasis on the pattern which shapes what can otherwise appear a somewhat disparate collection of materials. Clearly, we can have confidence that chapters 56–66 do in fact constitute a carefully constructed unit and there is no need to have to posit multiple authorship or editorial malpractice! This establishes chapters 60-62 as the central core ingredient of the unit, with chapter 61 as

---

3. *IBID.* vol. 2, p464..

the centre of the centre, with its prophecy of the Messianic age so wonderfully fulfilled in the ministry of our Lord Jesus Christ. Luke 4:16-21 provides his word recorded in Scripture as the key to the understanding of this motif in our contemporary context.

It is often helpful for our congregations to see a clear-cut example like this, of the New Testament providing the authoritative interpretation of the Old. It exemplifies the Reformation principle that Scripture interprets Scripture, that the later revelation expounds and amplifies the former. It also helps us to see the Bible as one book, with one story-line of God's redemption purposes carried out in covenant grace, running through and uniting its sixty-six component parts. This gives greater confidence in the dependability of the Bible as those we teach begin to see 'how it all fits together'. In addition, the Isaiah 61–Luke 4 nexus can teach us not to look for only one historical fulfilment of predictive prophecy and so avoid some of the woodenness and confusion that can arise from too constricting an approach.

The significant fact is that Jesus stops reading the scroll of Isaiah 61 before the full run of the paragraph ends. He concludes with the phrase 'to proclaim the year of the Lord's favour' but does not read on further to 'and the day of vengeance of our God'. This is because the opening sentence of his exposition is, 'Today this scripture is fulfilled in your hearing' (Luke 4:21): clearly what he had read was being fulfilled in his Galilean ministry. But it was not yet the day of vengeance. Indeed that part of the prophecy would await a fulfilment in principle at the cross, when he bore God's wrath on our behalf, and in final execution when, as the risen and anointed conqueror of chapter 63, he will trample the rebellious nations in his wrath.

These considerations indicate how much chapters 56–66 relate to our own time. The declaration of the Messianic gospel ministry is enclosed by the two portraits of the sovereign conqueror. These highlight the alternatives of God's wrath and judgement and are in turn enclosed by Isaiah's appeal for godly living in the waiting time, before the final separation of the sheep and the goats at the end of this world. The theme of 'waiting' occurs on several occasions during the book, not as an example of passive resignation, but as an active commitment to live by God's promises before they are fulfilled and to prosecute God's purposes before they are actualised.

For Isaiah's original hearers, there was the waiting time before the exile, and for those who took the scrolls to Babylon, waiting for the promised return. But for both, as indeed for centuries afterwards, the real waiting was for the Lord to come, in the person of the Messiah, a waiting 'for the consolation of Israel', which constituted a 'righteous and devout' life, like Simeon's, down the years (Luke 2:25). It is this expectation which is the hallmark of a lively faith.

We too are in the waiting time, between the Lord's first coming and his promised return. The applications are clear and much needed today. We too are called to live holy lives, marked by ethical righteousness, conscious of the great day that is coming, for 'As the body without the spirit is dead, so faith without deeds is dead' (James 2:26).

That 'deadness' was Israel's majority condition in the waiting time, in spite of it being largely disguised by formal religion and external conformity. Its marks are exposed throughout these chapters, and the same dangers are never far from any of us in the twenty-first-century Christian church. There are challenges in this we need to hear today

– not least, our prayerlessness before a God who comes looking for his people, only to find them preoccupied with other things (66:4b). Where they will not listen to his word, they will have nothing to say to his face.

However, there is a major danger in all this, that such preaching may simply lay more and more heavy burdens on God's people, as though everything depended on our efforts, energy or abilities. This is perhaps particularly the case among 'keen' Christians, who want to live in the waiting time as citizens of heaven, seeking to bring others with them into the eternal kingdom. It can so easily degenerate into a form of works religion, motivated by guilt and characterised by frenetic activity and stress. We must not allow the preaching of Isaiah to contribute to those burdens. It should instead be liberating. For Isaiah is, par excellence, the prophet of justification by faith, and faith is the response to God's prior initiative in grace.

The message of this last part of the book is that while we have a responsibility to live godly lives, to God's glory, in God's world, while we wait for our hope to be fulfilled in Christ's return, the ability to do this is God's alone and is the free gift of his amazing grace. The external conformity of works-based religion is as much a spiritual dead end as the pagan idolatries Isaiah so fearlessly denounces. Godly living in the 'now' is all about developing our relationship of faith and obedience with our rescuing Lord in the light of the 'not yet' of his eternal reign.

He wants his people to seek him for himself, not merely for his blessings, great though they are. He wants us to realise that he is the one who calls the nations, as he is the one who governs history. He wants us to know that we are never stronger than when we are most aware of our weakness, and therefore most dependent on him. That is Isaiah's abiding message – the sufficiency of the God of grace, to whom our obedience is the sure evidence of our trust and with whom our abandonment to his limitless grace is the daily proof of a humble and contrite spirit which trembles at his word. 'This is the one I esteem' (66:2). So, in the light of these realities and their pressing contemporary relevance, let's be encouraged to preach Isaiah!

The sermon outlines which follow are not an exhaustive treatment of the whole of this unit, but six select passages which might form the basis of a series to introduce the major themes of this final section of Isaiah's book.

Similarly, there are nine Bible studies, giving overviews of multiple sections. These could easily be broken down further or combined. To make this easier, the application in these studies is distributed throughout the questions, rather than at the end of the study.

3. Working Through the Text
1. Grace for the foreigner (56:1-8)
These few verses highlight some astonishing outcomes of the servant's work and the widespread offer of the gospel (chs. 53–55). In a way that could hardly be comprehended under the Torah, the door is being opened for covenant relationship with Yahweh to the foreigner (vv. 3, 6) and the eunuch (vv. 3, 4). Not only the exiles of Israel, but 'still others' are going to be gathered into fellowship with God (v. 8). Those who were excluded under Old Testament legislation (Deut. 23:1) will be welcome because of the servant's work. 56:1 might seem to indicate that if the first part of the verse is observed ('do what is right') the second half will follow ('my salvation is

close at hand'). But it was never that way under the old covenant, and there is no change now.

We need to remember the Old Testament principle that God did not give the law to Israel as a ladder by which to climb up and make themselves acceptable to him. This is the way of all human religion, but all our ladders fall short and all our attempts to justify ourselves before God are like 'filthy rags' in his sight (64:6). The law given at Sinai was to people who had already been redeemed by the blood of the Passover Lamb. It was therefore preceded by grace and could only be kept by appropriating grace. Obedience is the mark of covenant membership and the channel by which covenant blessings flow into our lives, but never the means by which grace is extracted, much less merited. The emphasis here in 56:2 is that obedience to the law and ethical righteousness is the mark of receiving God's saving grace. It results in living a new life and entering into the enjoyment of a relationship with Yahweh.

2. Sneering at God (56:9–57:13)

The sudden shift of subject matter and, especially, tone almost seems to precipitate us back into the early chapters of the book with its devastating exposure of Judah's sins in the days of the Assyrian threat to her sovereignty. Although by this stage in the prophecy the focus is increasingly the far distant future: the post-exile return, the waiting for the Messiah, his coming and work, and the eschatological fulfilment of the new creation (65:17ff.), Isaiah is still speaking to his generation in eighth century Jerusalem with a particularity that is acutely penetrating. From our standpoint, as contemporary preachers, we need to find the veins that are common to all humanity and to allow the

Word to judge us, as we see so many repeated characteristics not only in our own outwardly different contexts but also in our own similarly sinful, rebellious hearts.

Verses 9-12 expose the sins of Judah's leaders, likening them to dogs – blind, mute, sleepy, greedy – who cannot guard their community, which is now open to being devoured by beasts. They should be watchmen and shepherds of God's flock, but they are drunkards and profligates. So, the righteous are attacked and even removed. No one realises that God is giving them deliverance through death – into peace, which the wicked can never have (57:21).

In verse 3, an attack is launched on the whole nation, which is sustained until verse 13.[4] The catalogue of adultery, mockery, religious prostitution, child sacrifice, rampant idolatry and alliance with pagan powers reaches its climax with the revelation by God that behind it all lies the terrifying reality 'that you do not fear me' (v. 11b). Destruction is the only possible outcome if we will not make God our refuge (v. 13).

In preaching this text, it would be important both to show what it meant to Isaiah's hearers, but also to move beyond that. Set it in its history, but do not bury it! The parallels in the contemporary church, by which we all too clearly disclose how little we really fear God, should be drawn out. We are certainly prey to a multitude of fears when we no longer honour God, which leads us to the obsessions of our culture to find meaning and security in God-substitutes, whether they are celebrity, money, sex or power. The end-point – a culture dedicated to sneering and

---

4. See Motyer's comments, which show that this denunciation must have been written before the exile, in the eighth century, and demonstrate the unity of this passage with earlier chapters. Alec Motyer, *Tyndale Old Testament Commentary on Isaiah*, p353.

sticking out its tongue to the living God (v. 4) – is chilling in the extreme.

Leading a Bible Study

1. 56:1 How does this opening verse combine the two great themes of the whole prophecy, so far? NB. Righteousness is indispensably required by God, but it is no more achieved by human effort than Babylon's defeat was.

2. 56:2 What is the chief characteristic of the 'blessed' man? How does this fit with the theme of the book?

3. 56:3-8 What promises are given here to foreigners and eunuchs, who were excluded from Israel's worship? What conditions must be fulfilled? Note how the privileges are explicitly related to their previous deprivation. What are the New Testament parallels to these Old Testament requirements and benefits?

4. 56:9-12 Why is God's flock so vulnerable? What are the sins of the watchmen/shepherds? Why do you think Isaiah introduces this note here?

5. 57:1-2 What is happening to the righteous? Why?

6. 57:3-13 These verses provide the explanation. In spite of the servant's work, evil is still rampant. Although the path to salvation is open, evil still has to be finally dealt with and destroyed. What are the characteristics of rebellion on which these verses focus? What will be the consequences of this continuing rebellion and disobedience?

3. The wicked and the contrite (57:14-21)

The necessity of repentance is clearly shown by the depths of Judah's depravity, but these verses also stress the possibilities presented by returning to the Lord. We are back now with the 'righteous' of verses 1-2, the remnant of those who avail themselves of the highway home to God, which he so graciously offers (v. 14). Contrition and humility, the prerequisites of repentance, lead to fellowship with 'the high and lofty One' and so to personal revival (v. 15). Beyond punishment and estrangement, there lie healing, guidance, new strength and peace (vv. 18-19). There is no explanation of how this can happen, at this point, but we must remember the dominant influence of chapter 53, as the theological focal point of all God's gracious activity, on the whole of this later section. We are certainly aware that it is because the servant was 'pierced for our transgressions' that we can affirm with assurance that 'by his wounds we are healed' (53:5).

Again, the contrast is drawn between the penitent and the wicked. The restlessness of a life from which God is 'excluded' is a terrible sentence in itself, which cannot be reversed while impenitent, since the only source of lasting peace is rejected. It is important to see the contrast here is between the wicked and the contrite. The peace of God's healing mercy is not acquired by merit; it has to be received by grace. Note the emphasis in the verbs on God's initiative from beginning to end ('I live...I will...I punished...I will restore,' etc). In contemporary terms, we need constantly to remind our hearers that God's peace, heavenly rest, is not for good people. If that were so, heaven would be unpopulated, for who could possibly be good enough for God? Rather, heaven is for forgiven people, and forgiveness is the free gift of God to the repentant.

4. *True or false* (58:1-14)

In this section, the inadequacies of God's people are clearly traced to their persistent rebellion, in spite of their superficial religiosity and hypocritical 'reverence' for God. But, as in the previous section, this is balanced with a gracious appeal to a better way, indicated by true heart devotion to Yahweh, confirmed in repentance and offering hope of a glorious future, in which the overflowing blessings of his covenant promises will be faithfully fulfilled and experienced.

Verses 1-5 contain strong echoes of 1:10-20, where the earliest diagnosis of Judah's spiritual ills revealed, not a failure to observe the external forms of worship, but a cynical adherence to the form rather than the substance. So, here, God calls for a trumpet voice to expose their sinful rebellion (v. 1) which is identified as outward form without inner substance. 'they seem eager to know my ways…and seem eager for God to come near them' (v. 2). So eager that when there seems to be no response to their fasting, they are quick to lay the blame at God's door (v. 3). This is always the essence of false religion, based on the 'quid pro quo' attitude of a business deal, fundamentally rooted in human works and self-justification. Their objection to God gives the game away. 'We've done our part [fasting], so why haven't you done yours [answering our requests]?'

God's answer is immediate and direct (vv. 4-5). Fasting which is merely external, for one day, and which leads to quarrelling and strife with no end of exploitation of their workers, is an offence to God's justice and truth. 'You cannot fast as you do today and expect your voice to be heard on high' (v. 4b). It is a much-needed reminder of the principle of Psalm 66:18. Unrepented iniquity makes prayer inaudible to God.

By contrast, verses 6-14 outline the qualities which God looks for in their fasting – justice, freedom from oppression, sheltering the stranger, feeding the hungry (vv. 6-7), an end to malicious talk (v. 9), the keeping of the Sabbath, not doing as you please and not speaking idle words (v. 13). When these realities indicate the inner heart-change of which their fasting is the external expression, then the grace of God will cascade upon them. The promises are strongly motivational, offering light, healing, righteousness, the Lord's protection (v. 8), answered prayer (v. 9), constant guidance, satisfaction, strength, refreshment (v. 11), rebuilding and restoration (v. 12), joy in the Lord, and feasting on the inheritance of Jacob (v. 14), the promises first made to the patriarchs.

The chapter illustrates very clearly the choice which Isaiah's ministry constantly presented and which found its theological roots in the covenant between God and Israel, when first they came out of Egypt. Covenant obedience is the channel of covenant blessing, not as a meritorious work, but as an appreciation of the rescuing grace of God. Having brought his people into relationship through the blood of the Passover, Yahweh prescribes how they can continue to live in fellowship with the God whose holy character the law expounds. It is all dependent on God's grace, which is limitless in its supply, so that there is no deficiency in God's provision. All the promised blessings really are available.

But God cannot be deceived. To imagine that observing the externals of covenant obedience will pay God off and excuse us from the requirement of heart-obedience and the discipline of growing in godliness is a tragic miscalculation. It reveals how far the heart is from God, whether the context is the old covenant order or the new. Heart-obedience is the only valid response, which authenticates in itself the repentance and faith for which God is looking.

Preaching an Teaching the Text

Title: **True or false?**

Text: **Isaiah 58:1-14**

Structure: Relate the text to the theme of chapters 56-57, that in spite of the servant's work, the people of God are unable to fulfill the imperative of 56:1 apart from responding to God's grace in repentance and obedience.

1. God exposes sin (vv. 1-3)
    – external conformity (v. 2)
    – inner self-centredness (v. 3)
2. God requires sincerity (vv. 4-7)
    – empty religion exists for its own benefit (vv. 4-5)
    – true faith exists to bless others (vv. 6-7)
3. God promises great blessings (vv. 8-14)
    – righteousness and glory (v. 8)
    – answered prayer (v. 9)
    – light in the darkness (v. 10b)
    – direction and provision (v. 11)
    – reconstruction and fulfilment (vv. 12, 14)
    – 'IF' . . . see verses 9b–10a and 13.

Application: God's exposure of sin and promise of blessing should lead us to action in a life of repentance and obedience.

Leading a Bible Study

1.   57:14-15 What new note is introduced in these verses? Note the echoes of chapter 40 in verse 14. What is God inviting his people to do?

2.   57:16-19 These are great verses revealing the heart of God as he deals with rebellious sinners. Following

the first-person singular verbs, what is revealed about God's attitudes and actions?

3. 57:20-21 Compare 48:22. Why is this repeated after the servant's work? How do these verses (57:14-21) guide the remnant as they await the ultimate victory? What should be the marks of the church as we wait?

4. 58:1-3a The outward religious behaviour looks so right. What is it? Is there a danger that we could be repeating this?

5. 58:3b-5 What does God expose as fundamentally flawed in their attitude to their fasting? What principle lies behind this and how might we succumb to the same error?

6. 58:6-9a List what God is looking for in terms of social righteousness within the community. What pointers does this give the church about how we live in covenant community (cf. Matt. 25:34-40)? Why is this not 'works' religion?

7. 58:9b-14 Put together the picture of the godly life, in these verses, which is pleasing to the Lord. How does this apply to us, as Christians (e.g. v. 13)? And what are the equivalent promises of God for us, as redeemed people?

5. Cast yourself on God's mercy (59:1-8)

This section echoes the theme of 56:9–57:13, and is a further exposure of the sins which hinder God's blessings on his people. It reminds us that these persistent and recurrent evils are the most telling evidence of our inability, as human beings, to rescue ourselves. The aim of the passage is to move the hearers to confess, repent and cast themselves on the mercy of God, which is indeed the response we encounter in 59:9-15a.

Verse 1 picks up the accusation of 58:3 that God does nothing to help his people, but establishes that there is no shortage of power with him and no deafness to his people's cry. The problem is their iniquities which hide God's face, like a thick cloud, and stop his ears (v. 2). Again, the catalogue is detailed and precise – bloodstained hands, lying lips (v. 3), unjust government (v. 4), violent evil deeds (v. 6), ruin and destruction (v. 7). The use of 'they' throughout this section indicates how widespread such attitudes and behaviour were in the culture of Jerusalem and Judah.

In the middle of the list, the threatening and disillusioning nature of such rebellion is vividly portrayed in the metaphors of verses 5-6. They are the viper's eggs and the spider's web. What this sinful society produces is life-threatening and full of foreboding. Such 'eggs' poison the eater, and even breaking them results in the hatching of a dangerous adder. The 'clothing' which a godless society relies on for its warmth and security is as ineffective as dressing oneself in a cobweb. These are startling and effective images, because they show the intense danger and folly of the headlong plunge into evil which the rest of the paragraph exposes. The casualties are peace and justice, since there can be no peace except on a basis of righteousness (48:22; 57:21). What is supremely true of humans in relationship with God is equally true of human relationships with one another. Love for God will always result in love for neighbour.

6. *Repentance of the remnant (59:9-15a)*
The sequence of repetition ends, not just with the need for repentance but with the expression and recognition

of their situation by at least some of Isaiah's hearers, who from the content of these verses must be identified as the righteous remnant. 'Our offences are ever with us, and we acknowledge our iniquities,' is the key idea in the paragraph (v. 12b), which balances the section 57:14-21, with its emphasis on contrition and humility as the pathway to restoration. Sadly, we cannot see these verses as expressing widespread or national repentance, which Isaiah must have longed for, but they do indicate that God's word does not return empty (55:11). A remnant is being gathered through the prophetic revelations and these verses provide a model response. This is how God's people should react in the waiting time, when they are made aware of how far short of his standards they fall, through the ministry of the Word.

'They' changes to 'We' and, as the verses unfold, they reveal the characteristics of the repentant remnant, which unite them. Crucially, the speakers assume personal responsibility for the lamentable state of affairs in Judah, insofar as each one is individually part of the general indictment. True repentance always acknowledges the situation as God sees it, without excuse or denial. Verses 9-11 reinforce this strongly. They begin and end with the absence of justice and, therefore, of rescue. Instead there is darkness, shadows, blindness, weakness, frustration and depression (vv. 10-11). The images of the blind groping their way, the growling bears and mournful doves all need to be used in our preaching to heighten an appreciation of their true state (and ours, without God's grace). Verses 12-13, however, move from the human symptoms to the divine reckoning with regard to sin. The four descriptions of verse 13 are all devastating confessions of what has really been happening under the façade of their hypocrisy.

Similarly, the four consequences in verse 14 indicate that the lesson has at last been accepted and learned. The social consequences are traced to the root sins. The disintegration of the community is the result of the rejection of their covenant Lord and his covenant requirements. As Motyer observes, 'moral action' only arises out of 'moral principle'.[5] Where the principle of allegiance to the covenant Lord is rejected, there can ultimately be no continuation of social righteousness. And while the primary application was to the theocracy which was historical Judah, the lessons for the contemporary church as the New Covenant community are equally stark and penetrating. It is precisely at this point that God intervenes.

Where God's people accommodate God's law to the demands and norms of a secular culture, its principles will first be ignored and then dismissed. In consequence, we lose not only our distinctiveness, but also our unity. The church becomes a diluted religious version of society, at war with herself and paralysed in her mission, because her centre of unity (God's self-revelation in his word) has been abandoned.

We have now completed the first third of this final section of Isaiah. Sinful rebellion and human inability to change have again played a leading role in Isaiah's revelatory preaching. Equally, there have been many threads of divine promise, motivational calls to repentance, and gracious promises of better days and overflowing blessings for those who turn back to Yahweh in repentance, faith and obedience, the only sure mark of covenant commitment. All the way through the book, these two ways to live and their two destinations dominate the theological teaching and its application.

---

5. Alec Motyer, *Tyndale Old Testament Commentary on Isaiah*, p368.

But we have seen not only the generosity of God's grace, but also its absolute necessity if ever the situation is to be lastingly changed. There is nothing that a human being can achieve to overcome the down-drag of his fallen sinful nature. God must intervene if ever there is to be hope. And he does! We have already witnessed the Immanuel promises of a king in David's line, whose kingdom of righteousness and peace will ultimately be shown to be both universal and eternal. We have been summoned to 'behold the servant', whose Word ministry comes to its climax in a substitutionary sacrifice for the sins of the world. Now, once again, God is about to intervene, but, in this final picture of the sovereign conqueror, in a final way.

7. Portrait of the sovereign conqueror (59:15b-21, preached with 63:1-6)

Our next section, 59:15b–63:6, forms the central core of this concluding unit of the book. Topped and tailed with a portrait of the conqueror, it focuses on the eschatological hope of the transformation God will bring, in the image of the new Zion, or Jerusalem, finally accomplished by the vindication of the Messiah whose completed sacrificial work makes it all possible.

We are taken behind the scenes, as it were, to see what Yahweh's own assessment of this desperate situation is. He is displeased (v15) and appalled (v16). The absence of righteousness is the cause of his displeasure, and the absence of anyone to do anything about it is what appals him (vv. 15b-16a). So, he will do what is needed himself. God commits himself to bring about a work of salvation founded on righteousness (v. 16b). Note 'his own arm' and 'his own righteousness'. We know that the servant has already provided righteousness for the 'many' (53:11), but what about those who have rejected him and his gracious work? What about the continuing antagonism and rebellion against the Lord and his purposes, which characterise the waiting years? There has to be a final climax or showdown, in which the servant's victory is applied to all his foes in a final judgement, with its inevitable destruction of all evil. That is what Yahweh is preparing for in verses 17-18.

The apparel which the Lord puts on (breastplate, helmet and garments) is indicative of his protection and his authority as he moves against his enemies. This is not so much a last battle as a final execution of sentence on all the hostile powers, which were already defeated through the servant's atoning sacrifice and resurrection. His work now is both rescue and vengeance. The final complete salvation of his people equally spells the final liquidation of his foes. Only that can open up the glory of Zion, in all its fullness (chapters 60–62). Protected by, and motivated with zeal for, his own righteousness, the Lord comes with wrath and retribution, bringing about a universal recognition of his glory and fear of his name (nature). It is the Spirit, or breath, of the Lord who provides the energy for this work of conquest to be accomplished (v19b).

Verse 20 provides the link to the focus on Zion in the next three chapters. The conqueror now comes as the liberator-redeemer to his city and his people, but only to those who are repentant, the righteous remnant we saw identified in 59:9ff. Not all the sons of Abraham are truly sons of Abraham, in terms of their faith in God's justifying grace. Not all the outwardly professing members of the New Covenant people of God are truly citizens of the heavenly

Jerusalem. Repentance is the mark of membership and is surely a life long experience.

But for those who do turn and trust, verse 21 is the most magnificent promise. Echoing his words to Abraham in Genesis 17:4, God now addresses his repentant people, first the remnant and then the whole community of the redeemed, to outline the covenant blessings which are theirs. They concern the Spirit and the Word. Endowed with the Spirit and proclaiming God's Word, his people fulfil their God-given role, partly here in time, and fully throughout eternity. In this, they reflect the characteristics of their Redeemer, since these great blessings of covenant membership come to them only through the One uniquely equipped with the Spirit and the Word of Yahweh. We shall meet him again in chapters 61 and 62, before the final portrait of his person and work will close the section in 63:1-6. For a stimulating comparison of these pictures with the servant songs and their commentaries, see Motyer,[6] whose conclusion cannot be bettered. 'Here is a third messianic figure, completing the portrayals of King (chapters 1–37) and Servant (38–55). The King reigns, the Servant saves, and the Anointed One consummates salvation and vengeance.'

Preaching and Teaching the Text
Title: **Portrait of the sovereign conqueror**
Text: **Isaiah 59:15b-21 and 63:1-6**
Structure: Bring together the two portraits of the one who will bring about the blessings of chapters 60-62, by his total conquest of all that is evil, i.e. opposed to the will of God.
1. 'Who is this …?'
    – a regal conqueror (63:1)

---

6. Alec Motyer, Tyndale Old Testament Commentary on Isaiah, p.371

– a righteous rescuer (63:1; 59:17)

– the arm of the Lord (59:16)

2. What does he come to do?

– to repay wrath to his enemies (59:18)

– to trample the nations (63:3, 6)

3. Why does he do it?

– no man can remedy the situation (59:17b-18; 63:5)

– to ensure the total destruction of evil (59:18; 63:4, 6)

– to guarantee the security of a world-wide and eternal redemption (59:20-21; 63:4)

Application: 'Fear him, you saints, and you will then have nothing else to fear.' We need to take seriously the coming judgement, live in light of it and warn others of its reality.

Leading a Bible Study

1.   59:1-2 What wrong thinking among God's people is exposed here? What is the corrective?

2.   59:3-8 Paul uses verses 7-8 in Romans 3:15-17. What is his point in that context and how can that help us to apply these verses to ourselves today?

3.   59:9-11 Note the shift from 'They' to 'We', which implies that recognition of sin is the beginning of penitence. What else in these verses prompts a penitent response?

4.   59:12-15a Notice that the confession and repentance are primarily in social, relational terms. Is this corporate response equally appropriate for us today? If so, what might it involve?

5.   59:15b-19 What does verse 15b tell us, in summary, about the human inability we have witnessed in the last three chapters? What is God going to do about it? What is the significance of the armour he puts on? Identify what he will do (v. 18) and what will be the result (v. 19).

6.   59:20-21 Why is the focus on the redeemer so essential
      at this point? What is God promising in verse 21 and
      why is it so significant for us?

8. God's glory revealed (60:1-22)

This chapter and the next two constitute the central
teaching section of Isaiah's final unit. As such, they bring
out very clearly the essential focus of God's purposes in the
great rescue mission of the Messiah, which is the heartbeat
of the whole prophecy. We are not surprised to find themes
like righteousness and glory resurfacing here, as they have
often been the burden of Isaiah's message earlier in his
book. Here is a glorious fulfilment-vision of all that God
purposes to do through the work of the servant-king.

Picking up on the vivid description of 59:9-10, with
its imagery of darkness and blindness characterising our
human condition apart from God's intervention, 60:1-3
announce the penetration and dispersal of the darkness
and gloom with the arrival of God's light, which is 'the glory
of the LORD'. The glory of God is the outshining of the
inner essence of God's person and character, so that he
himself is the light illuminating the world's 'thick darkness'.
Here, chapter 60 echoes chapter 40 in its emphasis on
the God who comes. As verses 19 and 20 make clear, at
the end of the chapter, 'the LORD will be your everlasting
light'. The striking factor is the connection between God
and his people. The prediction is not just that God will
reveal himself as the light of the world, though that was
what happened in the incarnation (John 1:4-5), but that
the glory rises upon God's people, appearing over them.
The light of God is seen on Israel and through Israel, which

explains the consequence of verse 3, as the nations and their rulers, seeing the light, are drawn towards its source.

The outcome is described in some detail in verses 4-9, where the vision is of God's scattered people returning to the land, which is now prosperous beyond belief (vv. 6-7), as the wealth of the nations is brought home to Zion. The two fold motivation in verses 6 and 9 is the proclamation of Yahweh's praise and the honour of his person, but the reason why it happens is equally God-centred. He has endowed his people with splendour (v. 9b). That is why the nations are attracted to his light and why their rulers come to serve the 'Mighty One of Jacob.'

Verses 10-14 continue to explore the outcome of God's glorious self-revelation, but this time in terms of a renewed city, where those who had previously oppressed God's people come now to bow themselves before them, because they at last acknowledge Israel's king. Hostility and exploitation are no longer options.

The chapter closes with a section (vv. 15-22) in which God continues to address his people with a wonderful series of promises, focusing on his own work to accomplish their fulfilment. In fact, the relationship between the Lord and his people dominates the passage. His restoring and enriching work declares his commitment to them as Saviour and Redeemer (v. 16), and it is his very name (the LORD), with all its echoes of covenant faithfulness and dependability, which is the signature guaranteeing the promises made. 'I am the LORD; in its time I will do this swiftly' (v. 22b). Perhaps verse 21 brings together the whole section most powerfully with its declaration, 'Then will all your people be righteous...for the display of my splendour'. God shows his glory when he makes his sinful people righteous, because they have no ability to do this themselves. The fact of their godly lives proves to be the greatest attraction to their God that the world has ever witnessed.

The question for the expositor is what time-scheme Isaiah had in mind when he preached this oracle, because these latter prophecies have never been literally fulfilled (see verses 18-20). Clearly they point to the final culmination of God's purposes in the eternal kingdom, when his people will live in perfect fellowship with him, unhindered by sin and failure, unrestricted by time and space. There are two ways in which our preaching might apply this truth to Christians today. Firstly, it gives perspective to our present experience, since we are now members of God's 'faithful city', the heavenly Jerusalem, and therefore 'our citizenship is in heaven' (Phil. 3.20). This acts as a motivator and establishes our priorities on this basis.

Secondly, this has spin-offs in God's use of his people to reflect his light in our present context of this world. Whenever Christ, the light of the world, shines into his people's lives, the effective response is both repentance and a deep dependence on his grace alone. The result is people who become more and more like the Lord Jesus and who are used by God to attract men and women from all the nations to the light of Christ, the sovereign and redeemer of his people. The characteristics of the eternal kingdom can be seen, at least in some measure, here in time in God's people, but that is only possible through his grace. If we are to fulfil these possibilities, we have to be entirely dependent on God and his grace, which is Isaiah's emphasis in this final section of his book. However, it is always true that a holy church will produce a hungry world.

Preaching and Teaching the Text

Title: **God's glory revealed**

Text: **Isaiah 60:1-22**

Structure: Set the chapter as the first of the three, which form the core of the unit, expressing the eternal realities which are the fruit of the sovereign conqueror's triumph over evil. Explain that the Old Testament land-blessings find their fulfilment in the spiritual blessings of the gospel (e.g. Eph. 1:3ff.) which belong now to God's worldwide people.

How will God's glory be revealed?

  1. In transforming his people (vv. 1-3)
  – he is the light of the world and he shines through his people (John 8:12, Matt. 5:14).
  2. In bringing his people home (vv. 4-9)
  – from every part of the world
  – endowed with wealth and honour
  3. In causing their enemies to submit (vv. 10-14)
  – service and security
  4. In accomplishing a perfect salvation (vv. 15-22)
  – 'your God will be your glory'

Application: Commit your life and resources to this great gospel.

Leading a Bible Study

1.   1:1-3 Who is being addressed in this section and what is being promised? What does the content of the prophecy teach us about the nature of the darkness and the light?

2.   60:4-9 Look at the predictions in their own detail. What would this mean for Isaiah's original hearers or for the exilic community? What would life in

Jerusalem be like when these prophecies are fulfilled? How do they relate to life in the New Covenant?

3. 60:10-12 The opposition of the nations has been a constant theme in Isaiah. How will God change the situation? What might this have to say in encouragement to the persecuted church today?

4. 60:13-14 What is central to the joy of the faithful city, Zion?

5. 60:15-22 Clearly these verses have never been fulfilled in the history of the earthly Jerusalem, nor can they be. They must therefore be an earthly picture of the heavenly city as Revelation 21:22-27 (especially) indicates. What can we learn of the glories of heaven from these verses? How should they encourage our faith and focus our service? Note the emphasis on salvation and righteousness as the keystones of the faithful new city.

9. Gospel realities (61:1-11)

In this chapter, we begin to see more clearly the transforming effects of God's light as a new speaker is introduced. He is anointed by the Lord to proclaim his message, for which the Spirit of God rests upon him. There has been a good deal of scholarly discussion about the identity of the speaker, but if we believe that Scripture interprets Scripture we need be in no doubt about it. Even within the immediate context of Isaiah, the natural assumption would be that the anointed conqueror or divine warrior figure we met in chapter 59 and who will reappear in 63:1-6 is a strong candidate to be declaring his ability and ministry. However, the New Testament leaves the matter beyond question when in the synagogue at Nazareth, our Lord Jesus Christ applied these verses to himself (Luke 4:16-21).

This is the light which enables his people to arise and shine (60:1), demonstrated and fulfilled in the earthly ministry of the Messiah. It is this Spirit-empowered preacher of the gospel who proclaims restoration and deliverance (v. 1), grace and retribution (v. 2). The benefits he brings are described in the wonderful contrasts of verse 3 and their outworking in the practical daily lives of God's people (vv. 4-7). Again the theme which underlies it all is 'the display of his [God's] splendour' (v. 3b), as in chapter 60. The Old Testament imagery of prosperity and security also echoes the previous chapters. This is all about rebuilding, restoration and renewal (v. 4), and the 'double portion' is an everlasting inheritance of joy (v. 7).

All of these land images of Isaiah translate for us into the 'spiritual blessing in the heavenly places', which belong to his New Testament people, in Christ alone (Eph. 1:3ff., ESV). But they are no less real for that. Indeed, they are the only blessings which are guaranteed eternal currency in the new heavens and the new earth, our only lasting good. This explains why we cannot be content with any interpretation focused only on this world's geography and history. Both the content and the context demand an eternal and spiritual application.

Verses 8-9 return to the theme of covenant righteousness, so often highlighted by Isaiah, and emphasise that the Lord is able and willing to provide what he requires of his people. Again, it is his splendour and glory which are revealed in his gracious blessing of his covenant people (v. 9b). So, the section concludes with a song of praise on the part of the recipients of God's favour (vv. 10-11), delighting in the covenantally faithful Yahweh, who is the source of their clothing, adornment and fruitfulness. John Oswalt draws attention to this repeated motif in Isaiah, that 'when the work of the Servant/Messiah is presented, the response is a paean of praise', citing as examples 12:1-6; 42:10-13; 49:13-21 and 54:1-17.[7] These could well provide the preacher with a stimulating and valuable sub-series in Isaiah, looking at how the Lord's work reveals the Lord's glory and stirring our own response of praise.

From the standpoint of contemporary relevance to the twenty-first-century people of God, it will be helpful to underline the causal connections within the text, which provide important theological pointers to our own situation. The passage emphasises that the great gospel blessings are the gift of a gracious God, reminding us that it is only by divine intervention that we can ever be rescued and changed. But alongside that, there is also the insistent theme that such grace needs to be responded to in repentance and faith, which indicate a total and unreserved dependence upon that grace and its compassionate giver.

Our problem may well be that 'we would like to be "better" Christians, but are unwilling to become bondslaves'[8]. Perhaps our reluctance to depend fully on God and on his grace alone keeps us from reflecting God's glory to a sceptical culture. It may be that we need to recognise that the greatest single contribution any of us can make to the evangelisation of our generation is our personal holiness, because godly living, in the waiting time, is the greatest possible authentication of the gospel's truth.

---

7. John N. Oswalt, *Isaiah: The NIV Application Commentary*, p651.
8. *IBID*. p653.

Preaching and Teaching the Text

Title: **Gospel realities – now and forever**

Text: **Isaiah 61:1-11**

Structure: The glorious vision of chapter 60 needs to be lived out in time so that as God's people reflect his glory in lives that are holy, the nations will be drawn to him. Chapter 61 explains how.

1. The Messiah and his mission (vv. 1-3), see Luke 4:16-21.
    – anointed by the Spirit (v. 1)
    – to preach the liberating gospel of grace (vv. 1-2)
    – to declare God's righteousness (v. 2)
    – to transform God's people (v. 3)
2. His people and their experience (vv. 4-11)
    – restoration and security (vv. 4-5)
    – service and fulfilment (vv. 6-7)
    – God's faithfulness to his covenant (vv. 8-9)
    – righteousness and praise (vv. 10-11)

Application: Thank God for Christ's finished work and celebrate his character by living for his glory.

Leading a Bible Study

1.   61:1-3 Like the servant (42:1), the speaker is not introduced and not named. Rather he is defined by his task and his enabling. Look at his work in detail and identify its elements of comfort (cf. 40:1), vengeance and righteousness. Luke 4:16-21 establishes beyond all question that this is a portrait of Christ. What was fulfilled in Nazareth, what at Calvary and what still awaits fulfilment?

2.   61:4-7 Here are more great promises of what the conqueror's work will achieve for God's people.

Identify what the Lord says he will do for his own. In what senses have we entered into this already?

3. 61:8-9 How does the emphasis on the character of the Lord undergird confidence in the fulfilment of his promises?

4. 61:10–62:5 Under the extended marriage imagery (61:10; 62:3-5), God paints a picture of the intimate relationship of love and care which he will exercise towards his people. What does God do for them/us?

5. How are we to respond? Note that the new name of 62:2 indicates the new status into which God brings his people. Note too the repeated emphasis on salvation and righteousness (62:1-2).

10. Envy of the world (62:1-12)

The general theme of God's final fulfilment of his covenant promises continues in this chapter, but with the immediate question as to the identity of the speaker, in verse 1, who 'will not keep silent'. The 'I' of 61:10 (the Lord's redeemed people) now seems to change to God himself, since the people of God are addressed as 'you' in verses 2-9. Although some suggest 'I' must be Isaiah, perhaps because the verse seems to speak about constant prayer and/or preaching, by verse 6 it is clear that Yahweh is the speaker. His affectionate compassion for Zion and Jerusalem (v. 1) is God's constant concern throughout the book, as is its outcome in terms of righteousness and salvation, which always run in parallel.

If this is so, then verses 2-9 comprise God's personal message to Israel concerning the new state of affairs he will bring about, as his people are displayed to the watching world as 'a crown of splendour', 'a royal diadem' (v. 3). The new name(s) of verse 2 are 'Hephzibah' and 'Beulah' (v. 4), indicating a totally new state of affairs, since downtrodden Israel now becomes the envy of the world. All this reflects God's delight in his people, as a bridegroom in his bride (v. 5). Verses 6-9, however, focus on the responsibility the people must play if the waiting time is to culminate in glorious completion. The watchmen (or overseers) are the committed guardians of the city, whose most important role is to be entirely dependent on God for the city's blessing and to be unceasing in their prayers to him to act (vv. 6-7) in the faithful fulfilment of his promises (vv. 8-9) to preserve the city in security and prosperity.

The concluding verses (vv10-12) may seem to break in rather unexpectedly, but they form a very significant conclusion to the whole section which is chapters 60–62. The preceding verses have reminded us again of how greatly God values his people and what a joy and delight they give him. If the scenario of these chapters reveals God's eternal purposes, then it is not so surprising that Isaiah, in his own context, preparing God's people both for the exile and for the return, summons his people (in all ages) to leave their Babylon and to head home on the highway to Zion. The language of verse 10 seems to echo 48:20-21 and 52:11-12 and repeats their urgency. The imagery of the highway without barriers also reflects the restoration pictured in 40:3-4, as the exile ends.

The physical return to Jerusalem, as a result of the decree of Cyrus, was, however, only a pale foreshadowing of the end of the spiritual exile, in the arrival of God's Kingdom, when the Saviour came into Galilee, preaching the good news of salvation (see Mark 1:14-15; Matt. 3:1-3). Moreover his 'reward' and 'recompense' (v. 11) are those redeemed through his great rescue mission, now a people of righteousness and holiness, because of the servant's work. In the light of these eternal realities, the theological appeal of this whole section is to put our Babylons (all the ways and attitudes of a world in rebellion against its creator) behind us. To move from the city of destruction (ch. 47) to the 'City No Longer Deserted' (v. 12) by the lifelong journey along the highway to Zion, is God's proclamation 'to the ends of the earth' (v. 11a) in the gospel of his grace.

11. Redemption through wrath (63:1-6)

The central revelation of God's eternal purpose, the New Covenant or heavenly city in chapters 60–62, is now immediately enclosed by a second portrait of the conquering hero, to whom we were first introduced in 59:15b-21. Here, the emphasis is upon the completion of his work, by which the nations are judged and all rebellion destroyed, so that nothing can challenge or hinder the implementation of his righteous, eternal reign. This is the last great portrait in Isaiah of the Lord who is the shepherd-king and the suffering servant, now exalted as the divine conqueror, triumphing over all his enemies.

As with the other portraits of Christ in Isaiah, this section begins with an air of mystery ('Who is this coming from Edom?' v. 1). The unknown figure comes from Edom, the traditional archetypal opponents of God's people and God's purposes, and from Bozrah, its major city. His splendid garments and vigorous strength indicate a figure of authority and power (v. 1). His answer to the question of identity immediately links righteousness and salvation together and points to his divine person. But why are his regal garments 'stained crimson'? He must have been 'treading the winepress' in Bozrah, which means 'vintage', although he seems not to be at all exhausted by such strenuous activity. How is it all to be explained?

Verses 3-6 provide the awesome answer from the warrior's own lips. The winepress he has trodden 'alone' is that of his own wrath, against all evil, defined as rebellion against his sovereign rule. His garments are stained not with the juice of Bozrah's grapes, but with the blood of the nations. This explains why he is alone in this strange work of judgement. As verse 4 explains, this is 'the day of vengeance,' when the Lord's final righteous judgement on his enemies will bring the fullness of redemption to his people.

Note the contrast involved between the act of judgement (the day of vengeance) and the long-term, eternal outcome (the year of redemption). This all-powerful conqueror is, in fact, the righteous rescuer of his people. Always, in Scripture, judgement and salvation are the two sides of the one coin, which is divine intervention. When God comes, he comes to judge and to rescue from his judgement, for in the execution of his righteous wrath there is also delivering grace. Think of Noah and the ark, the crossing of the Red Sea and, supremely, the cross of Christ.

Only God could do this work (v. 5) because there is only one who is perfectly righteous, the divine Son. And it is a necessary work, because only with the total destruction of all that is evil could the eternal security of the redeemed people of God, in the everlasting kingdom of righteousness, be guaranteed. This is what we are waiting for in the waiting time. It will come and its effects will be total. The wrath of God confirms and secures for all eternity the salvation of his repentant, believing people. Chapters 60–62 could not happen without 63:1-6.

Leading a Bible Study

1. 62:6-7 Why have the watchmen been posted by the anointed one? What does this say about the ministry of prayer as God's people await the last day?

2. 62:8-9 How do the typical 'land blessings' of verses 8-9 encourage faith? What do they say about the God who promises them?

3. 62:10-12 The conqueror arrives at his city. Verse 10 details the preparations (rebuilding) and verse 12 the consequences of his kingly rule. The 'reward' and 'recompense' of verse 11 probably refer to the remnant redeemed community who come with him to settle the faithful city. They are the people referred to in verse 12. Apply these verses to Christ's first and second comings.

4. 63:1-6 The questions of verse 1 may be on the lips of the 'watchmen' (62:6). They are answered by a testimony from the conqueror, matching 59:15b ff. Compare the two passages and build up a pen-picture of the conqueror and his work.

5. What does the conqueror teach us about how the work of righteousness, salvation and vengeance has been carried out? Why is this work necessary if the Zion of chapters 60 and 62 is ever to come into existence? What is the timescale?

12. The prayer of faith (63:7–64:12)

We now come to the closing sections of prophecy, which can perhaps best be divided into three constituent parts. From 63:7 to 64:12 is, in effect, one extended prayer in which Isaiah the prophet, as the spiritual leader of God's people, assumes the role of intercessor, on their behalf. There is a great deal here, not only to instruct us as to how we should pray, but also to open our eyes to the theological realities which undergird true intercession.

This is followed by the Lord's response in 65:1-25, which, beginning with rebuke, moves into challenge and promise as the vision of 'new heavens and a new earth' opens up before us. Finally, 66:1-24 sets before us the criteria by which God will include in or exclude from membership of the New Covenant. It will no longer be on the basis of ethnicity, or even outward conformity to a form of religion, but through repentance and obedient faith. That is the only way the faithless city of chapter 1 can ever become 'the Faithful City' and the choice is as starkly drawn and uncompromisingly presented in the last chapter as it was in the first.

The prayer begins indirectly, with Isaiah talking about God and his faithful covenant love and mercy; but in view of the direct petition in verse 15, we are surely meant to set verses 7-14 in the context of his approach to God. It is part of his reminding God of all that he did in the past for his people. He is a God of action, revealing his kindness and compassion, demonstrated in his saving grace (vv. 7-8).

Verses 9-10 recall the time of the Exodus, with its contrast between God's faithful provision and Israel's rebellion. The chilling reality of God fighting against his people (v. 10b) as in the days of the judges, for example, was designed to bring them to a realisation of what they had lost and to long for something better – a return to 'the days of old' (vv. 11-14). The parallel to the situation of Israel in Isaiah's day is clear and plain, as the book has made obvious from its very beginning.

Chapter 63:15-19

On the basis of all this past revelation of God's faithful character, the first petition is then presented at verse 15. 'Look down from heaven and see...' There is no diminution of God's 'holy and glorious' character, but a plea for his 'zeal and ... might' to be revealed, in transforming grace, on several grounds (v. 15). These include his proven character of 'tenderness and compassion' (v. 15b) and his relationship with his people as Father and Redeemer (v. 16) which makes them his, by right (v. 19a).

Verse 17 does not attribute responsibility for Israel's state to God, which would be unbelieving arrogance. Rather, it acknowledges that wandering, hardening hearts are often confirmed in that perilous condition by God's quiet withdrawal of his presence, and therefore of his enabling grace. The plea is for him to return, to rule actively over what is rightly his. To continue in their present state, which Isaiah has so graphically exposed and rebuked over and over again in the prophecy, would be a practical denial of God's covenant election of his people. They may be faithless, but surely, Yahweh cannot be content to leave things in such a parlous state! This is why the emotional expression of the prayer deepens and intensifies with the next section.

Chapter 64:1-12

The opening exclamation is redolent with the deep emotion which has been building up in the preceding section, although the chapter division here can easily obscure this. The sigh of longing in the anguished plea of verse 1 is primarily for God to come down, returning to his people, to restore the covenant relationship. There is a backward look (v. 3), probably to Sinai (Exod. 19:16-20), which recognises the unique character and ability of the only living God to intervene, as he wills, in the affairs of his world. So why is it not happening now?

Verses 4-7 face up to the question with disarming candour. God looks for faithful dependence ('wait for him' v. 4b), godly behaviour from a joyful heart and the pursuit of holiness of character (v. 5a). This is the spiritual sincerity which casts itself on God, in dependent prayer, and which he answers. But verses 5b-7 illustrate just how far the present position of Israel is from this happy state of affairs. Isaiah wants his readers to be in no doubt as to why God hides his face, and the equivalent applications to members of the New Covenant community are strikingly clear.

What, then, is to be done? The response of verses 8-12 is that those who are aware of these spiritual realities must take the lead in turning to God to ask for mercy. Once again, the relationship which God has initiated and established, is the ground of Isaiah's prayer (vv. 8-9). The desolate cities and temple, which Isaiah foresees, must surely touch Yahweh's heart and rouse him to action, as they touch the prophet's heart and move him to prayer (vv. 10-12). For the dating of this passage, as a prophetic vision of Isaiah and not post-exilic factual reporting, see Motyer's helpful discussion.[9]

Clearly there is much here for a believing 'remnant' to seize in our current context of widespread denials of God's character and rejection of his Word in the contemporary, visible church. The point at which things begin to change is when we start to seek God for himself, to renew our own repentance on a daily basis and to demonstrate our total dependence on God's mercy and grace, in the place of our habitual self-reliance.

---

9. Alec Motyer, *Tyndale Old Testament Commentary on Isaiah*, p251.

Preaching and Teaching the Text

Title: **The prayer of faith**

Text: **Isaiah 63:7–64:12**

Structure: See the prayer as the true faithful response of God's people in the waiting time, when the mixed spiritual nature of the visible covenant community seems to preclude God's blessings. There are clear parallels to our own contemporary situation.

1. Talking to God about God (63:7-14)
    – God's faithfulness towards Israel (vv. 7-9)
    – their faithlessness towards him (v. 10)
    – longing for something better (vv. 11-14)
2. Crying to God to intervene (63:15–64:3)
    – because you are our Father (vv. 15-17a)
    – because we are your servants (vv. 17b-19)
    – because you rule the world (64:1-3)
3. Recognising before God the roots of the problem (64:4-7)
    – God's righteous demands (vv. 4-5a)
    – Israel's sinful disobedience (vv. 5b-6)
    – God's inevitable distance (v. 7)
4. Turning back to God in total dependence (64:8-12)
    – submission to his lordship (v. 8)
    – suing for his mercy (v. 9)
    – seeking his compassion (vv. 10-12)

Depending on the next sermon, it would be good to highlight 65:1 as God's response to chapter 64.

Application: Take these lessons and follow their pattern in our individual prayers and as congregations of God's people.

Leading a Bible Study

1.   63:7 How were God's actions in the early history of Israel conditioned (a) by his unchanging character

and (b) by their behaviour? What implications can
we draw from this about when we 'rebel and grieve his
Holy Spirit?'

2.   63:11-14 What is the spiritual purpose of recalling the
'glory days' of the Exodus? What do these verses have
to say about why they are days to be remembered?

3.   63:15-19 What arguments does the prophet use in his
approach to God to implore him to be gracious to his
people again? What patterns for our own praying can
we derive from this section?

4.   64:1-4 What is the prophet asking God to do? Why?
What does it mean to 'wait for him' (v4b)? How can
these verses motivate us to ask 'large petitions' of God?

5.   64:5-7 Analyse the ingredients of these verses which
reveal a proper preparation in the person who prays.
How does this relate to 'waiting' for God?

64:8-12 These verses express the resolution of the
tension as the one who prays learns to relate his
desires to the reality of God and his purposes. What
right attitudes to God are described here? Is this how
we think about him, while we wait?

13. Two ways to live (65:1-25)

This response of Yahweh, which follows the prayer, might
at first seem strangely ironic. It would be easy to assume
that verse 1 refers to Israel, in that God's self-revelation
was always available to them and his promises were always
accessible to faith. However, in interpreting the Bible it is
an important principle that the later revelation of the New
Testament should govern our understanding of the Old
and in this case we have an apostolic key to unlock the
prophet's message. In Romans 10:20-21, Paul quotes both

verse 1 and verse 2 of Isaiah 65. But he refers verse 1 to the Gentiles and verse 2 to Israel.

Here is evidence, then, of the great shift brought about by the servant's work and the expectation, throughout the unit, of the worldwide expansion of the gospel into the Gentile nations. The thrust seems to be that God is never in the business of hiding himself. He even reveals himself 'to those who did not ask for me'. How else would any sinner ever be saved? There is no deficiency of revelation or accessibility with God. It was Adam who was hiding from God (Gen. 3:8-10), not the other way round.

Verses 2-7 apply to 'an obstinate people', first unbelieving Israel in Isaiah's day, but by extension all who provoke God to his face through their disobedience, as they reveal the ways in which the relationship which he offers is spurned and avoided. To use imagery from Genesis 3, these are the trees of the garden behind which human beings habitually try to hide. This obstinate provocation is exemplified in evil behaviour 'ways not good' (v. 2) but rooted in the rejection of God's revelation in the Torah and later in all the Scriptures.

'Pursuing their own imaginations' is always the nub of the problem of human rebellion. We will not let God be God in our lives. We would much rather create our own fictional alternatives. That is why so many people still cling to the attitude, 'I like to think God is...', or more defiantly, 'I cannot believe in a God who...', as though personal capability was the measure of anything eternally significant! The list from verses 3-7 is literally damning – unauthorised, do-it-yourself worship (v. 3), pagan and occult practices (v. 4), religious elitism (v. 5), outrageous idolatry (v. 7). To all of this God's reaction is unequivocal – judgement must come (v. 6). The answer to 64:12 is shown therefore to be that God 'holding himself back' is an act of incredible mercy, in the light of the inevitable tidal wave of judgement which must eventually be released (v. 7b). That mercy now becomes the dominant theme of the next section.

Chapter 65:8-16

In a direct word from the Lord (vv. 8, 13), the remnant of faithful believers is encouraged to go on trusting and obeying, serving and praying by this great declaration of assurance. Destruction will not be total, since God's purposes will still prevail and his covenant promises will most certainly be fulfilled. There will be descendants and an inheritance for them (v. 9). The land will be restored to its fertility and security (v. 10). The exile will not be the end; the covenant will endure.

However, in Isaiah's insistent way, verses 11-12 show us the other side of the coin, as the equally inevitable consequences of pagan idolatry are once again spelt out in terms of terrifying destruction. This division between light and darkness, faith and unbelief, service and rebellion runs through the remaining verses, as it has dominated the contents of the book. There are only two cities – one made faithful, solely by grace, and the other faithless and doomed to destruction. There really are only two ways to live.

The contrast is developed in verses 13-16, which are addressed to the unbelieving majority, those who scoffed at Isaiah's simplistic and unsophisticated teaching (28:9-10). These are the diametrically opposite outcomes of the choices made in life. They are real choices and they have eternal effects.

Chapter 65:17-25

This great, climactic revelation of God's eternal purposes of grace is one of the mountain peaks of Isaiah's prophecy, as indeed of the whole Old Testament. The emphasis is on the newness of what God will create.'God will"create"something that, while being in continuity with what had been, will yet be a completely new expression of that reality'.[10] Verses 17-18a focus on the new creation while verses 18b-22a unpack the realities of the city, the New Covenant and its people. Here is the beginning of the answer to the dilemma posed back in chapter 1. The faithless old Jerusalem can only be changed by a new, creative act of God which will produce a new environment and community, where death and destruction have no more place. It has been Isaiah's agenda to explain how that can happen.

The concluding verses, 22b-25, explain the nature of these eternal blessings in terms of continuing vitality and fruitfulness (v. 22b), guaranteed security (v. 23), close relationship with Yahweh as he recognises and meets their needs (v. 24), and the peace and harmony of the entire new creation (v. 25). All the old enmities disappear in a world that is like a new Eden, because everything in it is new – except for the sudden appearance of the serpent in verse 25.'The only point in the whole of the new creation where there is no change ... is in the curse pronounced on sin, which still stands (cf. Gen. 3:14)'.[11]

The difference is that no harm or destruction is possible any longer, since God now dwells with his people on his holy mountain, the new creation. Revelation 21 and 22 expands our understanding of these realities so much more,

---

10. John N. Oswalt, *Isaiah: The NIV Application Commentary*, p687.
11. Alec Motyer, *Tyndale Old Testament Commentary on Isaiah*, p531.

but their inclusion here is designed to assure faith and to inspire righteous living. Our preaching of this glorious section should major on encouraging our hearers to believe these realities and to make them the critical factor in our use of time, money, talents and energy in this world.

Preaching and Teaching the Text
Title: **Two ways to live**
Text: **Isaiah 65:1-25**
Structure: Verses 1-16 constitute God's response to Isaiah's prayer on behalf of the nation, while verses 17-25 paint the picture of the eventual solution: the new creation which God will bring about. The perspective is changed when the present is understood in the light of the future.

1. Unexpected response (v. 1)
    – God does not hide himself (see also v. 2a)
    – He will bring in the Gentiles
2. Continuing problems (vv. 2-7)
    – Israel's provocation by unauthorised worship (v. 3)
    – occult practices (v. 4a)
    – flagrant disobedience (v. 4b)
    – religious pride (v. 5)
    – God's righteous judgement (vv. 6-7)
3. Divergent possibilities (vv. 8-16)
    – the 'remnant' will be preserved (vv. 8-10)
    – the rebels will be destroyed (vv. 11-12)
    – the contrast explained (vv. 13-16)
    – 'my servants … but you'
4. Amazing Prospects (vv. 17-25)
    – new creation (v17-18a) cf. Rev 21:1-3
    – new city (vv. 18b-25), 'my holy mountain'
    – joy in security, vitality, intimacy with God

– old curse (v. 25) – evil (serpent) excluded

Application: There are only two destinations, reached by two divergent lifestyles, the result of choices we make every day. So, which way shall we live?

Leading a Bible Study

1. 65:1-5 These verses explain why the sense of God's distance and alienation expressed in chapter 64 is in fact a reality. The fault is not on God's part. What has he been doing all the time? What does the non-response of his people indicate (vv. 1-2)?

2. Verses 3-5 elaborate the problems in some detail. What do they reveal about obstinate Israel's attitude towards the sacrifices God requires (v. 3b), their sources of revelation (v. 4a), their attitude to the law (v. 4b), their false spirituality (v. 5)? What parallels can we see in the external performance of religion today?

3. 65:6-7 How will God react to such 'smoke in my nostrils'?

4. 65:8-12 In typical Isaiah style, we now have the remedy of grace to the judgement of verses 6-7. What is God promising to do in verse 8? How does this relate to the righteous remnant (vv. 9-10)? Explore the contrast between 'my people who seek me' and 'you who forsake the LORD' (v. 11a). What are their differences in belief, behaviour and ultimate destiny?

5. 65:13-16 The contrast continues, with the emphasis on the future (vv. 15-16) which should control right living in the present. What motivation to more consistent godliness in our own lives do these verses provide?

6.   65:21-25 In verses 21-23, the blessings of heaven are
     again expressed in Old Testament land categories,
     compared with the fruitlessness and frustration of
     so much of Old Testament Israel's rebellion. What
     elements of the blessings of heaven are these verses
     pointing towards?

7.   What does verse 24 add about the joys of heaven?
     How does verse 25 relate to the curses of Genesis 3?
     What is transformed and what is not? Why?

14. The final choice (66:1-24)

The continuity of thought and parallelism of themes between
these two concluding chapters, 65 and 66, is established
not only by the content, but also by the quotation of 65:12
again at 66:4. The prayer of chapter 64 asked why the Lord
seemed not to answer his people's cries. Here, in chapters
65 and 66, the answer is given: far from God not answering,
he has been calling out to his people constantly, only to
encounter their deafness and disinterestedness, since they
have chosen the path of disaster. 'They did evil in my sight
and chose what displeases me' (66:4b).

By means of contrast, verses 1-4 expose for one final
time the roots of the chronic spiritual situation, which
Isaiah was called to address. The reality is that God is the
glorious sovereign and creator of the universe, so how could
he possibly be confined to a man-made temple (v. 1)? He is
not a God who can be contained, much less manipulated.
But as chapter 1 revealed, that is precisely what Israel was
trying to do with her naïve confidence in empty formalism
and religious ritual. All of this is useless; worse than that,
they actually incur God's wrath (vv. 3-4a). God looks not
for empty forms which act as religious substitutes for a real

encounter with him (v. 4b), but for humility and contrition springing from a deep reverence for his word and therefore for his person (v. 2b).

It is those who 'tremble at his word,' the remnant gathered by Isaiah's ministry, whom God calls his servants in 65:13ff., who are now addressed in verses 5-6. He assures them that though they suffer now at the hands of their enemies, they will be vindicated and God's judgement will fall because their enemies are his enemies.

Chapter 66:7-14

The assurance of verses 5-6 is now expanded with a further vision of hope: Zion has many children without the pain of labour (vv. 7-9). This is God's miraculous activity as he multiplies his people. The emphasis is not on the faithfulness, or worthiness, of the remnant to see such growth and expansion, but entirely upon God's gift of grace, the cause of enormous rejoicing (vv. 10-11). Just as a baby is secure in the loving care and provision of its mother, so God's people have only to receive his 'overflowing abundance' (v. 11) seen in peace, sufficiency, tender care and strengthening ('comfort'), as described in verses 12-13. All this is a stimulus to joy, but for one last time Isaiah must also show us the tragic alternative.

Chapter 66:15-24

'See, the LORD is coming with fire' (v. 15a). Everything depends on our relationship to this sovereign creator, king and judge. Are we his 'servants' or his 'foes' (v. 14b)? For the latter, the future can only ultimately hold fury, fire and sword, judgement and destruction (vv. 15-16). This is the inevitable outcome of their rejection of the LORD for worthless idols, however sophisticated their syncretistic 'worship' may have seemed to them (v. 17).

The tragedy is only deepened by the glorious alternative they have chosen to ignore or reject. Verse 18 provides great textual difficulties, discussed in the commentaries, but the gathering of the Gentile nations into God's eternal kingdom of glory is undoubtedly the big idea. It is the continuing agenda between the Lord's first and second comings. Might there be an echo of verse 18 in Acts 28:28, at the end of Luke's book, where after quoting Isaiah 6:9-10 in the face of Jewish unbelief in Rome, Paul affirms, 'Therefore I want you to know that God's salvation has been sent to the Gentiles, and they will listen!'?

The 'sign' of verse 19 must surely refer to the cross, since the context here is the far-distant future (to Isaiah) of the gospel age, which is our place in the timeline of God's purposes. This is what gathers new believers from around the Mediterranean world (v. 19a) and as we now know from 'every nation, tribe, people and language' (Rev. 7:9) across the whole wide world to the worship of Yahweh (v. 19b). This is what creates a new brotherhood of believing people (v. 20). This is the fruit of the servant's sacrificial death as he died 'for the scattered children of God, to bring them together and make them one' (John 11:52). That unity consists in the eternal endurance of all those who 'come and bow down before me,' the Lord says (v.23).

But the final word (v. 24) is reserved for the dreadful alternative destiny of those who rebelled against God and who refused to tremble at his word. It is Isaiah's final appeal: escape from such an end while there is still opportunity, because its effects are eternal. There can be no room for compromise or complacency and our preaching of Isaiah must reflect that, in both our compassion and our clarity.

In the words of Immanuel, who is the servant-king and the anointed conqueror, 'Enter through the narrow gate. For wide is the gate and broad is the road that leads to destruction, and many enter through it. But small is the gate and narrow the road that leads to life, and only a few find it' (Matt. 7:13-14). So, preach Isaiah!

Leading a Bible Study

1. 66:1-2 What does a right relationship with God look like, in view of the revelation of the heavenly, eternal kingdom of chapter 65?

2. 66:3-6 Why is God as angry with the externally orthodox as with those who follow pagan gods? (vv. 3-4). What do verses 5-6 show about the attitude of those cynics to those who 'tremble at his word' (the remnant)? What is God's response?

3. 66:7-13 What is the essence of these amazing promises? How do they help us to answer the key Isaiah question, 'How is the faithless city to become the faithful city' (1:21-26)?

4. 66:14-17 This paragraph matches verses 5-6, in showing us the other side of God's renewing work. What do verses 14-16 add to our understanding of God's judgement? How does verse 17 underline why it is both necessary and irresistible?

5. 66:18-21 How do these verses ultimately fulfil the great covenant promise to Abraham (Gen. 12:1-3)? Again the language and thought-forms are predominantly Old Testament, but what do they reveal about the

ultimate purposes of God's grace in the gospel? Note the centrality of God's glory.

6.   66:22-24 Why is the ending so characteristic of Isaiah's whole book? What are its continuing implications for life today and for eternity?

Appendix: One Isaiah, or More?

The far distant nature of the prophecies in chapters 40-66 has led to a great deal of discussion about their purpose and significance, as well as a questioning of their authenticity. Many of these arguments are primarily academic and are built on presuppositions about the nature of Scripture which evangelical scholars and preachers certainly do not share. These are not issues we shall want to focus on in our expository preaching, since they do not impinge on the lives of most of our hearers.

However, many preachers have lost confidence in the text because they were unsettled by these critical approaches during their theological training and have never been able to settle them satisfactorily since. There is always a nagging uncertainty at the back of their minds that prevents them from preaching what would seem to be the plain meaning of Scripture with conviction and authority. So, it may be worthwhile here to attempt an outline of how to deal with this issue, while recognising that there is a great deal more available in the introductions to commentaries, Bible dictionaries and specialist books such as *The Unity of Isaiah* by Oswald T. Allis.[1]

Second or Deutero-Isaiah was a hypothesis of nineteenth-century scholarship to deal with the problems of chapters 40–66. Basically, the issue is how Isaiah could have prophesied before the exile in such historical detail, even to the mention of the name of Cyrus as the conqueror of Babylon, a century or more before the events. The presupposition, often unspoken and unrecognised, is that God could not have given Isaiah such knowledge to enable such a detailed predictive prophecy. Either God could not know, since he does not actively govern the world according to the purposes of his will, or God could not inspire a prophet with such detail, since he would not transcend natural human limitations.

In effect, such views are anti-supernaturalist and deny the biblical doctrine of inspiration. The position is that the prophets were simply religious geniuses who saw a little bit further than their contemporaries did – 'seers' or sages, who projected into the future. But that they 'spoke from God as they were carried along by the Holy Spirit' (2 Pet. 1:21) is precisely what the presupposition denies. This would mean that there must be a second Isaiah, writing after the exile with precise knowledge of what had happened, or perhaps a school of Isaianic 'disciples', whose work provides a multiple authorship, which is the more favoured contemporary view.

This position is supported by two critical criteria, which are usually claimed to be self-evident. The first is that a prophetic writer always builds his predictions on the

---

1. Oswald T. Allis, *The Unity of Isaiah*, (Phillipsburg, USA: Presbyterian and Reformed Publishing Company, 1972)

facts of the time in which he himself lives. The second is that his purpose is to bring ethical instruction to his own contemporaries in that same historical time, so that their lives and behaviour are amended in their present, in the light of what he foresees of the future. Of course, there is truth in both of these observations. The prophet addresses his own generation where they are in order that their attitudes and actions may be changed, but to make this norm the ground of denial that God can provide extraordinary and detailed information about a long-distant future (as with Messianic prophecies, for example) is to attempt to shut God up in a box, for reasons of our own theological convenience. Parallels with the Pharisees' rejection of Christ's teaching come readily to mind.

So what are the main arguments for the unity of Isaiah?

(i) The book was received into the canon as a whole. Each of the 'latter' Prophets begins with a heading such as we find in Isaiah 1:1, which states the name of the prophet, often the origin (father's name, home town) and, in all but three of the books, the time or period of the prophecy. None are anonymous. So, for an unknown, unnamed prophet, or school of prophets, to begin at chapter 40 would seem to be quite irregular and distinctly odd.

(ii) There is no manuscript evidence to support the thesis that the book was not written as a single unit. On the contrary, in the text of Isaiah discovered among the Dead Sea scrolls in 1947, chapter 40 begins on the last line of the last column of the scroll containing chapter 39. Dated c.150 BC this evidence is almost as old as that of the Septuagint (LXX) translated c.200 BC which also treats the book as one. There is no objective textual or literary evidence for separating the two sections.

(iii) The unity is attested by other texts in both the Apocrypha and the New Testament. The author of Ecclesiasticus 48:24ff. (dated c.180 BC) refers to 40:1 and 61:2, affirming Isaianic authorship in these terms: 'Isaiah saw what should come to pass at the last and he comforted those who mourned in Zion.' The New Testament quotes Isaiah by name nearly twenty times – more than all the other writing prophets put together, and from both 'halves' of the book. Matthew's Gospel, for example, quotes Isaiah – in Matthew 4:14-16; 13:14-15 and 15:7-9, referring to Isaiah 9:1-2; 6:9-10 and 29:13, respectively – all from the first 'half' of the book (1-39). But the same attribution is also given to references from the second 'half' (40-66), in Matthew 3:3; 8:17 and 12:17-21, quoting from Isaiah 40:3, 53:4 and 42:1-4, respectively. In the fourth Gospel, John cites Isaiah 53:1 and 6:10 in consecutive verses, both as 'Isaiah', in John 12:38-40. Luke quotes Isaiah 61:1 as 'the scroll of the prophet Isaiah' in Luke 4:17. Paul has three references from the first 'half' of the book in Romans 9:27-28; 9:29 and 15:12, quoting Isaiah 10:22-23; 1:9 and 11:10, respectively. But he also affirms that his quotations of Isaiah 53:1 and 65:1 in Romans 10:16 and 10:20 respectively are equally the words of the prophet Isaiah. These references are well worth looking up both to illustrate how New Testament writers interpret and use Isaiah and also to realise how central this book is for New Covenant theology.

(iv) There is a perfectly good link in the text between chapters 39 and 40. Isaiah's contemporary situation is perfectly clear. In 39:1 Merodach-Baladan, heir apparent to the Babylonian kingdom, attempts to enlist Hezekiah's support against their common enemy, Assyria. Hezekiah, in his pride, seems to have been only too pleased to show the Babylonian envoys the extent of his treasure-store, but receives the divine rebuke, through Isaiah, that all this will be carried off to Babylon one day, along with his own royal descendants (39:5-7). That is the ominous future judgement which the people of Judah are facing. No wonder then that the focus turns in 40:1 to God's message of 'comfort' or new life, where the scope of what Yahweh will achieve in and through the exile and beyond it is shown to be so much greater than the immediate. The appearance and naming of Cyrus as the Lord's shepherd and servant is but a pale reflection of the great shepherd who is the suffering servant and whose own work of rescue, redemption and restoration will be both universal and eternal in its effects.

FURTHER READING

Over the last few years, a number of excellent commentaries on Isaiah have appeared, and every preacher will benefit from working through one of them thoroughly.

If you can only buy two commentaries on Isaiah, then Alex Motyer's Tyndale, 'Isaiah: An Introduction and Commentary' (Leicester: IVP 1999) provides excellent, accessible, commentary on the text, synthesising many of the conclusions from his larger commentary (see below). John Oswalt's NIV Application Commentary, 'Isaiah' (Grand Rapids: Zondervan 2003) is a mine of useful ideas for relating the text to a modern congregation.

Both Oswalt and Motyer have also written longer commentaries, which are very thorough. Motyer's magisterial 'The Prophecy of Isaiah' (Leicester: IVP 1993) is endlessly helpful, especially on the structure and historical context. Oswalt's two volume NICOT, 'The Book of Isaiah' (Grand Rapids: Eerdmans 1986, 1998) is surprisingly accessible for its size, and his ability to not only see the structure, but also to discern its theological purpose and didactic power is invaluable for the teacher. Preachers will find his rich introductory section on the themes of Isaiah particularly useful.

At a more accessible level, Barry Webb's excellent BST 'The Message of Isaiah'(Leicester: IVP 1996) is suitable both for study and personal devotions

For the most in-depth, academic engagement with the Hebrew text, the older three-volume NICOT by Edward J Young, 'The Book of Isaiah' (Grand Rapids: Eerdmans 1965, 1970 1972), engages well on philological issues. The volume in Keil & Delitzsch's set, *Commentary on the Old Testament* (Translated by James Martin - Grand Rapids: Eerdmans 1986, vol. 7) is also extremely thorough.

Finally, those wanting a full engagement with the problem of the unity of Isaiah will find 'The Unity of Isaiah' (Philadelphia, PA: Presbyterian & Reformed, 1950 ,various reprints available) by Oswald Allis both helpful and thorough.

PT MEDIA

RESOURCES FOR PREACHERS AND BIBLE TEACHERS

PT Media, a ministry of The Proclamation Trust, provides a range of multimedia resources for preachers and Bible teachers.

Teach the Bible Series (Christian Focus & PT Media)
The *Teach the Bible Series*, published jointly with *Christian Focus Publications*, is written by preachers, for preachers, and is specifically geared to the purpose of God's Word – its proclamation as living truth. Books in the series aim to help the reader move beyond simply understanding a text to communicating and applying it.

Current titles include: *Teaching 1 Peter, Teaching Romans, Teaching Acts, Teaching Amos* and *Teaching the Christian Hope*.

Forthcoming titles include: *Teaching Ephesians, Teaching Daniel, Teaching Mark, Teaching 1,2,3 John, Teaching Nehemiah* and *Teaching 1&2 Samuel.*

DVD Training

Preaching & Teaching the Old Testament:
  4 DVDs - Narrative, Prophecy, Poetry, Wisdom

Preaching & Teaching the New Testament
  3 DVDs - Gospels, Letters, Acts & Revelation

These training DVDs aim to give preachers and teachers confidence in handling the rich variety of God's word. David Jackman has taught this material to generations of Cornhill students, and gives us step-by-step instructions on handling each genre of biblical literature.

He demonstrates principles that will guide us through the challenges of teaching and applying different parts of the bible, for example:

- How does prophecy relate to the lives of its hearers – ancient and modern?
- How can you preach in a way that reflects the deep emotion of the psalms?

Both sets are suitable for preachers and for those teaching the Bible in a wide variety of contexts.

- Designed for **individual** and **group** study
- Interactive learning through many **worked examples** and **exercises**
- Flexible format ideal for **training courses**
- Optional **English subtitles** for second-language users
- Print as many **workbooks** as you need (PDF)

Audio
PT Resources has a large range of mp3 downloads, nearly all of which are entirely free to download and use.

Preaching Instruction
This series aims to help the preacher or teacher understand, open up and teach individual books of the bible by getting to grips with their central message and purpose.

Sermon Series
These sermons, examples of great preaching, not only demonstrate faithful biblical preaching but will also refresh and instruct the hearer.

Conferences
Recordings of our conferences include challenging topical addresses, discussion of preaching and ministry issues, and hard-hitting exposition that will challenge and inspire all those in ministry.

Practical Preaching Series
(Christian Focus & PT Media)

We need help not just in 'how to preach bible books', but also clarity and encouragement on the point and purpose of preaching and teaching. The books in this series are short and accessible, ideal for personal use, group study or training.

Bible Delight
Delight in God's word is key to preaching well, and indeed to living well. By guiding us through Psalm 119, Christopher Ash invites us to understand and deepen that delight. It is an invitation to be refreshed, in our lives, our study, and our teaching.

Priority of Preaching
Most ministers preach to congregations that are smaller than they'd wish and tougher than they'd hoped. Christopher Ash not only encourages us to keep going, he sets out a charter for preaching that draws from the very roots of the Old Testament. He shows us that nothing in the world is more worthwhile, because preaching is God's strategy to rebuild a broken world.

Other titles from
Christian Focus and PT Media

Teaching Acts:
Unlocking the book of Acts for the Bible Teacher
David Cook
ISBN 978-1-84550-255-3

Teaching Amos:
Unlocking the prophecy of Amos for the Bible Teacher
Bob Fyall
ISBN 978-1-84550-142-6

Teaching 1 Peter:
Unlocking the book of I Peter for the Bible Teacher
Angus MacLeay
ISBN 978-1-84550-347-5

PROCLAMATION
TRUST MEDIA

TEACHING
THE CHRISTIAN HOPE

Unlocking Biblical Eschatology
for the Bible Teacher

DAVID JACKMAN

SERIES EDITORS: DAVID JACKMAN & ROBIN SYDSERFF

Teaching the Christian Hope:
Unlocking Biblical Eschatology for the Expositor
David Jackman
ISBN 978-1-85792-518-0

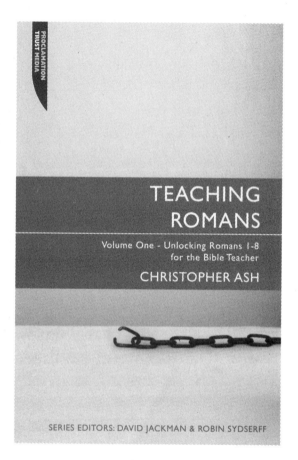

Teaching Romans
Volume 1: Unlocking Romans 1-8 for the Bible Teacher
Christopher Ash
ISBN 978-1-84550-455-7

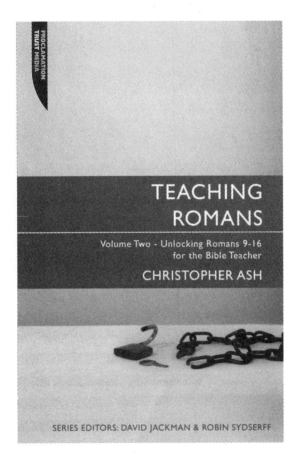

Teaching Romans
Volume 2: Unlocking Romans 9-16 for the Bible Teacher
Christopher Ash
ISBN 978-1-84550-456-4

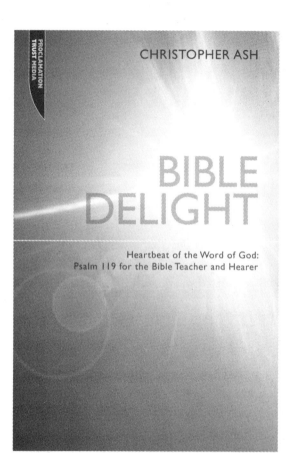

CHRISTOPHER ASH

BIBLE
DELIGHT

Heartbeat of the Word of God:
Psalm 119 for the Bible Teacher and Hearer

Bible Delight:
Psalm 119 for the Bible Teacher and Bible hearer
Christopher Ash
ISBN 978-1-84550-360-4

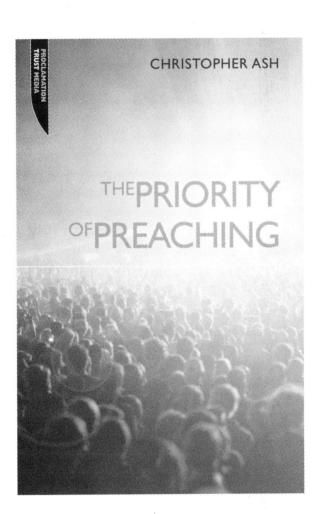

The Priority of Preaching
Christopher Ash
ISBN 9781845504649

Spirit of Truth:
Unlocking the Bible's Teaching on the Holy Spirit
David Jackman
ISBN 978-1-84550-057-3

Christian Focus Publications
publishes books for all ages

Our mission statement –

STAYING FAITHFUL
In dependence upon God we seek to impact the world through literature faithful to His infallible Word, the Bible. Our aim is to ensure that the LORD Jesus Christ is presented as the only hope to obtain forgiveness of sin, live a useful life and look forward to heaven with Him.

REACHING OUT
Christ's last command requires us to reach out to our world with His gospel. We seek to help fulfil that by publishing books that point people towards Jesus and help them develop a Christ-like maturity. We aim to equip all levels of readers for life, work, ministry and mission.

Books in our adult range are published in three imprints.

> *Christian Focus* contains popular works including biographies, commentaries, basic doctrine and Christian living. Our children's books are also published in this imprint.

> *Mentor* focuses on books written at a level suitable for Bible College and seminary students, pastors and other serious readers. The imprint includes commentaries, doctrinal studies, examination of current issues and church history.

> *Christian Heritage* contains classic writings from the past.

Christian Focus Publications Ltd,
Geanies House, Fearn, Ross-shire,
IV20 1TW, Scotland, United Kingdom
info@christianfocus.com
www.christianfocus.com